Born in Detroit in 1945, Woody Haut grew up in Pasadena, California, attended San Francisco State University, and has lived in Britain since the early 1970s. At present he is a London-based freelance journalist and disgruntled habitué of record shops and book shops. He has worked as a lecturer, taxi-cab driver, recordshop assistant, cinema programmer and Labour Editor for *Rolling Stock* magazine (US). His new book, *Neon Noir: Contemporary American Crime Fiction*, is also published by Serpent's Tail.

Praise for *Pulp Culture*

'Literature percolates society, and fiction, says Woody Haut, has been refracted by the class war and Cold War of this century. As the American yellowbrick road became an urban mean street, the likes of Dashiell Hammett and Raymond Chandler enunciated the paranoia and guilt of the American nightmare. Reds were under beds, UFOs were in the skies; a president was pulped, and culture turned decidedly noir. Fiction was full of trench coats and trilbies, square jaws and handguns. The Cold War may have thawed, but Haut recreates its chill, and brilliantly analyses the paperbacks that preempted the dystopian worlds of film directors David Lynch and Quentin Tarantino.' **Tobias Jones**, *Observer*

'A fascinating insight into the history of American hardboiled fiction and its origins in the Cold War. It will become a major work of reference in the field, encompassing as it does thorough analysis of the works of Jim Thompson, David Goodis, Chester Himes, Charles Willeford and many other vital writers who are only now getting the appreciation they failed to get when they were alive. Essential reading for all crime readers.' *Time Out*

'Haut examines the hardboiled novel in the context of postwar American politics – the anti-communism paranoia and the Cold War (Dashiell Hammett appeared before Senator McCarthy's committee) and also the liberal resistance to right-wing excesses. He charts, too, the economic and social development of the private eye in a rapidly changing America. *Pulp Culture* has a serious intent, but it is easy and fun to read.' ***The Times***

PULP CULTURE

Hardboiled Fiction and the Cold War

WOODY HAUT

Library of Congress Catalog Card Number: 95–69753

A catalogue record for this book is available from the British Library on request

The right of Woody Haut to be identified as the author of this work has been asserted by him in accordance with the Copyright, Designs and Patents Act 1988

First published in 1995 by
Serpent's Tail, 4 Blackstock Mews, London N4
Website: http://www.serpentstail.com

Set in 10pt Baskerville by Avon Dataset Ltd, Bidford on Avon, Warwickshire

Printed in Finland by Werner Söderström Oy

10 9 8 7 6 5 4 3 2

Contents

Acknowledgements   vii

I   **Introduction: Better Dead than Read**   1
Hardboiled writers, fear of a mass readership; finding the
crime; locating guilt

2   **A Knife that Cuts Both Ways**   14
State paranoia and paranoid states in the fiction of David
Goodis, Chester Himes and Jim Thompson

3   **Taking Out Contracts**   65
The origins of detection; the privatization of the investigatory
process; the politics of Philip Marlowe, Lew Archer, Paul Pine
and Mike Hammer; wages, conditions and inflationary
tendencies of fictional private eyes

4   **Femme Fatality**   106
The portrayal of women in pulp culture fiction; women
hardboiled writers; Leigh Brackett's *The Tiger Among Us*,
Dolores Hitchens's *Sleep with Strangers* and Dorothy B.
Hughes's *In a Lonely Place* as tacit critiques of a male-
oriented genre

5   **Profits of Crime**   132
The crime novel as social critique: William McGivern's *Odds
Against Tomorrow* and *Death Runs Faster*; Gil Brewer's *13
French Street*; Lionel White's *The Killing* and *The Big Caper*

6   **Beaten to a Pulp**   164
The end of an era, reflected in Charles Williams's *The Big Bite*
and Charles Willeford's *Pick-Up* and *The Woman Chaser*

Appendix I: Primary Pulp Culture Texts   192

Appendix 2: From Pulp to Noir   195

Notes   204

Index   227

Acknowledgements

Thanks to Mavis who not only read the manuscript at various stages, but remained tolerant of my obsession with *Pulp Culture*; to Asia whose work methods deserve emulation; to Mike Hart for reading the manuscript and offering his expertise; to Laurence O'Toole at Serpent's Tail for persevering; and to Allison & Busby, who tolerated my incursions into their bookshelves.

INTRODUCTION: BETTER DEAD
THAN READ

Hardboiled writers; fear of a mass readership; finding the crime; locating the guilt

The Thin Man Takes the Stand

It is no coincidence that Dashiell Hammett's *Red Harvest* was first published on the eve of the Wall Street Crash. Arguably the original hardboiled novel,[1] *Red Harvest* was written in a period of active left-wing political dissent and remains the genre's definitive statement regarding political corruption. Likewise, it is significant that Mickey Spillane's *Kiss Me, Deadly*, a blatant depiction of right-wing values, should have hit the newsstands in 1953, at the height of Cold War hysteria.

While in 1953 Spillane could only fantasize about ridding the world of communists, Hammett, in the context of the Cold War, had become politically suspect. Still struggling to complete his never-to-be-finished novel *Tulip*, Hammett would be called before Senator Joseph McCarthy's congressional sub-committee which was investigating charges that pro-communist books, including Hammett's, had been found on the shelves of the State Department's overseas libraries.[2]

It was a year in which teenagers were dancing to Bill Haley's *Crazy, Man, Crazy* and watching *Abbott and Costello Go to Mars*. The senator from Minnesota fixed his eyes on his adversary, and said, "Mr Hammett, if you were spending, as we are, over a hundred million dollars a year on an information program allegedly for the purpose of fighting communism, and if you were in charge of that program to fight communism, would you allow your shelves to bear the work of some seventy-five communist authors, in effect placing our official stamp of approval upon those books?"

Hammett responded laconically. "Well, I think – of course, I don't know – if I were fighting communism, I don't think I would do it by giving people any books at all."

McCarthy, realising that Hammett had just exposed his fear of a literate population, laughed uncomfortably. "From an author, that sounds unusual." With those words Hammett was excused. But it wouldn't be long before he'd be paying for his irony and the implication that the availability and consumption of books are political issues. Shortly afterwards three hundred copies of Hammett's books were removed from overseas libraries. Three years later the author who helped create a literary genre was sued by the government for back taxes, and eventually billed for $140,000. Financially ruined and suffering from inoperable lung cancer, Hammett died in 1961.

The year after Hammett had appeared before McCarthy, the National Security Council would, on five different occasions, discuss using atomic weapons against China. Society had become obsessed by the bomb; so much so that the means of retribution in Spillane's ultra-violent *Kiss Me, Deadly* would be altered. In his screen adaptation, director Robert Aldrich updated Spillane's signifier, changing it from a localized device capable of blasting Lilly, "a horrible caricature of a human",[3] off the face of the earth, to the more universally destructive "great atomic whatsit".

Despite political differences, Hammett would have done well to note Mike Hammer's comments in *Kiss me, Deadly*. "There's no such thing as innocence", says Hammer. "Innocence touched with guilt is as good a deal as you can get."[4] Dashiell Hammett's innocence had been waylaid somewhere between Los Alamos and the Ashland Federal Correctional Institution where he had served a six-month sentence in 1951 for refusing to answer questions in a case involving eleven indicted communist leaders facing deportation under the Smith Act. Moreover, Hammett was un-innocent enough to know that books are, in themselves, investigations, and, if one seeks mass distribution and a mass readership, one acknowledges the dominant cultural narrative or suffers the consequences.

In Pursuit of the Marginal

The meeting between Hammett and McCarthy is crucial to the development of pulp culture, for it highlights on the one hand the political potential of hardboiled writing and, on the other, the creation of a mass readership. Though by the end of the Second World War Hammett's literary output had ground to a halt, his work would remain an important influence on subsequent hardboiled fiction. Between 1945 and 1960 numerous hardboiled novels were published, many of which successfully captured the paranoia and urban reality of the Cold War years.

Still considered low-brow and throwaway, hardboiled writing has remained marginal in its relationship to mainstream literary criticism. Given the tediousness of mainstream literary criticism, there may be little reason to regret this. At the same time, it indicates a class-based separation between writers who have the status of literary *artists* and those who have been relegated to the status of literary *workers*. Tied to contracts and deadlines and obliged to include obligatory scenes of sex and violence, these writers, many of them refugees from other professions, were subject to the vagaries of the market.

Not surprisingly, literary workers like Jim Thompson, David Goodis, Geoffrey Homes, Charles Williams, Dolores Hitchens, Leigh Brackett, Dorothy B. Hughes, and Horace McCoy continue to be omitted from mainstream or post-modern literary criticism. Regardless of subjective notions concerning what constitutes "good" writing or the tenuous relationship that exists between popular literature and literary criticism,[5] hardboiled writing has been marginalized precisely because it is a class-based literature. Yet this marginalization has, in turn, provided hardboiled writing a perspective from which to continue its reflection and critique of society.

Pulp to Pocket

"OUT TODAY – THE NEW POCKET BOOK THAT MAY REVOLUTIONIZE AMERICA'S READING HABITS" (from a 1939 Pocket Book advertisement).[6]

"BOOKS ARE WEAPONS – in a free democracy everyone may read what he likes. Books educate, inform, inspire; they also provide entertainment, bolster morale . . . Read them and pass them on" (from a Dell wartime advertisement).[7]

The genre of pulp fiction has become synonymous with cheap paperbacks whose gaudy covers invariably portray men with guns and women with low necklines. Strictly speaking, the genre consists of stories written for pulp magazines published, for the most part, prior to the Second World War.[8] In fact, the heyday of pulp magazines would last only until the introduction of pocket (paperback) books. Thus pulp fiction, when used to describe post-war crime writing, is a slightly misleading, though useful, term.

Paperback fiction began tamely enough. Amongst Pocket Book's first ten titles were such steamy writers as Agatha Christie, James Hilton (*Goodbye Mr Chips*) and Dorothea Brande. The war, with its captive market, would take the production and consumption of cheap paperbacks into a higher gear, forcing publishers to cultivate, and respond to, a mass readership. Since paperbacks had yet to reach their popular peak, many hardboiled writers, having contributed to pulp magazines like *Black Mask*, were first published in hardback. This was the case with two of the era's most adept writers, Jim Thompson and David Goodis.

Though between them they published some twenty-five paper-back novels during the 1950s, their outstanding early work, including Thompson's 1949 *Nothing More Than Murder* and Goodis's 1946 *Dark Passage*, initially appeared in hardcover editions.

By 1949, nine companies had ventured into the paperback market. In 1951, production hit a peak, when 886 titles were published, eight times the number that appeared in 1945. Yet this increase coincided with a slump in sales – the influence of television perhaps causing a miscalculation of the market – prompting publishers to opt for more lurid formats. This, in turn, would lead to attacks by anti-pornography campaigners. According to one US senator, "alien-minded radicals and moral perverts" had infiltrated the pocket-book market, while, in 1952, the House Select Committee on Current Pornographic Materials concluded: "Some of the most offensive infractions of the moral code were found to be contained in low-cost, paper-bound publications known as 'pocket-size books' . . . which . . . have . . . degenerated into media for the dissemination of artful appeals to sensuality, immorality, filth, perversion, and degeneracy." Since pocket books also published the likes of Theodore Dreiser, D. H. Lawrence, Aldous Huxley, and Jean-Paul Sartre, pocket books were being judged not merely by their covers. For these accusations, like those voiced by Joseph McCarthy, could have been prompted by the fact that ordinary people were reading books once thought the province of an educated middle class; or the fear that, with the advent of the paperback original, these same people were about to create their own literary genre.

Though Dashiell Hammett, Raymond Chandler and Jonathan Latimer were published in paperback before 1945, it wouldn't be until after the Second World War that hardboiled writing became associated with the paperback industry. Many readers, demanding more than mere "whodunnits" preferred fiction that portrayed the reality of post-war urban life. As attacks on paperbacks grew, the number of mysteries actually fell from 50 per cent of the market in 1945 to 26 per cent in 1950 and 13 per cent in 1955. Having become something of a cliché, traditional mysteries would be replaced by crime and low-life fiction – particularly that which emphasized violence, sex and paranoia. Culturally more interesting and varied than mysteries, this new form of hardboiled paperback published by companies like Gold Medal, Ace, Signet and Dell would not only portray US society as inherently criminal but would also reflect the woof and warp of the Cold War at a time when America's yellow-brick road had turned into a mean and ultimately dead-end street.

Consequently, the term pulp culture denotes an era dominated by the excesses of disposability, and marks the relationship between pulp fiction and a historical period that begins with the 6 August 1945 bombing of Japan. This was an event closely followed by the publication of such pulp culture classics as *The Big Clock* (Fearing), *Dark Passage* (Goodis), *Nightmare Alley* (Gresham), *Build My Gallows High* (Homes), *Ride The Pink Horse* (Hughes), *Seven Slayers* (Cain), *If He Hollers Let Him Go* (Himes) and *Heed The Thunder* (Thompson). The era culminates sometime between 1960 and 1963, with the election and eventual assassination of John F. Kennedy, accompanied by the publication of books indicating a nation in transition – *The Heat's On* (Himes), *The Hustler* (Tevis), *The Woman Chaser* (Willeford). With reality appearing to overtake fiction, hardboiled writing would soon turn, for the most part, into pastiche and parody. Meanwhile, a macabre connection might be made between the pulping of books, the pulping of a nation and the pulping of a president.

Morbid Symptoms

Best remembered as the author of *The Big Clock*, Kenneth Fearing was, like Dorothy B. Hughes, a poet and writer of crime fiction. In this dual position, Fearing was able to examine the relationship between crime, narrative, language and culture, noting, in his poem *Sherlock Spends a Day in the Country*, "The crime, if there was a crime, has not been reported as yet; / The plot, if that is what it was, is still a secret somewhere in this / wilderness of newly fallen snow."[9]

The essential investigation, according to Fearing, is to locate the crime and find the plot – a political act that entails the writer taking into account the prevailing conditions of an era. Regarding the effect of the mass media on crime writing and culture, Fearing says, "The revolution that calls itself The Investigation had its rise in the theaters of communication, and now regularly parades its images across them, reiterates its gospel from them, daily and hourly marches through the corridors of every office, flies into the living room of every home."[10] Thus the mass media helped create a narrative context for pulp culture writing, as it too focused on individual rather than state crimes.

With the old world dying and the new one about to abort, the morbid symptoms suggested by pulp culture were becoming apparent. Their impact and effect soon placed a topical spin on Horace McCoy's description of the historical process in *No Pockets in a Shroud*: "A man goes to bed tonight a fool and tomorrow morning he wakes up a wise man. He can't explain what's happened in between; all he knows is it's *happened*." Indicative of the era, and hardboiled fiction's uneasy transition from pre-war to post-war hardboiled fiction, McCoy's *No Pockets in a Shroud* would, in 1948, be altered by a New American Library editor who, fearing a Marxist interpretation, found it necessary to change the heroine from a communist to a sex pervert.

Meanwhile, the Marshall Plan,[11] the establishment of the CIA, the federal loyalty program, the Taft-Hartley Act (depoliticizing the CIO), the House Committee on Un-American Activities, and military intervention in Guatemala, Lebanon and Korea contributed to the era's paranoia. This condition would be epitomized by Mike Hammer who, in *One Lonely Night*, declares, "I killed more people tonight than I have fingers on my hands. I shot them in cold blood and enjoyed every minute of it . . . They were Commies . . . red sons of bitches who should have died long ago."[12]

Despite a period of industrial unrest, a war-rejuvenated economy juiced productivity to an unprecedented level. The result was an expanded middle class and an increase in suburban dwellings (between 1950 and 1960 suburbs grew forty times faster than central areas). Yet, as portrayed in many pulp culture novels, there remained a considerable amount of economic and social disparity.[13] For those able to do so, relocating to the suburbs was a means of ignoring, or at least escaping, this disparity. As the nuclear family – a portentous term considering how social conditions would shatter many dreams of suburban utopia – replaced the extended family, the values underpinning suburban life were prefigured in post-war advertisements in which women were told, "You're living for this minute . . . the day your man comes home for keeps. You want a house . . . a garden. All the happy dreams you laid away in rose leaves come bubbling back to life." Or shown to be saying, "He's coming home – and I'm throwing away the book."[14] These dreams and values existed alongside pulp culture texts which viewed this social shift with unease. In William McGivern's brilliant portrayal of suburban versus urban angst, *The Big Heat*, the mob blows apart Detective Bannion's cosy middle-class home not long after "dick" and soon-to-be-deceased wife discuss child development over gin and tonics. Here suburbia must not only be defended, but urbanism, with its incipient problems, must be attacked.

Against the background of an expanding middle class and encroaching consumerism, pulp culture writing, with notable exceptions (Dorothy B. Hughes, Dolores Hitchins, Leigh Brackett, Vera Caspary, Mildred Davis, Margaret Millar), represents male fantasies in which the suburbs are a last refuge. In these texts, invariably written from a male perspective, women with children are kept in the background and only occasionally allowed to intrude into the narrative. More often than not, it is the *femme fatale*, often an urban throwaway or product of a wealthy family, who must carry the narrative to its doom-ridden conclusion.

Whatever their political orientation, the subtexts of hardboiled fiction reveal as much about the culture as the author. In the best, though bleakest, hardboilers – those of Thompson, Goodis, McCoy – characters, faced with cultural apprehensions regarding the "Red Menace" and nuclear devastation, commit, with minimal moral intrusion from the author, any number of antisocial acts for seemingly inexplicable reasons. The implication is that protagonists know others better than they know themselves. In *Many A Monster*, published in 1949 and an early example of what would become a post-modern crime cliché – a novel about a serial killer – Robert Finnegan writes, "Although he could no longer understand himself, he still understood other people."[15] While Thompson, in *The Killer Inside Me*, writes, "We might have the disease . . . or we might just be cold blooded and smart as hell; or we might be innocent of what we're supposed to have done."[16] For both writers – Finnegan a former radical trade unionist and Thompson a former communist – human behaviour, warped by conditions and circumstances, can be extreme and unpredictable. Neither, however, offers a coherent cure for society's ills. Yet this, and the narrative objectivity of many hardboiled writers, might have had more to do with avoiding the wrath of McCarthyism than believing that political explanations had become irrelevant. While pulp culture fiction contains few overt political statements, its subject matter – capitalism's relationship to crime, corruption, desire and power – remains highly political.

In either case, these critiques, or their absence, found favour with the reading public. *Cassidy's Girl* by David Goodis, published in 1951 by Gold Medal, sold over a million copies. Such novels attracted the attention of Hollywood movie studios, already feeling the pressure of McCarthyism. With a number of pulp culture writers working as scriptwriters, it was often easier to insinuate that all was not perfect in America through the ambiguities of *film noir* rather than confront the system and risk having one's message co-opted.

Nevertheless, while propaganda, the staple of much proletariat writing, was not a primary feature of hardboiled crime or low-life investigation, many pulp culture writers had been influenced by their proletariat predecessors (London, Kromer, Anderson, Conroy), especially when portraying those characters marginal to the dominant culture. Pulp culture writers were not only familiar with magazines like *Black Mask*, but they were within a tradition whose writing, according to David Madden, is "as terse and idiomatic as the news headlines and people who speak the language of the streets, the pool rooms, the union halls, the bull pens, the factories, the hobo jungles . . .".[17] Consequently, pulp culture writing retained the basic themes of proletariat writing: the corrosive power of money, class antagonism, capitalism's ability to erode the community, turning its citizens into a disparate band of self-centred and alienated individuals – the only difference being that this was an era in which paranoia and suspicion had become public commodities. This was summed up nicely by Robert Finnegan in *Many A Monster*, when the book's narrator comments drolly, "The presence of a lunatic in the restaurant gave her a sense of personal insecurity".[18] Chandler, centring on inter-personal relationships, takes an equal-sized bite from the culture, saying, "We looked at each other with the clear innocent eyes of a couple of used car salesmen".[19]

Pulp culture writers would respond to the era in different ways. But few were openly political. While it was hardly necessary for Mickey Spillane to be ambiguous, William McGivern's work, particularly *The Big Heat*, can be read as an attack on organized crime or as a veiled critique of McCarthyism. On the other hand David Goodis, known for reading *The Daily Worker* for its jazz listings rather than its line on current events, would, after retreating to his native Philadelphia and family, write numerous pulp culture classics that exuded alienation and paranoia. Likewise Chester Himes who, weary of America's racism and having offended everyone – communists, New Dealers, Jews and bourgeois blacks – in *If He Hollers Let Him Go* and *Lonely Crusade*, would move to Europe where he would write the famous Harlem detective novels which are eloquent statements regarding urban black culture between the wars.

It was left to a prairie populist like Jim Thompson to portray the disfigurements of capitalism, identifying it as a national, rather than local, disease. In the last section of his 1958 novel *The Getaway*, capitalism is represented by the kingdom of El Rey – a dystopia with a "climate to suit every taste" and the "largest per capita police force in the world"[20] – a place to which thieves and capitalists escape, but from which there is no escape; where cannibalism is an everyday and logical act: "A smell filled the air. The odor of peppery, roasting flesh ... 'Quite fitting, eh señor? And such an easy transition. One need only live literally as he has always done figuratively.' "[21] Here paranoia is essential for survival:

> Most immigrants travel to the kingdom in pairs. In the begin-
> ning, each will handle his own money, carefully contributing
> an exact half of the common expenses. But this is awkward, it
> leads to arguments, and no matter how much the individual
> has he is never quite free of the specter of want. So very soon
> there is a casual discussion of the advantages of a joint account,
> and it is casually agreed that they should open one. And from
> then on – well, the outcome depends on which of the two is
> the shrewder, the more cold-blooded or requires the least
> sleep.[22]

But the kingdom of El Rey is also a post-pulp culture world where the extremes of capitalism destroy anything human. Whichever, the male protagonists of these narratives are frequently seduced by the kindgom's promise of wealth. Inarticulate, avaricious, subversive or paranoid, they attempt to claw their way into the kingdom only to be pulped along the way. The process of their destruction is a primary subtext in pulp culture fiction.

Losing the Narrative

Currently repackaged out of a sense of nostalgia and a need to profit from the past, it's not surprising that original pulp culture paperbacks have become consumer objects fetching extraordinary prices. At the same time, pulp culture reprints are avidly consumed, allowing *fin de siècle* readers both to investigate the past and, in noting the literature's language, place, attitudes and politics, make connections with the present. This, in turn, has helped create a new generation of crime writers – James Ellroy, Walter Mosley, James Crumley, Sara Paretsky and Elmore Leonard, for example – who have gone beyond parody to examine the new urban reality in which they find themselves.

With its fellow travellers, informers, infiltrators and misogynists, the 1950s was an era of psychotic behaviour and suicidal impulse, of shadows, square jaws and dangerous women. Whether liberal (McGivern), radical (Himes), populist (Thompson), nihilist (Goodis) or fascist (Spillane), pulp culture writers produced a class-based popular literature, which, with its compelling tales of corruption, violence and obsessive behaviour, indicated a nation struggling with itself.

Limited by format but sharing a mood, style and historic juncture, pulp culture plots were inevitably secondary to the obsessional world they created. Likewise the set pieces and solutions to crimes – for so long a part of the detective novel tradition – grew less important than the perceptions gathered along the way. As the present-day reader becomes entrapped in that process the crimes mount, and are eventually lost within the fabric of an imagined society. It's here that pulp culture stories begin to merge and the genre takes the shape of a single narrative, and it is through this narrative that a contemporary reconstruction of the pulp culture era is possible.

Pulp Culture examines this narrative while focusing on the era's most interesting and energetic writers and texts. Though the chapters explore relevant themes they vary in approach, moving from a survey of the genre and its two basic components – paranoia and private detection – to placing specific texts in political and historical contexts. The first chapter delves into the dark and paranoid worlds of David Goodis, Chester Himes and Jim Thompson, situating their bleak and violent narratives in the social and political framework of their time. The second chapter investigates the politics of private investigators: Raymond Chandler's Philip Marlowe, Howard Browne's Paul Pine, Ross Macdonald's Lew Archer and Mickey Spillane's Mike Hammer. It goes on playfully to explore the effect of inflation on the rates of fictional private detection. The third chapter discusses the portrayal of women in pulp culture fiction through Leigh Brackett's *The Tiger Among Us*, Dorothy B. Hughes's *In a Lonely Place* and Dolores Hitchens's *Sleep With Strangers*. Not only are these books indicative of the era, they also illustrate how female pulp culture writers were able to negotiate their way through a male-oriented genre. The fourth chapter examines the crime novel as social critique, exemplified by William McGivern's *Odds Against Tomorrow* and *Death Runs Faster*, Gil Brewer's *13 French Street* and Lionel White's *The Killing* and *The Big Caper*. The final chapter considers the final days of the Cold War era as portrayed in Charles Williams's *The Big Bite* and Charles Willeford's *Pick-Up* and *The Woman Chaser*. With fiction unable to stand comparison to the era's events and policies, these novels illustrate the destruction of pulp culture protagonists and the texts in which they appear. Lastly, with pulp culture fiction and *film noir* inextricably linked, the book concludes with a filmography, listing the contributions of relevant writers and a selection of twenty films based on pulp culture narratives.

2

A KNIFE THAT CUTS BOTH WAYS

State paranoia and paranoid states in the fiction of David Goodis, Chester Himes and Jim Thompson

"With a new face I won't need to worry." (David Goodis, *Dark Passage*)[1]

"All I can do is wait until I split. Right down the middle." (Jim Thompson, *The Killer Inside Me*)[2]

"I could always feel race trouble, serious trouble, never more than two feet off." (Chester Himes, *If He Hollers Let Him Go*)[3]

Fear of a *Noir* Planet

Paranoia is essential to pulp culture writing and an agent capable of energizing and corrupting both narrative and nation.[4] Pulp culture paranoia drives the narrative, creating an emotionally charged atmosphere in which fear, suspicion, greed and violence are commonplace. This was at a time when US obsessions ranged from post-war insularity to the Cold War and the bomb, and coincided with the publication of novels – Kenneth Fearing's *The Big Clock*, Cornell Woolrich's *Waltz Into Darkness*, Gresham's *Nightmare Alley*, for example – whose claustrophobic paranoia reflects such obsessions. In 1947, the recent attack on Pearl Harbour and Congress's decision to centralize the armed forces and establish the Central Intelligence Agency gave notice that paranoia would soon become a nationwide condition. One manifestation of this paranoia, and indicative of irrational concerns regarding an alien invasion, would be the sudden mania for flying saucers.

The lurid covers of pulp culture paperbacks – often showing an anxious man holding a bottle and a svelte woman holding a gun – were emblematic of the era's dis-ease. Simplistic images, but no more so than the cover of a 1948 *Look* magazine showing foreign soldiers and a caption which reads, "Could the Reds seize Detroit?" Published in the same year, Horace McCoy's ultra-hardboiled and aptly named *Kiss Tomorrow Goodbye* investigates the era's paranoia and pathology. With a cover befitting the mood, the 1949 abridged Signet paperback depicts a half-disrobed woman, eyes closed, leaning against a bed, as a man sits watching her, a cigarette dangling from his mouth. Only a few years after Franklin D. Roosevelt's death, having "nothing to fear but fear itself" had become transformed into an epigram describing the era's paranoia, the specific object of which had been lost within the shadows of history.

Given the histrionics of the Cold War, with its need for political and economic scapegoats, fear was a recurrent theme. Representative is Geoffrey Homes's 1946 *Build My Gallows High* in which Red Bailey is blackmailed into abandoning his reconstructed life to become an accomplice in a job that recalls his shadowy past as a private eye. Here Bailey aligns himself with those working against the social order.[5] His situation was not unlike that of the 6.6 million people who, between March 1947 and December 1952, would be investigated for alleged communist links. For the fear that one's past might be scrutinized contributed to a climate of paranoia essential to the functioning of the Cold War.

Yet paranoia was an understandable reaction. In 1950, a year which saw the publication of Mickey Spillane's *Vengeance Is Mine*, Cornell Woolrich's *Fright* and Ross Macdonald's *The Drowning Pool*, the US quadrupled its defence expenditure and the National Security Council produced a document linking the Cold War with US economic and political requirements and outlining the terms on which the Cold War would be fought.[6] Moving between isolationism and expansionism, a space opened in which paranoid narratives could easily fit.

Considering the country's obsessive concern with national security, it's not surprising that communism was portrayed on television and film (*I Led Three, I Married A Communist*) as a mental illness rather than a political ideology. Yet just as money is the prime mover for Stanton Carlisle in *Nightmare Alley* – his moving from sideshow medium to big-time spiritualist could be likened to a McCarthyite witch hunter as he seeks to exploit those wishing to escape the object of their fears – so profit motivated the Cold War. As pulp culture private eye Max Thursday says in Wade Miller's 1947 *Fatal Step*, "Scruples never earn money."[7] Representing the dysfunction of a nation in transition, paranoia was so potent a subtext it blurred the narrative of both text and nation, causing readers and writers to lose track of plot and historical context. This was less disastrous for pulp culture fiction, concentrating as it does on culture, characterization and narrative progression, than for "who-dunnits", preoccupied with plot, linearity, order and detection.

Though it is futile to connect specific pulp culture texts to specific events, the relationship between text and era is more than metaphorical. Which is why paranoia, as a hardboiled ingredient, post-war phenomenon and basis of the American nightmare, makes for uncomfortable literary discussion. Whether the systematized delusions that comprise being "beside oneself" – paranoia's literal meaning – create the fear popularly known as paranoia; or whether the fear popularly known as paranoia causes the delusions, "paranoia" is both a social and a psychological condition, the rule rather than exception.

Even the act of reading, of going *outside* oneself to get *into* the book, could be interpreted as a paranoid as well as a liberating experience. The subversiveness of pulp culture literature lies in the way it uses textual paranoia to expose the limitations of a purely psychological critique and the extent to which it is culturally based. Yet the paranoia on which Jack Finney's *The Body Snatchers* is based does not come solely from McCarthyism and the atomic age; it was endemic to ambitions of the era, justifying expansion abroad and repression at home.[8] Sustained by guilt, paranoia – like the aliens in *The Body Snatchers* – can perpetuate itself. Consequently, the best examples of pulp culture texts are those which convey paranoia not so much by demanding the reader turn the page to see "whodunnit", but by creating an atmosphere which allows readers literally to be "beside themselves".

Pulp culture literature, without the restrictions imposed by cash-obsessed and depoliticized Hollywood studios, could afford to regard paranoia as both a social and a psychological phenomenon. The twisted thoughts and actions of the paranoid can be found in the behaviour of many pulp culture protagonists. This is apparent in their convoluted logic which attempts to prove what they already believe, an obsessive pursuit of hidden meanings and clues, a rejection of alternative interpretations, a subjective view of the world, a sexual anxiety based on fears concerning women and homosexuality, and an insistence on the right to question, deliberate and eavesdrop.[9]

Without overemphasizing the psychological origins and implications of paranoia, it is noteworthy that comments regarding *film noir* by French "schizologists" Gilles Deleuze and Félix Guattari are, in many instances, applicable to pulp culture fiction. For both focus on paranoid protagonists operating within a paranoid culture. As Deleuze and Guattari maintain, *noir* protagonists – not unlike characters in the work of David Goodis and Jim Thompson – inhabit a social field where power relationships and desires are territorialized by family, employers and the culture within a paranoic boundary.[10] Like *film noir* (Deleuze and Guattari cite Nicholas Ray's domestic-*noir* tale of addiction, *Larger Than Life*), pulp culture fiction explores a global rather than an analytical and regressive field of coexistence. With delirium existing within an economic, political, cultural and pedagogical framework, the origins of paranoia, according to Deleuze and Guattari, are neither purely psychological nor exclusively pathological, but a reaction to a pathological and cultural condition.[11] In many ways, this makes the paranoia that pervades the early work of the black pulp culture writer Chester Himes understandable. Likewise Jim Thompson and David Goodis, whose pathological protagonists cast their desires on the world only to have them fall back on the family. Filled with dark thoughts and contorted behaviour, their texts portray a world heading towards chaos. With transgression a necessity, the best pulp culture fiction is a reaction against the culture's acquiescence to the social factors that induce paranoia. Everywhere desire is manufactured and law is circumscribed by what it denies. As Deleuze and Guattari put it, "The law tells us: You will not marry your mother, and you will not kill your father. And we docile subjects say to ourselves: so *that's* what I wanted."[12] No wonder so many pulp culture characters exact revenge for dreaming the impossible.

Ostensibly a passive pursuit, the act of reading takes one through the text and into a world of possibility. Likewise a mass readership, assisted by the GI Bill, might well have noted the conditions perpetuated in a paranoid nation. Soon television emerged as the dominant cultural form, re-enforcing paranoia by manipulating information, internalizing political debate and contributing to an eventual decline in literacy. And, with paranoids needing to contain antisocial or foreign bodies, the CIA would begin investigating new ways of inducing paranoia, illustrated by their attempts to perfect a technique that would help obliterate the memory of former CIA agents. Their experiments included administering LSD to ordinary citizens without their knowledge or consent.[13] Back in the world of fiction, the cover of M.E. Chaber's 1957 anti-communist novel *The Splintered Man*, published in the year of Joseph McCarthy's death, shows a man in his underclothes held by soldiers as he's about to be injected with a "truth drug" which turns out to be LSD.

While not fearing anything but fear might be an equation for paranoia, fear of the outsider and the unknown is an American tradition, leading to and resulting from US expansionism. Such infringement can be noted in pulp culture texts that portray the invasion of public space, as in Lionel White's *The Killing,* or the takeover of small towns, as in William McGivern's *Odds Against Tomorrow.* Indeed, paranoia pushed people to the suburbs. As suburbia grew, cities, once circumscribed areas of protection, were represented as sites of potential danger, inhabited by immigrants and ethnic minorities. Poetic and streetwise, Nelson Algren, in a novel such as *Never Come Morning,* was particularly adept at portraying the paranoia of urban life: "How could you trust the barber, who was nobody's friend, when you couldn't trust Benkowski, who was anybody's friend? . . . You couldn't trust the ones with brains, because they had them, and you couldn't trust the ones without, because they didn't."[14]

As spatial and social disparity increased, pulp culture protagonists were suddenly walking the "mean streets". Meanwhile, suburban readers were able to derive vicarious pleasure from their literary descents into what was often foreign territory. Thus Philip Marlowe transgresses race and class boundaries as he traipses through "one of the mixed blocks over on Central Avenue, the blocks that are not yet all negro . . .".[15] This at a time when suburbia had insulated the fears of property owners and consumers who had willingly conformed to the revised labour and productive processes. In portraying and exploiting paranoia, pulp culture fiction allowed readers to recognize their contradictory situation, while its popularity and relevancy lay in the fact that it could subvert as well as re-enforce paranoia.

Undercover

In a culture permeated by paranoia, it's appropriate that three of the genre's main perpetrators should be members of groups that had cause to be paranoid. Roughly contemporaneous, and living in the Los Angeles area during the 1940s, David Goodis (1917–67), Chester Himes (1909–84) and Jim Thompson (1906–77) – a Jew, an African American, and a one-time member of the Communist Party – represent the apogee of pulp culture writing. Each had their own opinion regarding the social factors – poverty, racism or capitalism – producing paranoia. Even now their texts sizzle with alienation and antisocial activity.

Conversant in popular psychology and the realities of everyday life, Jim Thompson was influenced by Swift, Sophocles and Freud. According to Arnold Hano, his editor at Lion Books, "Jim . . . would take the classics . . . and turn them into modern suspense novels, in synopsis form." In fact, had not Sophocles already done so, Thompson might well have written *Oedipus*. Yet given the twisted behaviour of those inhabiting his work, one wonders if Thompson might not have read Freud back to front, reversing diagnoses and symptoms to portray a world turned inside out.

With tragedy the most likely outcome for a politically conscious black person, Chester Himes prefigures later *noirists* like Donald Goines, Iceberg Slim, Gar Haywood and Walter Mosley. In an era of segregation and lynchings, Himes certainly had cause to be paranoid. His attention drawn to the prevailing social, rather than literary, conditions, Himes found it unnecessary to cite literary influences other than fellow exile Richard Wright, Shakespeare and Camus, from whom he borrows the titles of his two-volumed autobiography, *The Quality of Hurt* and *My Life of Absurdity*. Though he also mentions reading Rimbaud, Faulkner and Joyce while attending the Saratoga Springs writers' colony in 1948.

More downbeat than his favourite writers – Steinbeck, Wolfe and Hemingway – David Goodis portrays the psychologically scarred without resorting to doctrine or social realism. This is exemplified by *The Moon In The Gutter*'s mock-proletariat opening: "At the edge of the alleyway facing Vernon Street, a grey cat waited for a large rat to emerge from its hiding place."[16] Meanwhile, Jim Thompson's tales of corrupt bloodlines illustrate the extent to which the accumulation of capital produces economic inequality and people twisted and pushed to such extremes that dissolution is all that awaits them. As for Chester Himes, the opening chapter of *If He Hollers Let Him Go*, filled with dreams of outcast dogs and people searching for work in wartime Los Angeles, indicates the extent to which social circumstances can affect one's conscious and unconscious life. Taken together, the common denominator for Goodis, Himes and Thompson is crime, the investigation of which results in a cultural critique, fictional paranoia and protagonists who threaten to veer out of control.

David Goodis

"I am not Dashiell Hammett", said David Goodis, probably with half a smile. But it is a comment which, as much as the war, his Jewish origins, social class, or his attitude towards women, suggests the source of Goodis's literary paranoia. For, given the history of the genre, even Goodis had to compare himself with Hammett.

As the author of nineteen novels, most of them paranoid reveries linked to some kind of identity crisis, Goodis was a master at conveying urban angst. After the muted reception of his first novel, the 1938 *Retreat to Oblivion*, Goodis, born to middle-class parents in Philadelphia, would have to reassess his own identity. Despite the romanticism attached to being a literary worker, Goodis must have concluded that, unlike Hammett, he would never be a "serious" writer, but would be forever condemned to pulps and paperbacks.

Moving to New York, Goodis supplemented his pulp writing with advertising work. Eventually *Dark Passage*, a novel which updates and revises Hammett, would appear, serving as Goodis's ticket to Hollywood. There he would churn out a half-dozen film scripts and two novels. In Hollywood, Goodis's behaviour fluctuated from the innocuous to the eccentric. Sleeping on a friend's sofa despite drawing a substantial salary as a scriptwriter, wearing second-hand suits or occasionally a bathrobe in which he would pass himself off as an exiled Russian prince, Goodis, despite his affectations, could never have been mistaken for Hammett. Apart from the fact that Goodis was short, stooped and furtive-looking, his writing is darker, more dreamlike and poetic than Hammett's worldly hardboiled style. Nevertheless, the suggestion that he might be mistaken for someone else, that he might not be himself, must have given Goodis cause to question his own literary identity.

Fed up with Hollywood, Goodis returned to Philadelphia in 1950, moved in with his family and cared for his mentally retarded brother, a situation mirrored in Goodis's novels of the period like *The Moon in the Gutter*, *Down There* and *Black Friday*. Whether retreating from or into oblivion, Goodis was prolific in Philadelphia, writing thirteen paperback originals, the majority of which are now pulp culture classics, unsurpassed in their portrayal of trapped and alienated individuals. Yet Goodis was always self-deprecating about his work. To a critic enquiring about his first novel, Goodis wrote, "It was nothing, and the same applies to most of the 16 others since then . . .".[17] Not surprisingly, Goodis's final years were characterized by bitterness and isolation, exacerbated by a lawsuit in which Goodis accused the producers of *The Fugitive*, a TV series, of plagiarizing the idea for the series from *Dark Passage*. Six years after Goodis's death, the case was settled out of court, with the Goodis estate relinquishing all rights to *Dark Passage* for a mere $12,000.

More adept at recycling characters with paranoid tendencies – sexual anxiety, obsessive behaviour and criminality – than depicting memorable individuals and storylines, Goodis invariably locks his characters into downwardly mobile and criminal cultures. Having rejected fame, fortune or artistic talent, Goodis's protagonists find refuge amongst tramps, thieves, whores and drunks. Yet no matter how self-destructive they become, their dis-ease remains a mask hiding their personal shortcomings. Reticent about making explicit social statements – though he once approached Jerry Wald at Warner Brothers regarding a project on civilization's entry into the atomic era – Goodis regarded paranoia as a by-product of the culture, the result of social deprivation, unrequited love, excessive demands and circumstance. Setting most of his work in working-class communities like Philadelphia and Atlantic City, Goodis preferred the romanticism of marginality over private investigation or public politicking.

Published as a Morrow hardback in 1946, and in a Dell paperback edition in 1948, *Dark Passage* exquisitely captures the fears of post-war America. One of Goodis's best-known novels, it is darker and more obsessional than anything written by Hammett. From its opening line – "It was a tough break. Parry was innocent." – and the description of Parry as "[a] decent sort of guy who never bothered people and wanted to live a quiet life", Goodis portrays a nation ill at ease and unsure of its post-war identity.

Escaping from San Quentin where he's been falsely imprisoned for killing his wife, Parry descends into an abyss of paranoia. A product of institutional life, Parry even has his doubts about Irene, a wealthy San Francisco artist who doggedly helps him. Staying in her apartment, Parry is "beside himself", certain she will phone the police. Unable to trust anyone, Parry says to Irene, "You're in on it. I know you're in on it."[18] That his paranoia is lifted momentarily when he discovers Irene's collection of Count Basie records (at Hollywood parties, Goodis used to sit at the piano and play his rendition of Basie's *One O'Clock Jump*) is indicative of Goodis's overly romantic notions regarding jazz, black culture and the healing power of music. Unable to alter the past, or control the present, Parry fears he will be recognized. In a taxi on his way to a plastic surgeon, Parry is paranoid enough to think the doctor might turn him in, slice him up or, at the very least, blackmail him. Yet Parry knows only a new identity will alleviate his fear and provide him with some breathing space.

After the operation, a heavily bandaged Parry returns to Irene's apartment to recuperate. Hiding in the bedroom, he is horrified when Irene, certain she will not be believed, admits to Madge and Bob that Parry had been in her apartment when Madge last visited. Unable to appreciate Irene's audacity or sense of humour, and paranoid enough to personalize anything sounding ambiguous, Parry concludes that he cannot afford to rely on other people:

> So now she was out with it, taking herself away from it as it came out. And now he was alone again and he couldn't take himself away from it as she could. He was alone with it, and she was going away from it, and it was part of the quiet that crushed him now. And he was alone, crushed by it. And he knew as long as he was alone he mustn't be alone here.[19]

Consequently, he prepares for a quick exit: "He decided to take a run at the window and go through the glass and finish the whole thing. He took a step toward the window and then stopped and turned his back to the window and looked at the wall. He stood there without moving for almost a full hour."[20]

When Parry finally examines his new identity, his paranoia eases and he fits together the pieces that will help him solve the crime. At the same time Parry, like other Goodis protagonists, is concerned with survival and escape: "I don't want to get even with anybody. All I want is to get away."[21] But when the blackmailer, Arbogast, is shot with his own gun after struggling with Parry, Parry realizes that now he too, like Madge, is a murderer. Looking at the body, he is unmoved by his misdeed, unable to "understand why he felt no regret, why he felt no horror at the sight of this dead thing on the ground, this thing he had killed". Neither glad nor sorry, Parry accepts his fate, knowing "it was one of those logical patterns. It was geometry. He was alive and the thing on the ground was dead." Making his paranoia work for him, Parry "was building the method, telling himself how he could prove the guilt of the other person, forcing the showdown that would display and clarify his own innocence."[22] But when Parry locates Madge, and tells her he knows she killed his wife, Madge, the only person capable of corroborating Parry's story, kills herself. With Parry's identity reconstructed, he and Irene prepare for a new life south of the border. Typical of Goodis's fiction, *Dark Passage* leaves the reader wondering if Parry's paranoia has been eradicated or if it will one day return to haunt him.

Nightfall, published in 1947, is another intensely claustrophobic novel, perfect in its construction, in which Goodis presents a paranoid fugitive with a precarious identity. Filmed a decade later by Jacques Tourneur, *Nightfall* begins with Vanning, a commercial artist, looking out of his window on a hot Manhattan night:

> . . . He wanted to go out.
> He was afraid to go out.
> . . . The realization brought him more fright. He rubbed his hands into his eyes and wondered what was making this night such a difficult thing. And suddenly he was telling himself that something was going to happen to him.[23]

A suspected bank robber and murderer, Vanning is an amnesiac who lives in a world of shadows and half-remembered images. Fraser, a police psychologist, follows Vanning obsessively, and soon realises he is inextricably linked to his adversary. Noting Vanning's fragmented personality, a perplexed Fraser tells his wife, "He's a killer and yet he's not a killer."[24] Suffering from blackouts and hallucinations, Vanning is "beside himself" enough to know that he must "get away from the negative side. Too much of it would lead to complete fear, and if he ever reached that point he might just as well take gas. Defeat was a whirlpool, and the only thing to do was swim away from it. . . ".[25]

Feigning compassion, Fraser, acting in a professional capacity, seeks to exploit Vanning. Capturing Vanning means he will receive not only the accolades of his peers, but also a reward and a promotion, which would allow him to be an even more upstanding member of the middle class. Yet his pursuit of Vanning causes the police psychologist to question his own identity: "There was so much he didn't know about Vanning. There was so much he didn't know about other men . . . So many madmen were walking around and fooling people."[26]

Conversely, Vanning's paranoia extends to the world Fraser inhabits, making the mere mention of bourgeois life cause for anxiety. When a surrealist artist confides in him about his marriage, Vanning, perhaps in deference to the artist's aesthetics, constructs his own fantasy marriage, insisting it is not without its problems. Given his fanciful nature, Vanning is unable to halt his flashbacks and hallucinations:

> A strange quiet became a bubble growing larger in the center of the table, and he could see through the bubble. He could see her face, and that was as far as he could see. It frightened him, and he didn't know why. There was no reason for fright. The situation held no immediate danger. But he was frightened, and gradually . . . he realized that it was not Martha he feared . . . And it was not the police. It was himself.[27]

With the absolution of past crimes, including those committed during the war, dependent on their recollection, Vanning's memory returns and he recalls where he dumped the money. This, in turn, allows Vanning miraculously to overcome his paranoia, expunge his criminal past and re-establish his crumbling identity.

In Goodis's world, men and women relate to one another on a primeval level. Here women aggravate male paranoia, which is in keeping with reports that Goodis, when frequenting jazz clubs on LA's Central Avenue, would search for large black women who were not averse to knocking him around.[28] Not surprisingly, Goodis's male protagonists cannot easily relate to women, who assume the role of *wife* or *waif*. Though both are one-sided *femmes fatales*, the wife is invariably a man-eater and a mother figure, while the waif is a surrogate daughter, sister and virgin. Inducing fear through sexuality, the wife is voluptuous, rapacious, foul-mouthed, and faithful to the protagonist so long as she believes he is faithful to her. Often more in love with the bottle than the man, the waif's tragic past makes her incapable of love. Though Goodis's heroes attach themselves to wives, whose sexuality they find erotic and repulsive, they fall in love with waifs, resulting in temporary liaisons that are asexual and obsessional.

In *Cassidy's Girl*, published in 1951 and the most popular of Goodis's novels, paranoia regarding women pushes the protagonist towards violence: "He wanted to open the door and rush downstairs and smash their laughter down their throats. His hand went up and found the cord that switched on the light, and he took a few steps toward the door. Then it occurred to him that they weren't worth it."[29] Married to Mildred, a voluptuous and powerful woman capable of dominating her husband physically, sexually and psychologically, Cassidy's sado-masochism only aggravates his paranoia:

> She sent the lighted cigarette against his bare chest and he
> didn't feel it. She scratched him again, she was punching and
> kicking but he didn't feel any of it . . . He threw her down flat
> on the cot . . . She tried to bite his hand and he took it away
> from her face and then his hands were on her wrists. She
> fought and fought, but his knees pushed hard against her
> thighs. She screamed and her screams clashed with the roaring
> of the storm and the wild clatter of the rain.[30]

For Cassidy, sex with Mildred is possible only after they fight, a situation he finds humiliating and stimulating: "He knew he was disappointed because the battle hadn't continued. Of course, he told himself, that didn't make sense. But then there were very few elements in his life with Mildred that made sense."[31] Unable to escape, Cassidy "stood looking at this woman to whom he had been married for almost four years, with whom he slept in the same bed every night, but what he saw was not a mate. He saw a harsh and biting and downright unbearable obsession."[32]

At Lundy's, Cassidy meets the waif-like alcoholic Doris: "She was looking at the glass as though it were the page of a book and she were reading a story."[33] Not surprisingly, Doris is Mildred's opposite: "The curves of her body were mild, scarcely apparent . . . and she was so . . . pitifully thin. And yet, that in itself was a stimulus for his need to caress her, to give her something of his strength."[34]

Yet Cassidy has little strength to give. With his desire for Mildred proportionate to his self-loathing, Cassidy's paranoia is rooted in a culture that entraps men as well as women. Though Goodis is not interested in exploring political or psychological states, Cassidy, coming from a middle-class family with high expectations, is unable to live with failure. Meanwhile, in Goodis's world, a single event in the past often causes debilitating problems in the future. Thus Doris's alcoholism is the result of her having accidentally set her home alight, killing her husband and children, while Cassidy's loss of self is caused by his having piloted an airplane that crashes and kills its passengers. As the lone survivor, Cassidy is blamed for the accident. Drifting from town to town and job to job, Cassidy has been working as a stevedore in Philadelphia. Mildred finds him a job driving a bus, which allows him to regain a degree of self-respect:

> He knew he had lost the ability to control Cassidy, and certainly he would never be able to control Mildred, but there was one thing left in this world that he could and would control. The one thing that was real, that had meaning stability and purpose . . . It was only an old, battered, broken-down bus, but it was a damn good bus.[35]

But disaster strikes again. As Cassidy is about to drive a group of children to school, Haney boards the bus. Drinking from a flask, he spills whiskey over Cassidy and the bus goes out of control, killing every child. Unable to explain himself, Cassidy runs away. When Mildred finally locates him, she claims Cassidy as her property just as Cassidy had once declared that Mildred belonged to him. The battle between the sexes, according to Goodis, often reverses the dynamics of power in the culture at large. As he assesses what little is left of his identity, Cassidy says, "I'm a letdown artist. I build it up and then I cut the rope and I let it fall down."[36] Though he'd like to run away with Doris, he knows his love for her is doomed: "His pity for Doris had been the reflection of pity that he felt for himself. His need for Doris had been the need to find something worth-while . . . within himself . . . She was perfectly and permanently married to her lover, the bottle."[37] This is Goodis the fatalist, whose characters are trapped in a nightmare from which they can't escape.

Goodis portrays the criminal gang – invariably murderous and inept – as an extended and somewhat dysfunctional family whose problems range from adultery to incest. But it's the relationship between gang members as much as the crimes they commit that exacerbates the paranoia and propels the narrative. Published in 1953 by Lion and adapted for the screen a decade later by Goodis's friend Paul Wendkos, *The Burglar* is another gem of a novel whose every line is drenched in emotion, and whose characters are moved towards their inevitable demise. Here Goodis centres on a group of second-rate house robbers headed by Harbin, whose precarious mental state relates to his feelings for Gladden to whom he is a surrogate father and brother. But his relationship with Gladden and the gang is undermined when he meets Della, a shakedown artist: "[O]ne side of Della was drawn to him . . . and the other side was out to louse him up."[38]

Realizing that her intentions are as criminal as they are amorous, Harbin is so hurt that he decides he'd rather torture Della than merely kill her:

> This was . . . the worst thing any man could do to any
> woman . . . because he was rejecting her without qualifying the
> rejection, throwing her into a gully of dismay, watching her
> flounder and choke, her brain seething, trying to reach reason

PULP CULTURE

while he held the reason just a trifle out of her reach.[39]

Allowing his emotions to get in the way, Harbin is about to transgress the limits of acceptable crime.

Moreover, Harbin is about to contradict the advice given to him by Gladden's father who passed on to him the art of burglary and his philosophy of crime. Here Goodis's preoccupation with crime and paranoia merge:

[E]very animal, including the human being, is a criminal, and every move in life is a part of the vast process of crime . . . If a man decided to be a burglar . . . and made his hauls with smoothness and finesse, with accuracy and artistic finish, and got away with the haul, then he was . . . an honorable man. But the haul had to be made correctly, and the risks had to be faced with calm and icy nerve, and if associates were involved, the associates had to be treated fairly, the negotiations with the fence had to be straight . . . There was no such thing as just a burglar. There were scientific burglars and daredevil burglars . . . There were gentle burglars . . . and of course there were the low-down sons of bitches who were never content unless they followed it up with a blackjack or switchblade or bullet.[40]

Though he sends her away, Harbin's feelings for Gladden remain unchanged: 'It was more than habit and it was deeper than inclination. It was something on the order of a religion, or sublimating himself to a special drug. The root of everything was this throbbing need to take care of Gladden."[41] In another example of Goodis's obsession with fated love, Harbin tells Gladden that circumstances have brought her back to the gang. But Gladden says, "No, not circumstances. You."[42] Even Della recognizes Harbin's unnatural obsession: "You're controlled by a dead man . . . His ideas became your ideas. His life became your life . . . his daughter became your daughter."[43] Not that Harbin and Gladden are oblivious to the semi-incestuous nature of their relationship: "He knew it was Gerald . . . causing him to say it as he said, 'I love you, Gladden.' "[44] When, after killing Della's accomplice, Gladden and Harbin attempt to swim away from trouble, Gladden says, "You hold me as if I'm a child and you're my father."[45] In the "center of nothingness",[46] Gladden drowns herself. Trying unsuccessfully to save her, Harbin, because it's "the honorable thing to do",[47] drowns himself as well.

Sometimes it's purely a matter of circumstance and environment. Goodis's *The Moon In The Gutter*, published in 1953 by Gold Medal and adapted for the screen in 1984 by Jean-Jacques Beineix, is a bleak but lyrical narrative set in the dockland slums of Philadelphia where love goes unconsummated and happiness can only be found in a bottle. To Bill Kerrigan, the neighbourhood reminds him of his sister who, after being raped, slit her throat with a razor, and whose blood stains Vernon Street. Unable to erase her bloodstains from his mind, Kerrigan is horrified when slumming socialite Loretta Channing insists the docks are "breath-taking":

> Take a closer look . . . See that green stuff? That's bilge from the holds of the ships. There's nothing dirtier. If it gets on your skin it crawls right through you. You never get it off you, no matter how hard you scrub. The smell . . . I'm only trying to give you the full picture. You come down to see the dirt, I'm showing you the dirt.[48]

Though supposedly apolitical, Goodis is perceptive in noting that the differences in social class invariably alter perception and generate paranoia.

In fact, Loretta Channing terrifies Kerrigan. Not only is she from another social class, Kerrigan associates her sexuality with his sister's death. Again Goodis equates incest with social immobility. Driven over the edge by his sister's death, Kerrigan allows himself to be controlled by Channing just as the rich invariably control the poor:

The need was so intense that he wondered what kept him from taking her into his arms. Then all at once he knew what it was. It was something deeper than hunger of the flesh. He wanted to reach her heart, her spirit. And his brain seethed with bitterness as he thought, That ain't what she wants. All she's out for is a cheap thrill.[49]

When Loretta shows up at pier and takes a photo of him, Kerrigan is insulted: 'You'll show it to your uptown friends. Picture of a man, stripped almost naked, like something on exhibition in a cage."[50] But, drawn by the thought of what he cannot have, Kerrigan is eventually seduced by Loretta. "It was like soft music drifting through the dream. And the dream was taking him away from everything he'd known, every tangible segment of the world he lived in."[51]

Though Kerrigan marries Loretta, they never share a bed. But it's Kerrigan's step-sister and would-be wife, Bella, who reminds him that Loretta has dumped him because she comes from a different social class:

The groom brings her to a house with the plaster chipping off the walls and the furniture coming apart and empty beer bottles all over the floor. It's a wonder she let herself sit on the sofa. This afternoon she'll be taking her dress to the cleaners . . . Another thing she'll do, she'll go to a beauty parlor and have her hair washed, an extra soaping just to make sure. After all, in these Vernon rat traps you never know, you can pick up anything.[52]

Without even the sense of the local whore who returns the engagement ring given to her by Loretta's brother, Kerrigan finally comes to his senses, telling Loretta: "We don't ride the same track. I can't live your kind of life and you can't live mine. It ain't anyone's fault. It's just the way the cards are stacked."[53] Walking out of Dugan's Bar, he returns home and assumes his place, yelling at Bella, "Get up . . . Make me some supper."[54]

Magnanimous regarding the Channings' propensity for slumming, the locals liken it to "a kind of ulcer in the head that gives him loony ideas . . . most of us are sick with it, one way or another. There ain't a man alive who don't have any problems."[55] As for who raped Kerrigan's sister, it's just something that happens to those unlucky enough to be caught outside when the moon shines on Vernon Street:

> [N]o matter where the weaker ones were hiding, they'd never get away from the Vernon moon. It had them trapped . . . Sooner or later they'd be mauled and battered and crushed. They'd learn the hard way that Vernon Street was no place for delicate bodies or timid souls.[56]

Yet the more Goodis's characters are haunted by their pasts, the more beatifically paranoid they become. Likewise, there is amongst Goodis's winos and derelicts a minimal amount of paranoia and a degree of democracy discounting the exigencies of ekeing out a marginal existence. At least that's the case in *Street of No Return*, also published in 1954, which begins when ex-singer Whitey, who is allowed to commit "slow-motion suicide",[57] goes off in search of a bottle of wine. Having stopped a race riot and been beaten up by the police, Whitey regains his identity enough to comment on the masochism involved in living on the edge: "You've played a losing game and actually enjoyed the idea of losing, almost like them freaks who get their kicks when they're banged around."[58] Finally returning with a bottle, Whitey and his friends find a wall to protect them from a cold wet wind. They have taken a long time to go nowhere and are now benignly indifferent: "They sat there passing the bottle around, and there was nothing that could bother them, nothing at all."[59] Paranoid regarding women and fearful of being pursued for past crimes, Goodis's defeated protagonists survive, only to keep on keeping on. As poetic investigations of the Cold War era, Goodis's fiction delves into the turbulent and troubled lives of those living on society's margins. Displaced and constantly questioning themselves, they represent an America unsure of its future. Hardly realistic, Goodis's fiction contains a tortured beauty that can take one's breath away. He may not have been Dashiell Hammett. But then Hammett was no David Goodis.

Chester Himes

If Goodis's literary paranoia can be extrapolated from a short quote, it is from a lengthy sentence – courtesy of the Ohio State Prison System – that Chester Himes's literary paranoia can be located. Indicting pre-war society and its treatment of African Americans, Himes would claim that "[n]othing happened in prison that I had not already encountered in outside life".[60] Yet serving seven and a half years for the armed robbery of a suburban couple shaped his life and writing:

> I knew that my prison term had left its scars, I knew that many aspects of prison life had made deep impressions on my subconscious, but now I cannot distinctly recall what they are or should have been. I find it necessary to read what I have written in the past about my prison experiences to recall any part of them.[61]

Paradoxically, being so "beside himself" that he could not recall his imprisonment gave Himes a blank sheet on which to write. Not that Himes was the only black writer to be paranoid or published in the era of pulp culture. The likes of Richard Wright, Ralph Ellison, Willard Motley and James Baldwin also had their "hurt" placed on paperback stands. But, spanning the era of pulp culture, Himes's writing is a virtual history of the US from the Depression through the 1960s, from his early prison stories to his Harlem-set novels.

Referring to Camus's statement "racism is absurd", Himes would imply that his paranoia was the result of an absurd, but not uncommon, situation: being black and in prison. Says Himes, "Realism and absurdity are so similar in the lives of American blacks one can not tell the difference."[62] With his mental state provoked by racism, Himes's work is more realistic, though no less personal, than the work of Goodis or Thompson.

Paroled in 1937, his inability to publish *Black Sheep*, a novel he wrote in prison, contributed to Himes's dis-ease: "When speaking of the reactions of Americans to my writing, I talked compulsively with sudden outbursts of paranoia."[63] Later, critics found it difficult to deal with Himes's anger, as well as the violence and politics of his work. But his 1947 *The Lonely Crusade*, with its ambivalent portrayal of the Communist Party – and its attempt to shift the politics of race away from leftist dogma – troubled the left as much as it did the literary establishment. Even Himes's wife, having read his portrayal of her, is said to have threatened divorce. Despite the modicum of notoriety derived from his 1946 *If He Hollers Let Him Go*, Himes was denied a George Washington Carver Memorial Award because, according to Himes, a Doubleday editor had been nauseated by the book.[64] Yet *If He Hollers Let Him Go* and *Lonely Crusade*, in which Himes's protagonists suffer such sexual anxiety they must incessantly assert their virility, were less offensive to critics than Himes's portrayal of prison homosexuality in his novel *Cast The First Stone*.

While Goodis could go to Hollywood and feel displaced, and Thompson could move there and become an inebriated rewrite man on the *Mirror*, for African Americans like Himes, Langston Hughes and Countee Cullen, LA was a nightmare. Says protagonist Bob Jones in *If He Hollers Let Him Go* – arguably the most accurate novel about being black in wartime Los Angeles – "It was the look on the people's faces when you asked them about a job. Most of 'em didn't say outright they wouldn't hire me. They just looked so goddamned startled that I'd even asked . . .".[65] A decade prior to the Supreme Court's Brown vs the Board of Education decision, LA for Himes was a metaphorical prison. Having taken twenty-three jobs in essential industries, he admits that living in wartime LA had taken its toll:

Los Angeles hurt me racially as much as any city I have ever
known . . . It was the lying hypocrisy that hurt me . . . Up to the
age of thirty-one I had been hurt emotionally, spiritually, and
physically as much as thirty-one years can bear . . . and still I
was entire, complete, functional; my mind was sharp, my
reflexes good, and I was not bitter. But under the mental
corrosion of race prejudice in Los Angeles I had become bitter
and saturated with hate.[66]

If He Hollers Let Him Go is the story of Bob Jones, an African
American who works as a leaderman in a southern California
wartime shipyard. Like Lee Gordon in *Lonely Crusade*, Jones is a
walking time bomb. Well educated but frustrated because he
cannot find appropriate employment, his paranoia comes from
living in enemy territory, not knowing where the next attack
will come from, or upon whom he will vent his anger. Not that
white racists are Jones's only enemy. For he is equally scathing
about the black bourgeoisie, particularly the middle-class father
of his girlfriend: "He was the kind of pompous little guy you'd
expect to have a hyphenated name, one of the richest Negroes
in the city if not on the whole West Coast."[67] Leading a life that
is both true and false, Jones cannot help being "beside himself".
Given LA's racism, including a curfew for blacks and segregated
seating at nightclubs, Jones has good reason to be paranoid.
    In fact, his condition engulfs him from the moment he awakes:

It came along with consciousness. It moved slowly underneath
my head first, somewhere back of my closed eyes, moved slowly
underneath my skull to the base of my brain, cold and hollow.
It seeped down my spine, into my arms, spread through my
groin with an almost sexual torture, settled in my stomach like
butterfly wings. For a moment I felt torn all loose inside,
shrivelled, paralysed, as if after a while I'd have to get up and
die.[68]

Not surprisingly, Jones's mental state soon affects his health: "I
lost twenty pounds in two weeks and my hands got to

trembling . . . I was even scared to tell anybody. If I'd gone to a psychiatrist he'd have had to put me away."[69]

Aware of the politics of race, Jones reduces it to a personal issue, saying, "Race was a handicap, sure, I'd reasoned. But hell, I didn't have to marry it. I went where I wanted and felt good about it."[70] Though he knows a black person is tolerated only as long as he stays in his place, Jones, despite attempts to toe the line – finding the right woman and having acceptable social aspirations – can't help breaking the rules, including his obsessive pursuit of Madge, a redneck who has trouble written all over her. After a series of racist indignities, his paranoia increases: "I was tensed every moment to spring."[71] Soon Jones wonders whether he should fight or switch: "I was tired of being ready to die every minute; it was too much strain. I had to fight hard enough each day just to keep on living. All I wanted was for the white folks to let me alone; not to say anything to me; not even look at me."[72]

Managing to hold on to his humanity, Jones stops short of raping Madge. Nevertheless, he is arrested and offered the choice of enlisting in the army or going to prison. Jones chooses the former, and joins other men of colour facing the inequities of the armed forces, and the likelihood of dying overseas. In effect, Jones has merely exchanged one prison for another.

From the rage of *If He Hollers Let Him Go* to the displaced criminality of *Cotton Comes to Harlem*, Himes, the former criminal and ex-con, was well positioned to develop the contradictions of pulp culture paranoia. But it was while in France during the late 1950s that Himes, encouraged by Série Noire editor Marcel Duhamel – "We don't give a damn who's thinking what – only what they're doing"[73] – began writing his famous Harlem detective novels. In fact Himes, while in prison, had subscribed to *Black Mask* and was well acquainted with hardboiled fiction. Moreover, in the 1930s, he was already dabbling in the genre, producing amongst other works a story, "He Knew", about a pair of black detectives. Encouraged by the response of the

French, the Harlem novels would become a long-term project. Though considered an invaluable portrait of urban ghetto life, Himes's Harlem is, nevertheless, an imaginary space:

> I didn't really know what it was like to be a citizen of Harlem; I had never worked there, raised children there, been hungry, sick or poor there. I had been as much of a tourist as a white man . . . The Harlem of my books was never meant to be real; I never called it real; I just wanted to take it away from the white man if only in my books.[74]

Even in these novels, paranoia remains an underlying, though less dominant, theme. Not surprisingly, Himes's detectives – Coffin Ed Johnson and Grave Digger Jones – are trapped by their colour, community, culture and employment. In their enforcement of the law, they personify social disorder disguised as order.[75] Yet they know the real criminals are not the small-time Harlem crooks and hustlers, but those with real money and power. Himes's shift from confessional to hardboiled fiction indicates the pressure placed on black writers. Yet Himes's detective novels, as well as denoting the final days of pulp culture, signify the changes that would occur in the black communities during the 1960s.

Published in 1957, *A Rage in Harlem* – originally titled *For Love of Imabelle* – is Himes's first Coffin Ed and Grave Digger novel. It is also Himes's only Harlem detective novel to be published in the US before appearing in France. And in 1991 it would be adapted for the screen by Bill Duke, whose glossy Harlem appears to be more influenced by Expressionist painter Edward Burra than Himes. *A Rage in Harlem* is also noteworthy for its humour and accessibility. Accordingly, the novel opens with a hilarious scene of jive alchemy, as Hank puts Jackson's money in the oven to transmute his bills from low to high denomination. Interrupted by a phoney law officer, Jackson pleads for leniency: "I'm a church man, I ain't dishonest. I confess I put up the money for Hank to raise, but it was him who was breaking the law, not me. I ain't done nothing wouldn't nobody do if they had a chance to make a pile of money." He envisions a prison term and the loss of his girlfriend:

> If he went to prison . . . she'd have another man and would have forgotten all about him. He'd come out of prison an old man, thirty-eight years old, dried up. No one would give him a job. No woman would want him. He'd be a bum, hungry, skinny, begging on the streets of Harlem, sleeping in doorways, drinking canned heat to keep warm.[76]

Though they make a late entrance in this particular novel, Coffin Ed and Grave Digger will occupy a special place in Himes's mythical Harlem. In the tradition of black tricksters and folk heroes like Honky-Tonk Bud,[77] the two detectives quickly become the stuff of legends: "Folks in Harlem believed that Grave Digger Jones and Coffin Ed Johnson would shoot a man stone dead for not standing straight in line."[78] Existing on the edge of criminality, they are prepared to use illegal means if and when necessary. As the narrator in *A Rage in Harlem* says, "They took their tribute, like all real cops, from the established underworld catering to the essential needs of the people." Despite their criminal methods, Grave Digger and Coffin Ed have a vested interest in maintaining the peace, telling those who work their beat to "Keep it cool . . . Don't make graves."[79]

But in Himes's Harlem anyone possessing anything has cause to be paranoid. When Jackson flashes a wad of bills in a crowded bar, every unsavoury character in Harlem closes in: "[T]he whores got there first, pressing their wares so hard against Jackson he couldn't tell whether they were soliciting or trying to dispose of surplus merchandise. The pickpockets were trying to break through. The muggers waited at the door."[80] When Goldy – Jackson's nun-impersonating dope-fiend brother – is hurt in a fight, his scream adds to the soundtrack accompanying Harlem's theatre of violence:

Shaking plaster from the ceilings . . . the rats between the walls, the cockroaches crawling over kitchen sinks and leftover food; shaking the sleeping flies hibernating in lumps like bees behind the casings of the windows. Shaking the fat, blood-filled bedbugs crawling over black skin. Shaking the fleas, making them hop. Shaking the sleeping dogs in their filthy pallets, the sleeping cats, the clogged toilets, loosening the filth.[81]

The Big Gold Dream, published in 1960, opens with another example of Himes's wicked humour. At Sweet Prophet Brown's revival meeting, Alberta testifies about her dream: "I was baking three apple pies . . . And when I took them out the oven and set on the table to cool the crusts busted open like three explosions and the whole kitchen was filled with hundred dollar bills."[82] Donating $50 to her church, Alberta, about to be baptized, is given water blessed by Sweet Prophet. She falls into a trance and is pronounced dead. Sweet Prophet must do some quick thinking, for "[n]ot only his career as an evangelist, but his personal fortune was at stake".[83]

In *The Big Gold Dream*, Himes portrays not only Harlem's religious scam artists, but also the relationships between the black community and the dwindling Jewish population of Harlem. When Rufus, Alberta's husband, sells his wife's furniture supposedly to pay for her funeral, the Jewish dealer offers a paltry sum. Removing his false teeth, Rufus says he might sell them as well. Examining Rufus's mouth, the Jewish dealer says, "Holy Mackerel, you got a red tongue, blue gums and white teeth . . . If anybody calls you a Communist, you just open your mouth and show them your national colors."[84] Not surprisingly, given Harlem's history, there's a hint of anti-Semitism when, after the dealer notices the mattress has already been ripped open, Rufus says, "Us colored folks ain't got no money to hide. You Jews got it all."[85] Though after the negotiations, Rufus and the Jew sit down and eat helpings of alligator tails and rice, washed down with beer: "By the time they had cleaned the pot, everybody felt lovey-dovey."[86]

After Rufus robs and kills the Jew, he himself is murdered. For this is capitalism at its most basic, in a culture where entrepreneurism and survival go hand in hand. At least this is the case with rent parties. Whereas during the Depression house parties were a common way for people to pay their rent, "most had quit the practice as industrial jobs opened to colored people and pay for domestic work increased".[87]

When it is discovered that Alberta is not dead, Coffin Ed and Grave Digger interrogate her. For, amongst the police, only they can read the community's signs and narrative. As for the white sergeant, Frick, "Every time he came to Harlem on a case, he got a violent headache."[88] Though "most people in Harlem consider the police as public enemies",[89] Coffin Ed and Grave Digger command respect. After all, they are part of the community. But they also generate fear. One look at Coffin Ed's acid-scarred face and you know he can be "as dangerous as a rattlesnake".[90] In fact, the scar is part of the legend that makes Ed the cop that he is. When Grave Digger asks Coffin Ed why he has no sense of humour, Grave Digger replies, "They burned it out of me."[91] Not dissimilar to the changing conditions and mood in Harlem, when the house-party humour of Red Foxx and Louis Jordan gave way to the anger and militant politics of the mid 1960s.

Having lost everything, and in a culture in which women control domestic life, Alberta's conniving boyfriend Sugar, becomes so marginal that even Harlem's rejects reject him:

> The jokers he played tonk with didn't have any more than he had . . . and that was only what their women gave them; and he knew they wouldn't lend him any if they had. He didn't have anything valuable enough to sell. He didn't have the talent to pick pockets, if there had been anybody's pocket to pick. He didn't have the nerve to rob anybody. He wasn't strong enough to mug.[92]

To find the murderer, Coffin Ed and Grave Digger follow a

line of enquiry suitable only in places where money is scarce. Coffin Ed says: "Let's find somebody with a roll of fresh money and work back from that."[93] Meanwhile, the task is simplified by the detectives' knowledge regarding the dynamics of religion. Figuring the murderer must have heard Alberta talk about her dream at the baptism, they know that "[a]ll kinds of hustlers hung around Sweet Prophet's activities, hoping some of the Prophet's money would fall off".[94]

Grave Digger and Coffin Ed's sole ally is Lieutenant Anderson. He depends on them even though he realizes they have their "own personal interpretation of law enforcement". Indeed they do, for Grave Digger and Coffin Ed turn a blind eye to "houses of prostitution, operators of orderly gambling games, people connected with the numbers racket, streetwalkers who stayed in their district. But they were rough on criminals of violence and confidence men . . . dope peddlers and pimps."[95] And as for Dummy – a deaf-mute, ex-boxer, now a pimp – they say, "If he didn't do that he would do something worse . . . He can't talk and he can't hear. He probably could get a job as a porter or a dishwasher; but he won't do that. He has been in the chips, and he figures those jobs are degrading." Ignoring the damage inflicted on women by Harlem's thriving sex industry, Grave Digger and Coffin Ed, still on the subject of Dummy, reveal their political shortcomings: "If these chippies don't work for him, they will work for some other pimp. At least he treats them better than most pimps would . . . And when a chippie makes up her mind to be a whore, there is no stopping her."[96] After all, Grave Digger and Coffin Ed are cops and, as such, work for the state, their function being to push the narrative, investigate the crime, fire their pistols and pick up the pieces.

The Heat's On, published in 1961 in France and five years later in the US, has an equally humorous opening. After setting off a fire alarm, Pinky, a giant black albino half-wit, and a white hunchback drug-dealing dwarf meet in the middle of a white neighbourhood. As the fire engines arrive, Pinky asks the dwarf,

"You're my friend, ain't you?" When they realize it's a false alarm, the firemen physically assault Pinky, and a white policeman pulls out his pistol and takes aim. Fortunately, Coffin Ed intervenes, saying, "You can't kill a man for putting in a false alarm."[97]

Aware that the economics of racism breeds suspicion and fear, Coffin Ed and Grave Digger, investigating Pinky's claim that his father has been murdered, realize they are being watched by white residents living in the apartment block where Pinky's father worked as a caretaker. Ed says, "They think we're burglars". Grave Digger replies, "Hell, what else are they going to think about two spooks like us prowling about in a white neighborhood in the middle of the night? . . . If I was to see two white men in Harlem at this time of night I'd figure they were looking for whores." Coffin Ed says, "You would be right", to which Grave Digger replies, "No more than them".[98]

Meanwhile, back in Harlem, the air is rife for crime and riots:

> It was too hot to sleep. Everyone was too evil to love. And it was too noisy to relax and dream of cool swimming holes . . .
> The night was filled with the blare of countless radios, the frenetic blasting of spasm cats playing in the streets, hysterical laughter, automobile horns, strident curses, loudmouthed arguments, the screams of knife fights.[99]

Significantly, the only difference between Harlem's streetfighters and the two detectives is that the latter are state employees. They have to make a living, and are aware of the hazards. Coffin Ed puts it bluntly, saying, "Blink once and you're dead", while Grave Digger adds, "Blink twice and you're buried".[100]

After the dwarf dies of a ruptured spleen, the detectives are charged with police brutality. "Routine procedure," says Grave Digger about the blows to the stomach which cause the dwarf's death. When the assistant DA reminds them their duty is to maintain the peace, and leave punishment to the courts, Coffin Ed says, "Peace at what price?", while Grave Digger adds, "You think you can have a peaceful city letting criminals run loose?"

The assistant DA says, "You've killed a man suspected of a minor crime, and not in self defense." Says an angry Grave Digger, "All the crimes committed by addicts . . . All the fucked-up lives . . . All the nice kids sent down hooked for life . . . that one lousy drug has murdered more people than Hitler. And you call it *minor*!"[101]

Nevertheless, the detectives are suspended. Anderson, like any good cop, blames the liberal press:

> We're suffering from the customary summer slack in the news. It'll blow over . . . The papers are on one of their periodic humanitarian kicks . . .
> "Yeah, humanitarian," Grave Digger said bitterly. "It's all right to kill a few colored people for trying to get their children an education, but don't hurt a mother-raping white punk for selling dope."[102]

In this narrative faith healer Heavenly Sister and her assistant Uncle Saint occupy a central position. As though indicating the extent to which he has lost his identity, Uncle Saint says, "Boy, I been throwing my voice so long I don't know where it's at anymore myself."[103] Here again Himes conveys his antipathy regarding religion. However, the state is another matter. A woman warns Pinky that two white policemen are in a bar he's about to enter: "She didn't know him from Adam's tomcat, but it was a rigid code of colored people in Harlem to stick together against white cops; they were quick to warn one another when white cops were around."[104] But Grave Digger has been wounded and Coffin Ed, armed and drugged, seeks retribution rather than rapport. On the warpath, he raids every shooting gallery in Harlem: "He was not a narcotics man; he didn't even have a shield. His entrance was illegal and he had no authority."[105]

By incorporating the language of the streets – modified for mass consumption – Himes indicates the era's concerns and the relationship between language and power. As Coffin Ed listens to his car radio:

A mealy-mouthed male voice . . . blabbed about domestic politics, the Cold War, what the Africans were doing, the latest on the civil rights front and a fistfight between two motion picture actors in El Morocco . . . The voice . . . blabbed on: ". . . when Queen Elizabeth passed over the bridge . . ." It sounded to Coffin Ed as though he said "when Queen Elizabeth *pissed* over the bridge . . ." and he wondered what did she do that for.[106]

After which Coffin Ed hears the news that Grave Digger is dead.

Despite the nature of the market for which he was writing, Himes tries to avoid over-romanticising black urban life. There is nothing pretty about Sister Heavenly disembowelling a dog in an attempt to reach a cache of drugs. However, neither is it entirely realistic. When Coffin Ed cuts the throat of a woman from whom he wants information, Himes, realizing the sensationalism of his subject matter, says, "He knew that he had gone beyond the line; that he had gone outside human restraint; he knew what he was doing was unforgiveable. But he didn't want any more lies."[107] When she offers to be Coffin Ed's slave, he says, "Is everybody crooked on this mother-raping earth? . . . You think because I'm a cop I've got a price."[108] Meanwhile, reports of Grave Digger's death have been greatly exaggerated, the police having spread the news merely to push Coffin Ed into action. Not that Coffin Ed is bothered by their unscrupulous behaviour. For it affords him the opportunity to note the resilience of his partner and, by implication, black culture: "Sometimes these minstrel shows play on when grand opera folds."[109]

Yet Coffin Ed remains concerned about the public's attitude towards the police: "Folks just don't want to believe that what we're trying to do is make a decent peaceful city for people to live in . . . People think we enjoy being tough, shooting people and knocking them in the head."[110] Unfortunately, Coffin Ed doesn't understand that he and his partner are on the wrong side. Having been contaminated by the state, no one trusts them.

Better off as private detectives, Coffin Ed and Grave Digger work inside the law by going outside it. Hiding behind their badges, they are on a personal mission, pursuing drug dealers, murderers and con artists. With a healthy tolerance for small-time crooks, neither addresses himself to the real criminals – those who control Harlem politically and economically – nor the origin of crime.

Despite the power of his narratives and his scathing attack on white culture, Himes's adherence to neatly concluded narratives reveals a structural, and political, weakness. Perhaps for spatial reasons, Himes tends to summarize, rather than depict, vital portions of his plot, giving the impression that he is more interested in order, law and pacification than radical social change. Encouraging voyeurism, Himes is often willing to provide his readers with a safety net, ignoring the fact that people kill for no reason, that justice is rarely done, or that some crime cannot be easily explained. Accessible to black and white readers, Himes's detective novels tend to be more conservative than they appear; but, at the same time, they portray a racist culture in a non-doctrinaire manner. Because his detectives do not investigate the origins of crime, Himes, perhaps for the sake of his audience, chooses to target drug dealers and con artists rather than make a thorough investigation of racism and that which produces and perpetuates it. Nevertheless, Himes was able to move the pulp culture hardboiled novel on to new political ground, maintaining that paranoia is the result of a specific state crime.

Jim Thompson

The smalltown greasy-spoon world of Jim Thompson is filled with monsters, real and imaginary. But the origin of Jim Thompson's literary paranoia can be found in the legacy of Manifest Destiny. Taking paranoia to an extreme, Thompson, born and raised in Oklahoma, explores the dark side of the Continental Divide. There he creates his warped characters. At first barely recognizable, they soon become uncomfortably familiar. For Thompson's literary paranoia finds expression through the manner in which his characters impose their delusions. In Thompson's fiction anything is possible, as his investigations disclose a world where sanity and insanity, right and wrong, good and evil, are indistinguishable; where external manifestations are used to explain the horrors of life ordinarily thought to be internal to those manifestations.

Not hitting his literary stride until the 1950s, when he was in his late forties, Thompson's fascination with paranoia might equally have been due to his intermittent financial insecurity. Though all he ever wanted to do was write, Thompson found it necessary over the years to work on oil rigs and in factories and to find employment as a baker, bellboy, caddy and newspaperman. No stranger to jails or hospitals, and having had numerous bouts with the bottle, Thompson's identity underwent various gut-wrenching permutations, such as his claim to have written his first novel, *Now and On Earth*, to obtain money for his father's release from an institution, only to learn on receiving a cheque for his book of his father's suicide.[111]

Thompson's investigation of paranoia could also have been the result of his involvement with the Communist Party. According to his sister, Freddie:

> Jimmie briefly belonged to the Communist Party in Oklahoma, those people were really, really smart and liked him . . . he didn't realize he could get himself in trouble . . . he just enjoyed talking to people on his level . . . Later, when he became intimidated to be more into it . . . we left San Diego. Later he was always a little afraid (it would hurt him), but it never came out.[112]

However, Thompson's politics must have warranted investigation on at least two occasions: as director of the Oklahoma Writers Project when, after coming to the defence of some Project workers who'd been dismissed, he put together a labour history of the state, including an account of a recent oilfield strike; and when, after driving west in a car belonging to a fellow Party member, he worked in a wartime factory in San Diego.

While Party involvement was sufficient cause for Thompson to leave Oklahoma, there's no indication of further political involvement. Drunk through a good part of the McCarthy era, Thompson, after working for the Los Angeles *Mirror*, was too busy for politics: if one goes by his publishing output, he was writing a novel every two months between September 1952 and June 1955. With the exception of his second novel, *Heed the Thunder*, Thompson never returns to the proletariat orientation of his early stories and sketches, exemplified by his 1931 story "Gentlemen of the Jungle": "Capital won the war... All the time Labor was out there on the front sweatin' and starvin', Capital was settin' back on his money bags, restin' and gettin' fat,"[113] Yet in novels like *Now and On Earth*, *Roughneck* and *Bad Boy*, Thompson makes use of his political past. Likewise, in portraying warped protagonists like Lou Ford or Nick Corey in *Pop. 1280*, Thompson constantly utilizes the language of prairie populism:

> We got controls all along the line, our physical make-up, our mental make-up, our backgrounds; they're all shapin' us in a certain way, fixin' us up for a certain role in life, and . . . we better play that role or fill that hole or any goddang way you want to put it or all hell is going to tumble out of the heavens and fall right down on top of us.[114]

Nevertheless Thompson, in his pulp culture writing, forsakes overt politics for an even more subversive line of attack.

The origin of Thompson's literary paranoia can also be noted in an incident that occurred in the West Texas oilfields.[115] When a deputy sheriff arrives to take a youthful Thompson to jail after failing to appear in court for disturbing the peace, Thompson, atop an oil rig, drops a section of a crown block, narrowly missing the deputy. Thompson climbs down and says he's ready to go, but the deputy looks at him and drawls, "What makes you so sure we're going anywhere?" Having unnerved Thompson, the deputy says, "Everyone knows me. No one knows you. And we're all alone . . . What do you think an ol' stupid country boy might do in a case like this?" Reading Thompson's mind, the deputy adds, "There ain't nothin' you can do with a gun that you can't do a better way." Believing he's about to be killed, Thompson apologizes, insisting he had dropped the crown block as a joke. Finally, the deputy says, "I'll tell you something . . . There ain't no way of telling what a man is by looking at him. There ain't no way of knowing what he'll do if he has the chance. You think maybe you can remember that?" Though he had wanted to write about the incident, Thompson could only make the deputy appear "solemnly irritated, not murderous". Moreover, Thompson, admitting to being "too prone to categorise – naturally, using myself as the norm", overestimates the deputy's complexity: "He had gone as far as his background and breeding would allow to be amiable. I hadn't responded to it, so he had taken another tack. It was simple once I saw things through his eyes instead of my own."[116] Almost thirty years later, Thompson was able to resurrect him as Deputy Sheriff Lou Ford, the sardonic, likeable and inscrutable murderer in *The Killer Inside Me*. Looking beyond the surface, Thompson was able to move "outside himself", to cultivate a literary detachment which enabled him to write about paranoia with greater veracity.

As early as 1946 (in his second novel, *Heed the Thunder*), Thompson examines in frightening detail the parameters of paranoia caused by incest, punishment and torture, and the ease with which a person can be turned into a psychotic killer:

> Courtland had hurt the Czeny boy more terribly than he ever knew, and when the boy reached home, he was beaten again by his father and locked in the stable for punishment . . . By morning he was raving, by that evening his head was puffed to twice its normal size; he was a festering, bleeding, sightless mess . . . When his insanity became uncontrollable, they

chained him in the cellar, and there he remained for three
months.

With love as a pretext for torture, the boy's wounds will be mental
as well as physical:

> By fall, he seemed completely normal again – except for his
> looks . . He was a monster; and a monster could not go back to
> school, he could not visit a sweetheart, he could never even as
> much as ride into town. He could only be kept out of sight, be
> hidden and given work to do. And so he was . . . And
> sometimes he would slip away from his drudgery and lie
> concealed near the road, peering at the infrequent passers-by
> out of his almost-blind eyes. Waiting . . .[117]

In fact, Thompson's fictional world has room only for victims
and paranoics. With a captive audience, Lincoln, a veteran of
the Civil War, philosophizes as he lies on his death bed:
"Hindsight's the only gift we got, except on one thing. On that,
we're all prophets . . . We know what's in the other fellow's mind.
It don't make no difference that we've never seen him before, or
whatever. We know that he's out to do us if he gets the chance."[118]
Capitalism, according to Thompson, exploits the land and its
inhabitants, while those living on the land reflect its condition.
In Thompson's world, working the land for short-term profit
inevitably results in warped individuals, rotting crops and
exhausted soil. Thus *Heed The Thunder* ends with an elegy which,
in re-stating the relationship between land and democracy, could,
but for its sense of foreboding, have been penned by a proletariat
writer during the Depression. Turning the optimism associated
with expansion into a paranoid vision of impending doom,
Thompson parodies the likes of Whitman, Wolfe and Agee:

> The good land, the bad land, the fair-to-middling land, the
> beautiful land, the ugly land, the homely land, the kind and
> hateful land; the land with its tall towers, its great barns, its
> roomy houses, its spring-pole wells, its shabby sheds, its

dugouts; the land with its little villages and towns, its . . . great cities, its blacksmith shops and factories, its one-room schools and colleges; the hunky land, the Rooshan land, the German land, the Dutch and Swede land, the Protestant and Catholic and Jewish land; the American land – the land that was slipping so surely, so swiftly, into the black abyss of the night.[119]

From this black abyss comes the paranoia that pervades Thompson's 1949 *Nothing More Than Murder*. Marking Thompson's farewell to hardcover publishing and the beginning of his paperback pulp culture career, *Nothing More Than Murder* is narrated by Joe, a psychotic who cannot control his desire for Carol, an unattractive, large-breasted woman. Here paranoia moves from effect to cause, as Carol manipulates Joe, pushing him to crime. Knowing others but unable to know himself, Joe's transgressions derive from an inability to recognize boundaries:

It wasn't the way she looked, but the way I did. Because all I'd ever seen in her was myself, the little of myself that was pitying and compassionate and unselfish or whatever you want to call it. And, now, in the ending, even that little was gone. And all that was left was what I could see here, in her eyes. Dead eyes, turning in slightly.

I shivered and tried to look away.

I thought, *They can't hang me. I'm already dead. I've been dead a long, long time.*[120]

Emerging from his drunkenness and failures of the 1940s, Thompson would publish a series of perverse and paranoid pulp culture classics. In his 1952 *Cropper's Cabin*, the dialogue is split into different voices, creating a community of paranoids in an upside-down world:

Hell, how could a man save something when he couldn't save himself? There was a great silence, and out of it came only one voice, yelling at me to run and keep on running forever.

Yelling at me not to do anything, not to try to rebuild. *You'll be disappointed, Tom. It just isn't worth the disappointment, and heartbreak. They'll never forget that trial, kid . . . They'll laugh at you; or worse, they'll pity you. And you're ignorant, uneducated, and your health isn't good and – What can you do anyway? . . . Think of everything you've got to fight. Keep thinking – that you'll lose even if you win. Then go and hide. Bury yourself. And stay buried. Run away from –* [121]

One of Thompson's best and most unnerving novels is his 1952 *The Killer Inside Me*. Here Deputy Sheriff Lou Ford is so beside himself that he must issue a psychological storm warning: "All I can do is wait until I split. Right down the middle."[122] As in many of his other novels, Thompson tacitly criticizes the psychological model of character motivation favoured at the time by Hollywood and prudent pulp culture writers. Paying lip service to popular psychology, Thompson rejects the notion that a person's actions can be explained, predicted or controlled. Just as well Thompson never offered a political line or explanation for his literary paranoia in a book such as *The Killer Inside Me*. Published in the same year that "I Was A Communist for the FBI" was being broadcast on national radio, it was not the best of times to lay one's political cards on the table.

Written in less than a month, *The Killer Inside Me*, which Burt Kennedy routinely adapted for the screen in 1976, began as a synopsis about a cop with sadistic tendencies. Though this hardly does justice to Lou Ford who, lacking an ideology to legitimize his actions, emerges as a kind of psychotic anarchist or trickster. A victim of circumstances and heredity, he exists in a dark and solipsistic world, seeking retribution by parody and sublimation. Thus his cliché-ridden conversation. "I began needling people in that dead-pan way . . . as a substitute for something else."[123]

No matter how hard he tries, Ford cannot comprehend his paranoia. Gradually it's clear his condition is linked to a boyhood sado-masochistic relationship with the family's housekeeper. Because Lou's father had been involved in a similar relationship with the same woman, Lou, spying on them, had concluded that such behaviour must be normal. Learning of Lou's relationship, his father's reproach throws Lou into a world of uncertainty. When Lou sexually assaults a young girl, for which his brother takes the blame, Ford's father must make a tough decision about his son's future:

> Dad had wanted me to be a doctor, but he was afraid to have me go away to school so he'd done what he could for me at home. It used to irritate him, knowing what I had in my head, to hear me talking and acting like any other rube around town. But, in time, when he realized how bad I had *the sickness*, he even encouraged me to do it. That's what I was going to be; I was going to have to live and get along with the rubes.[124]

With all avenues of escape closed, Ford must assume the role of a dumb small town deputy sheriff.

Unable to differentiate between his inner and outer self, he consults his father's medical texts, discovering: " 'Schizophrenia, paranoid type. Acute, recurrent, advanced. Incurable.' It was written, you might say, about – But I reckon you know, don't you?"[125] Yet naming his condition is no solution to his problems.

Ford is involved with two women: Amy, the local schoolteacher, and Joyce, a prostitute, with whom Ford renews his interest in sado-masochism. Afraid she will lose him, Amy tells Ford she's pregnant. But Lou informs her that his father, concerned about his condition, had demanded his son have a vasectomy. Worried that Joyce knows too much, he decides to kill her and her friend Elmer, the son of the man who killed Lou's half-brother. Seeing Elmer with a half-dead Joyce, he says, "I yelled with laughter, bending over and slapping my legs. I doubled up, laughing and farting and laughing some more. Until there wasn't a laugh in me or anyone. I'd used up all the laughter in the world."[126] Then Ford shoots Elmer in the mouth.

Ford pins the blame on Johnnie, a young hoodlum. Visiting him in jail, Ford, his own paranoia about to go into overdrive, begins by speculating on how a person can ever really know anything, which leads to his analysis of the human condition:

> We're living in a funny world, kid, a peculiar civilization. The police are playing crooks in it, and the crooks are doing police duty. The politicians are preachers, and the preachers politicians. The tax collectors collect for themselves. The Bad People want us to have more dough, and the Good People are fighting to keep it from us . . . It's a screwed up, bitched up world, and I'm afraid it's going to stay that way. And I'll tell you why. Because no one, almost no one, sees anything wrong with it.[127]

Having explained the world, Lou admits his guilt and kills Johnnie, using the teenager's own belt to make it look as though he's hung himself.

As the evidence mounts, Lou knows he must kill Amy: "Why'd they have to come to me to get killed? Why couldn't they kill themselves?"[128] About his mental state, Ford says, "We might have the disease, the condition; or we might just be cold-blooded and smart as hell; or we might be innocent of what we're supposed to have done."[129] But the killer inside Lou remains unknowable and unpredictable. When Ford is released from jail, his lawyer says, "[T]he name you put to a thing depended on where you stood and where it stood. And . . . and here's the definition, right out of the agronomy books: 'A weed is a plant out of place.' "[130] Implying the lawyer has either hit the nail on the head or cramped his style, Ford says, "You're in my yard."[131] With circumstance making people what they are, Ford's burden is to remain a rube and a killer. As the police surround Ford's house, Joyce walks in, and Ford tells her, "I reckon that's all unless our kind gets another chance in the Next Place. Our kind. Us people. All of us that started the game with a crooked cue, that wanted so much and got so little, that meant so good and did so bad."[132]

Lou Ford reappears in *Wild Town* and is indistinguishable from Tom Lord in *The Transgressors*. In the former Ford, though enigmatic, remains a rube only so long as it suits him. In control of the narrative, if not his actions, he dispenses with his downhome drawl and colloquialisms in serious moments. Likewise, Ford's paranoia might also be a front, hinted at in the following, which connects Ford to the deputy sheriff who visited Thompson in the oilfield.

> [H]e had to do something, and because he was "old family" he had been given a deputy sheriff's appointment. It was no job for a book learned dude, obviously. For a man with ambitions that would be interpreted as pretensions. You had to blend in with those around you, with the public's conception of a cowtown deputy. So Ford had blended. He had fitted himself into the role with a vengeance, exaggerating it until it bordered on caricature. And with this outward twisting of the man, there had been an inward one. In the brain – the intelligence – which could not be used as it had been intended to be.[133]

Wild Town ends with Ford alone, "his face tightened, pain stabbed through his head, flooded the jeering black eyes. For a moment his world had been penetrated – that private, one-man world – and he knew a sense of loss so great that it was almost overwhelming."[134] *Almost*, for even though Ford appears to lose Amy, "loneliness swept over Ford ... But only briefly; it was gone almost as soon as it came."[135]

In Thompson's frightening *A Hell of a Woman*, Frank "Dolly" Dillon, having committed a double murder, sits in a squalid shack with $100,000 at his side. Like a psychotic Horatio Alger, he believes his past excuses his crimes:

> I had won out in the unequal struggle with every son-of-a-bitch in the country, even my own father, giving me a bad time. I had forged onward and upward against unequal odds, my lips bloody but unbowed. And from now on it would be me and all this dough, living a dream life in some sunny clime – Mexico

or Canada or somewhere – the rest of the goddamned world could go to hell.

But though I seldom complain, you have doubtless read between the lines and you know that I am one hard-luck bastard. So now, right as I stood on the doorstep of Dreams Come True, my whole world crumpled beneath me.[136]

In another split-prose diatribe, Dolly, literally beside himself, fragments in front of the reader. As competing voices fight to control the narrative, Dolly is castrated and throws himself from the window.

She had a big . . . *she was all the women* pair of shears in her hand, and she sat snipping the *of the world rolled into one. So it was the very least I could* ends of her hair, staring down at me. And I looked at *do, and I'd have to do it fast* . . . She made herself . . . *I got up and shoved my foot through the window.* look like Joyce and then like Mona, and then . . . all the *it woke me up a little; the cold air, and those jagged* others. She said I'd disappointed her; I'd turned out *splinters of glass. but I probably wouldn't feel anything,* like all her other men. You deceived me, she said *the load I was carrying. and she was entitled to it. I poked.* You're no different from the rest. Don't you want me to *any forth, and it didn't take hardly any time at all. Helen* darling. I nodded and began unfastening and *came to the door of the bathroom, and she began* fumbling and then, then she lowered the shears and *laughing, screaming. I threw myself out the window.* then she was smiling again and letting me see. There, she said, that's much better, isn't it? And, then, nice as I'd been, she started laughing. Screaming at me.[137]

Savage Night, published in 1953, borders on the surreal, a kind of smalltown Oklahoma *Eraserhead*. The book is set in Peardale, a veritable breeding ground for paranoia: "The whole place had a kind of decayed, dying-on-the-vine appearance . . . There was something sad about it, something that reminded me of bald-headed men who comb their side hair across the top."[138] Once again women are the subject of Peardale's paranoia, as

Bigger, a consumptive hit man, finds a strange growth under Ruthie's skirt:

> I looked down, my head against hers so she couldn't see that I was looking. I looked, and I closed my eyes quickly. But I couldn't keep them closed.
>
> It was a baby's foot. A tiny little foot and ankle. It started just above the knee joint – where the knee would have been if she had one – a tiny little ankle, not much bigger around than a thumb; a baby ankle and a baby foot.
>
> The toes were curling and uncurling, moving with the rhythm of her body.
>
> "C-Carl . . . Oh, *Carl*!" she gasped.
>
> After a long time . . . I heard her saying, "Don't. Please don't Carl. It's a-all right, so – so, please, Carl. Please don't cry anymore."[139]

Bigger, who is also malformed, identifies with Ruthie. Receding into a pre-culture womb, Bigger, locked into a freezer at the bakery, begins to shrink. Eventually he is locked in a cellar where Ruthie chops at him with an axe until all that's left is a bloody torso. As he dies, there's little to separate reality and hallucination. After all, Bigger's savage night is partly his own creation.

> She was swinging wild. My right shoulder was hanging by a thread, and the spouting forearm dangled from it. And my scalp, my scalp, my scalp and the left side of my face was dangling, and . . . and I didn't have a nose . . . or a chin . . . or . . .
>
> I went over backwards, then down and down and down, turning so slowly in the air it seemed that I was hardly moving. I didn't know it when I hit the bottom. I was simply there, looking up as I'd been looking on the way down. . . .
>
> . . . The darkness and myself. Everything else was gone. And the little that was left of me was going, faster and faster.
>
> I began to crawl. I crawled and rolled and inched my way along; and I missed it the first time – the place I was looking for.

I circled the room twice before I found it, and there was hardly any of me then but it was enough. I crawled up over the pile of bottles, and went crashing down the other side. And he was there, of course.

Death was there.

And he smelled good.[140]

In *A Swell-Looking Babe*, published in 1954, Bill "Dusty" Rhodes's paranoia relates to his relationship with his mother. Supporting his family after his father is dismissed from his teaching position, Dusty meets Marcia, the incarnation of all women: "She was twenty. She was thirty. She was sixty."[141] In bed with her, Rhodes, adopted at age five, flashes back to his mother:

> She did not need to push him away, not physically. Her eyes did that . . .
> *"You're a very smart boy, Bill."*
> *"Am I, Mother?"*
> *"Very. Far ahead of your years. How long have you been planning this?"*
> *"P-planning what, Mother?"*
> *"You had it all figured out, didn't you? Your poor old Dad, sick and worn out so much of the time. And me, still young and foolish and giddy and loving you so much I'd do anything to save you hurt."*[142]

As in other Thompson narratives, *A Swell-Looking Babe* includes an enigmatic person capable of separating fact from fiction, and sanity from insanity. As usual, his motives are suspect, as he seeks to control others in the name of humanity. Kossmeyer, Dusty's father's lawyer, "was an expert at separating truth from lies . . . [Rhodes] had chosen to play the game on the strict ground of proof: to disregard the rules of right and wrong, truth and falsehood. Now Kossmeyer was playing the same way . . . He *knew*, and as long as there were no rules to the game . . ."[143]

In *The Nothing Man*, published in 1954, Clinton Brown's paranoia is apparently caused by the wartime loss of his penis. A newspaper rewrite man, Brown, an alcoholic, believes he has killed on numerous occasions. In the course of the novel, he discovers he is incapable of murder. But his unfortunate wartime wound has sentenced him to a hell in which he must torture those around him. Afraid she will discover his secret, Brown apparently "kills" his wife, making him realize that his impotency extends further than he believed. Though shown the error of his ways by a kindly sheriff, Brown's paranoia permeates the novel: "The two-way pull had taken hold and he wasn't looking at the real me – the me-in-charge-of-me. I'd moved off to one side, and I was moving faster every second. I was miles away and ahead of him."[144] Meanwhile, Brown explains his need to torture, and, in doing so, gives us a glimpse, be it slightly facetious, into Thompson's notion of the narrative:

> In a way I liked him; I felt sorry for him. Yet there was another side of me that hated him, that was determined to make him go on suffering for what he had done to me. I wanted to steer clear of trouble for two reasons. Because I liked him – because I hated him. . .
>   . . . It's hard to be specific about one's emotions. It is difficult to stop a story at a certain point and give a clear-cut analysis of your feelings . . . Personally I am a strong believer in the exposition technique as opposed to the declarative. It is not particularly useful . . . when employed on an of-the-moment basis, but given enough time it invariably works. Study a man's actions, at length, and his motivations become clear.[145]

Though extreme, *The Nothing Man*, in its implication that human nature is explicable and redemption possible, is actually one of Thompson's more conventional narratives.

Filmed in 1990 by James Foley, *After Dark, My Sweet* concerns Kid Collins. Whether paranoid, or merely living in a paranoid world, "Collie" has spent his life traipsing between institutions and boxing rings. Supposedly stupid and violent, he, like Lou Ford, is a complex and ambiguous individual. Though Collins is intelligent enough to perceive any aspect of a given situation, he is unable to choose any one aspect over another. "They said that my thinking was one-sided, and, hell, compared with theirs, mine had more sides than a barn. They knew all about me . . . But they knew me as something kind of isolated, something set off by itself and not really a part of the world. I was a case, not a person."[146] As innocence and guilt become too fragmented to be distinguishable, Collie's paranoia gives him a unique perspective: "When a man stops caring what happens, all the strain is lifted from him. Suspicion and worry and fear – all the things that twist his thinking out of focus – are brushed aside. And he can see people as they are, at last.[147]

But is Collie's mental state merely an act?

> I guess I had you fooled, didn't I? Well, I guess I should have, all the practice I've had. I started in almost fifteen years ago – I was up for a murder rap, see, and it was the only thing I could think of. So I went into the act, and it got me out from under. And then I went into the Army, and it got me out of that. It looked like such a sweet deal that I started working the act full-time.

When Fay asks what he means, Collie replies:

> The crazy stuff . . . Hell, it's better than a pension. I could just roam about doing what I pleased – acting stupid, and cracking down when people fell for it . . . I don't know why people never get wise . . . You do all sorts of things to give yourself away – to prove . . . that you're plenty good at looking after yourself. But somehow they never seem to catch on.[148]

Though not so deluded as to think he must save the world, Collins seeks to foil the kidnap, save the boy and redeem Fay. Convincing Fay he plans to kill the boy, Collins pretends to lose his gun, at which point Fay shoots him.

Despite not knowing whether Collie is a lunatic, genius, saint or idiot, one realizes it is unwise to make hasty conclusions about those inhabiting Thompson's literary terrain for, as the alcoholic pornographer in Thompson's unpublished *A Horse In the Baby's Bathwater* says, "There ain't but one plot in the whole world . . . *Things're not as they seem.*"[149]

In *The Kill-Off*, published in 1957 and convincingly filmed by Maggie Greenwald in 1989, Thompson again divides his chapters according to various voices and so establishes a community ridden by guilt. One such character, Bobbie, demonstrates how a dose of pulp culture paranoia can turn to violence:

> [H]er lips were stiff and lifeless, and her body was like ice. And the glow was leaving me. The life and the resurrection were leaving me.
>
> "D-don't," I said. "I mean, please. I only want to love you, only to love you and have you love me. That's all. Only sweetness and tenderness and – "
>
> Suddenly I dug my fingers into her arms. I shook her until her silly head almost flopped off.
>
> I told her she'd better do what I said or I'd kill her.
>
> "I'll do it, by God!" I slapped her in the face. "I'll beat your goddamned head off! You be nice to me, you moronic bitch! Be sweet, you slut! Y-you be gentle and tender and loving – you love me, DAMN YOU, YOU LOVE ME! Or I'll . . . I'll . . ."[150]

Conversing with his dead grandmother, Marmaduke Gannder in the same novel places things in an unusual historical context:

> Once upon a time, there were two billion and a half bastards who lived in a jungle, which weighed approximately six sextillion, four hundred and fifty quintillion short tons. Though they all were brothers, these bastards, their sole occupation was fratricide. Though the jungle abounded in wondrous fruits, their sole food was dirt. Though their potential for knowledge was unlimited, they knew but one thing. And what they knew was only what they did not know. And what they did not know was what was enough.[151]

When his friend denies suggesting he and Marmaduke should

pull a fake hold up to collect some insurance money, Marmaduke sheds some light on Thompson's take on the world:

> I went out . . . wondering if this after all was not the original sin, the one we all suffer for: the failure to attribute to others the motives which we claim for ourselves . . .
> . . . We were both disguised. The materials were different, but they had all come from the same loom. My eccentricity and drunkenness. His roughness, rudeness, and outright brutality.
> We had to be disguised. Both of us, all of us. Yet obvious as the fact was, he would not see it. He would not look through my guise, as I had looked through his, to the man beneath. He would not look through his own, which would have done practically as well.
> It was too bad, and he would be punished for it – as who is not?[152]

Thompson's final pulp culture novel, *The Grifters*, glossed on to the screen by Stephen Frears in 1990, focuses on the paranoia between Roy, a short-term con artist, and his mother who works for the syndicate. Only thirteen years younger than she is, Roy is psychosexually obsessed with his mother. Despite their feelings for one another, it's money, rather than perversion, that corrupts their relationship:

> Roy sighed; tried to explain . . . acceptably the most difficult of propositions; i.e., that the painful thing you are doing for a person is really for his or her own good. And yet, talking to her, watching her distress, there was in his mind, unadmitted, an almost sadistic exulting. *Harking back to childhood, perhaps, rooted back there, back in the time when he had known need or desire, and been denied because denial was good for him.* Now it was his turn. Now he could do the right thing . . . simply by doing nothing. *Now now now the pimp disciplining his whore listening to her pleas and striking yet another blow. Now now now he was the wise and strong husband taking his frivolous wife in hand. Now now now his subconscious was taking note of the bond between them, the*

*lewd, forbidden and until now unadmitted bond. And so he must
protect her. Keep her from the danger which the money would
inevitably lead her to. Keep her available.*[153]

After saving Roy's life, Lilly, his mother, kills him.

Politically disillusioned, Thompson, sticking close to his
individual and eccentric readings of Freud, would continue
creating extraordinary paranoia-filled texts – *The Getaway Pop.
1280, Texas by the Tail, South of Heaven, King Blood, Child of Rage*
– until the early 1970s. In Thompson's world, there are no heroes
or detectives capable of solving every case and wittily countering
every remark. Though his world is neither pretty nor romantic,
Thompson's dark narratives viciously attack the morality of the
era and, in portraying murder and insanity as unpredictable and
commonplace, are not afraid to suggest the indiscriminate
"pulping" of its protagonists.

A Final Twist of the Knife

Goodis, Himes and Thompson approach paranoia in different
ways. Goodis's Vincent Parry runs away from himself. Himes's
Bob Jones is so angry that he is beside himself. While
Thompson's Lou Ford, as a product of a distorted environment,
goes beyond himself. If pulp culture literature is about the pulping
of protagonist, text and narrative, then the separation of self
from culture, or self from self, implies a recycling and remaking
of person, text and nation. However, paranoia, whether in the
form of fear or delusion, can be used either to reorder or unhinge
the world.

Goodis, Himes and Thompson were not the only writers to
use pulp culture paranoia to their advantage. Paul William Ryan
was paranoid enough to adopt two pseudonyms, writing thrillers
like the previously mentioned *Many a Monster* as Robert Finnegan
and labour articles under the name Michael Quin. As the military-
industrial complex shifted into a higher gear and the propaganda

machine became ever more sophisticated, pulp culture literature, with an increasingly dispersed readership and a fragmented working class, found it difficult to stay in tune with the nation's latest obsessions, and so turned from paranoia to suspense as the basis of their texts. The foremost practitioner of this would be Charles Williams, whose novels set the tone for the early 1960s. But Williams was too accomplished a writer to immerse himself in paranoia at the expense of an orderly narrative. Others, knowing this was an era in which there was more to fear than fear itself, had no such misgivings about examining society through the sharpened and often distorted perceptions of those who inhabit their fiction. The problem is, as Jack Finney points out in *The Body Snatchers*, "Fear – a stimulant at first, the adrenalin pumping into the blood stream – is finally exhausting."[154]

3

TAKING OUT CONTRACTS

The origins of detection; the privatization of the investigatory process; the politics of Philip Marlowe, Lew Archer, Paul Pine and Mike Hammer; wages, conditions and inflationary tendencies of fictional private eyes

The Investigation

"Is the richest prize of the Investigation its absolute power to prevent investigation?" (Kenneth Fearing)[1]

Crime-ridden, corrupt, and oppressive, the post-war era witnessed the decline of the private eye as a cultural and literary icon.[2] On the verge of being "pulped" fictional private eyes had saturated the market, having become fragmented leftovers of an era when concerned citizens, wisely or not, sought their expertise and moral commentary.

Enclosed within a political strategy consisting of containment abroad and repression at home,[3] pulp culture private eyes were rarely at ease negotiating the rapids of post-war political waters. As investigators drifted towards privatization – typified by secrecy, enclosure and financial agreement – their emblematic "eyes", no longer open as they had been when the insignia of the strike-breaking Pinkerton Agency, had begun to wink in the direction of the state. With the Cold War contributing to an atmosphere of fear and suspicion, public investigation was best avoided. Amidst a shrug of the shoulders and a shot of rye, private eyes plying their trade on anyone who failed to represent the interests of the state risked engaging in a subversive activity. As for private eye writers, their precarious situation meant following one of two paths – the classicism of Raymond Chandler, or the manic right-wing fantasies of Mickey Spillane.

Yet pre-pulp culture private eye writers had envisaged a range of options regarding their mode of operation. Though the privatization of their investigatory process began in the 1920s, coinciding with the Palmer Raids[4] and the subsequent rise of the FBI, hardboiled private eye writing remained both public and accusatory until the beginning of the Cold War.

Though the relationship between politics and crime has always been close its modern permutation was explored as early as 1916 by Jack London in *Assassination Bureau Ltd.* Committing suicide before he could finish the novel, London presents two related but contrasting philosophical and political trends: a Nietzschean anarchist who believes social evil can be eliminated by murder, and a Marxist who seeks to solve the world's problems through self-organization and emancipation. With the world on the brink of revolution or barbarism, the investigations and ethics of the two protagonists, themselves guilty, echo those of future private eyes:

> "One of the first things done is to give a candidate an unimportant and unremunerative murder – say, a brutal mate of some ship, or a bullying foreman, a usurer, or a petty grafting politician . . ."
> "You are an anarchist?" the visitor asked . . .
> The Chief of the Assassination Bureau shook his head.
> "No; I am a philosopher."
> "It's the same thing."
> "With a difference. . . the anarchists mean well; but I do well. Of what use is philosophy that cannot be applied?"[5]

With state crimes so public, private detectives were allowed to be adversarial in their investigations. Likewise, readers eagerly awaited those willing to investigate state crime. Publishing Dashiell Hammett, Horace McCoy and Steven Fisher – writers who retained an adversarial approach to state power – *Black Mask*, in pursuit of a mass readership, remained pragmatic: namely, if it sold, print it. Treating all writing as potential pulp, *Black Mask* easily moved from one extreme to another, introducing, in 1923, both Hammett's Continental Op and Carroll John Daly's Race Williams, who, hardboiled and right wing, prefigured the likes of Mike Hammer.

A private investigator, newspaperman, cameraman and gambler, Williams's speciality was meting out justice. In "Knights of the Open Palm" – the first Williams story and an example of the magazine's early obsession with the Ku Klux Klan – Daly's hero begins his fight against foreign-born corruption: "I'm what you call the middle-man – just a halfway house between the dicks and the crooks . . . But my conscience is clear; I never bumped a guy off who didn't need it."[6] And when, in *The Third Murderer*, The Flame – an early femme fatale – complains about the state of society – "Honesty – the one thing that the rich leave for the poor to fatten on" – Williams replies, "You didn't bring me here to fill me up on Communism." The Flame counters with her own ideological warp: "No . . . Communism is a hatred of the poor for the rich – not simply an envy."[7] Without a moral code and positing envy rather than hatred as democracy's motivating force, Daly, unlike Hammett or McCoy, would rather acquire wealth than redistribute it.

From its inception, *Black Mask* was adept at rendering pseudo reality and violence. Meanwhile, "a generation who 'smelt fear' in their world read Raoul Whitfield when it couldn't tough out the more refined anxieties".[8] Introduced by *Black Mask* in 1925, Whitfield is interesting in his depiction of a non-Anglo private eye. Jo Gar is an inscrutable Filipino whose fight against crime is impassive and hard edged. Says Gar, "I am never aggressive . . . Manila is a city of heat – heat breeds laziness."[9] One wonders if the world might not have been better off had Race Williams or Mike Hammer confined their narratives to the tropics. For in a more temperate climate, only crime jolts Whitfield's protagonist into action. Set in Hollywood, Whitfield portrays a culture that on the surface appears calm but underneath is seething with crime, corruption, violence and possibility.

Pre-pulp culture fictional private eyes – Hammett's Continental Op and Sam Spade, Whitfield's Jo Gar and Ben Jardinn, Frederick Nebel's Dick Donaghue, Norbert Davis's Max Latin, Robert Leslie Bellem's Dan Turner, Jonathan Latimer's William Crane – were invariably private in performance but public in attitude. More interested in a perceptual than a political process, these writers would cultivate – and many would succumb to – what would become known as objective realism. With snatches of light-hearted subjectivity creeping into their narratives, a context was provided in which public attitudes could be expressed. This was well expressed in 1930 when Nebel's Dick Donaghue reminds the reader that private eyes are no different from other workers for whom tedium is an occupational hazard: "I'm just a plain everyday guy trying to make a living – as honestly as possible. There's not a hell of a lot of romance attached to my business. I'm no drawing-room cop. One day I'm here – the next day, somewhere else. That's not romance. It's damned monotonous."[10]

But as the years progressed their employers – often mistakenly referred to as clients by private eyes confused over who controls the narrative and the culture – were increasingly those financially capable of hiring private eyes rather than those who merely needed their services. Having little to do with mass movements or organized protest, the perceptions of private eyes were credible not because they were objective but because they retained links with a social class to which they could no longer belong. As pulp culture detective Johnny April, in Mike Roscoe's *One Tear for My Grave*, says, "Sometimes it pays to have the right blood type."

Without a working-class background, Raymond Chandler could personalize his narrative and single handedly reinvent the genre. He accomplished this through a sophisticated parody of *Black Mask* fiction. Concerned less with the state of society than with the society of the state, Chandler, once a businessman and a director of independent oil companies, guided his narrative down a cultural and literary cul de sac, successfully decoding the culture until his style turned into a literary cliché.

In a culture saturated with crime and corruption, one wonders why anyone, regardless of pay, would risk investigating the culture, much less track down petty criminals for the ruling class. But the private eye was perhaps the last concerned citizen in an increasingly apathetic era. Which prompts Marlowe to say:

> I'm a romantic . . . I hear voices crying in the night and I go see what's the matter. You don't make a dime that way. You got sense, you shut your windows and turn up more sound on the TV set. Or you shove down on the gas and get far away from there. Stay out of other people's troubles. All it can get you is the smear.[11]

Who wasn't a potential criminal? As post-war organized crime sought to maintain its Prohibition profits by moving from illegal alcohol to illegal drugs,[12] those returning soldiers who could not adapt to civilian life were able to use their experience of the European black market to gain access to the criminal world. Moreover, unemployment, especially amongst the young, was rising.[13] Soon petty crime – car theft, drug dealing, house-breaking – would become an integral part of the "underground" economy and a permanent feature of late capitalism.[14] When profits began to exceed expenditure, organized criminals began to divert their money into "clean" businesses. Inevitably, petty crime became less lucrative through its overexpansion. This decline of the petty crook parallels the decline of the private eye. While petty crooks and private eyes remained nostalgic subjects of pulp culture texts, the increase in criminal activity helped create an atmosphere in which crime fiction – not necessarily with private eyes as protagonists – flourished, a continued part of America's long-standing fascination with crime, violence and corruption.

Living in a society in which crime had become more centralized at the top and pervasive at the bottom, discerning readers might have preferred their private eye narratives to be more adventurous, moving on from Hammett's critique of free enterprise exploitation and political corruption in *Red Harvest* to investigate the criminal class, solve political crimes and re-write the nation's narrative. However, this was beyond the scope of most fictional private eyes who, according to Hammett, possessed too few clues, compared to real detectives who possessed too many. Thus it was easier to be nostalgic about pre-war private eyes and criminals than to consider the state's guilt regarding its policies at home and abroad.

Increased militarization[15] and the scapegoating of suspected subversives[16] meant that the state had entered another stage of the investigative process. This would be described by Dalton Trumbo, one of the Hollywood Ten, in the following way:

> If a man is a Communist and denies his affiliation before the committee, he has committed perjury and will go to jail. If he answers affirmatively, the second question will be "Who else?" If he refuses this answer he is in contempt in the same degree as if he had refused the first, and he will go to jail. If he answers the second, he will be confronted with the third: "Who are your relatives? Your business associates? Your acquaintances?" At which point, if he complies, he is involved in such a nauseous quagmire of betrayal that no man, however sympathetic to his predicament, can view him without loathing.[17]

Because many were guilty by association, the investigation had turned into a political double bind, which meant that only the likes of Mickey Spillane could afford to make overt political statements. Thus readers were assured that both commie and criminal would be contained by the state. But the purpose of investigation, as Fearing maintained, is to *prevent* further investigation. This was aided by the growing popularity of television, and its ability to spectacularize and depoliticize events. With private licence rarely leading to public benefit, Fearing enumerates the benefits of investigation: "[It] . . . lists the proscribed . . . unveils the confessions rehearsed in its secret trials, proves that its trials are not trials . . . specifies those demons for the coming season, then relaxes and performs the cheerier task of erasing memories, of arranging far better horizons for all of us."[18]

Investigating the Investigators

Gumshoe, shamus, peeper, private eye, private dick: whatever the epithet, fictional detectives have based their investigation on the notion that the world is knowable and can be decoded through logic or intuition. Not even two world wars, prohibition, depression, Cold War or McCarthyism could alter their belief that investigation would yield solutions rather than precipitate further investigation. It was again Hammett who articulated the predicament of private detectives, likening their situation to a "blind man in a dark room hunting for the black hat that wasn't there".[19]

Despite the conditions surrounding the investigative process, the pulp culture era saw the appearance of numerous private eyes: Harold Q. Masur's Scott Jordan, Bret Halliday's Mike Shane, Wade Miller's Max Thursday, Bart Spicer's Carney Wilde, Richard Prather's Shell Scott, Thomas B. Dewey's Mac and William Campbell Gault's Brock Callahan. But the private eyes who typify the era, and those examined more closely here, are Raymond Chandler's Philip Marlowe, Ross Macdonald's Lew Archer, Howard Browne's Paul Pine and Mickey Spillane's Mike Hammer. Arguably the best known of these, Philip Marlowe, has become a template for private eyes from the pulp culture era to the present. Yet Chandler's clever parody of the genre meant Marlowe would eventually become a cliché. Meanwhile, his followers, having studied Chandler's privatization of the investigative process, and his use of wit, observation and moral perspective, would produce facsimiles, or parodies of parodies. What does separate Marlowe from his various scions, however, is his expositional style and attitude:

> Until you guys own your own souls you don't own mine. Until you guys can be trusted . . . to seek the truth out and find it and let the chips fall where they may – until that time comes, I have a right to listen to my conscience, and protect my client the best way I can.[20]

A Private Dick in Public Places

Centring on local and domestic crime, Philip Marlowe's conscience does not prevent him from selling his services to those wealthy enough to employ him. Hardened by disillusion – caused by a case of downward mobility acquired even before being fired from the DA's office – Marlowe's work jettisons him, like his namesake, into capitalism's heart of darkness. Having descended into a hotbed of free enterprise, Marlowe privatizes the investigative process, refines his means of expression, and delves further into a commodity-filled culture. So private is his investigation and so adept is he at decoding the culture, Marlowe invariably locates crimes within crimes and investigations within investigations. Though obfuscating the crime he's hired to solve, Marlowe's process of investigation results in, and ultimately professionalizes, a deconstruction that permeates future investigations of Los Angeles and late capitalist culture. In it for the money, Marlowe acknowledges the subjectivity of his investigations and solutions: "Proof", he says, ". . . is always a relative thing."[21]

Underrated by some, overrated by others, Chandler sought to create "emotion through dialogue and description".[22] An interesting but subjective notion. Consequently, when Marlowe solves a crime it is the result of an investigation only he understands. Often unable to follow, much less summarize, a

Chandler narrative, the reader, while admiring the wit, becomes the victim of a displaced paranoia regarding the comprehension of crime. This is why Chandler, privatizing both process and solution, tends to perpetuate social unease and corruption. As for Marlowe, he is more a reaction to an era of state intervention – specifically, the New Deal. But, despite his apolitical conservatism, he is too manic and observant for the 1950s. Dislocated, Marlowe comments on civilization and its discontents:

> [L]ong before the atom bomb, civilization had created the machinery for its own destruction, and was learning to use it with all the moronic delight of a gangster trying out his first machine gun. The law was something to be manipulated for profit and power. The streets were dark with something more than night.[23]

Despite his perception of corruption and crime, Chandler can never quite come to grips with the political climate and moral ambiguity of the post-war era, and so notes the effect, rather than the causes, of cultural change. While Marlowe "can be trusted to keep his mouth shut",[24] he's willing to invoke sociopolitical perceptions should he feel threatened. This despite the fact that, according to Chandler, Marlowe has "as much social conscience as a horse".[25] At least Marlowe does not create a cosy nuclear family, or seek solace in the suburbs. A fallen exile from another era, Marlowe is a man without attachments who lives in rented accommodation, works in a shabby office, is unconcerned about money, choosy about his clients and free to speak his mind.

Consequently, Marlowe can afford to take liberties when confronting others, particularly women, who are often portrayed as villains in Chandler's work: "It was a nice face, a face you get to like. Pretty, but not so pretty that you would have to wear brass knuckles every time you took it out."[26] Not surprisingly, Marlowe is unable to treat women as equals, or become too involved with them.

"You're a little old fashioned, aren't you?" She looked down at the hand I was holding.

"I'm still working. And your Scotch is as good it keeps me half-sober. Not that I'd have to be drunk – "

"Yes." She drew her hand out of mine and rubbed it. "You must have quite a clutch – in your spare time . . ."[27]

So long as interacting with others consists of verbal sparring, Marlowe remains secure. Keeping *I* and *dick* private, Marlowe's preferred mode of self-defence is his linguistic wit, which is often as preposterous as it is imaginative. Nevertheless, Marlowe's manipulation of language keeps him detached and in his own self-enclosed world.

Marlowe's occasional disorientation and unconsciousness, usually the result of a knock on the head rather than any pulp culture phobia, is in keeping with the era's political apathy and lack of power. Losing touch with reality, Marlowe searches for excuses, saying, "A gun slid into my hand all by itself."[28] Prone to fragmentation, Marlowe, hearing voices, says, "I was trying to figure the thing out subconsciously."[29] As he plays with his pipe, Marlowe knows Anne Riordan "watched that with approval. Pipe smokers were solid men. She was going to be disappointed with me."[30] Not the tough guy he pretends to be, and post-modern in his capacity for dissolution, Marlowe, caught in situations over which he has no control, reverts to humour and childlike petulance: "Just lay off carrying me . . . I'm all grown up. I go to the bathroom alone and everything."[31]

With a dubious attitude regarding women and an identity less defined than it appears, it's not surprising – given an era which amalgamated the Yiddish *gantzel* (a sexually vulnerable boy) and *gonif* (thief) to create *gunsel* (gunman), to associate thievery with sodomy – that Marlowe is ambivalent when it comes to homosexuals. Yet his intolerance doesn't stop Chandler from locating them – Lavery in *The Lady In The Lake* or Geiger in *The Big Sleep*. While in *The Long Goodbye*, Roger Wade offers the following rant: "Word got around that I was a homo. The clever boys that write book reviews because they can't write anything else would have caught on and started giving me the build-up . . . The pervert is the top guy now." To which a disingenuous Marlowe replies, "That so? Always been around, hasn't he?"[32]

Paranoid about anyone who cramps his style – including the reader, who is always kept at arm's length – Marlowe maintains a cordial relationship with the criminal class. Portraying them as businessmen, Marlowe feels they at least work for a living, unlike the wealthy inhabitants of LA who employ him, or those on the periphery of the culture – blacks, Mexicans, the poor – who are credited with supplying colour rather than wealth or labour. Explaining how he got on with Potter in *The Long Goodbye*, Marlowe says, "He explained civilization to me . . . He's going to let it go on for a little while longer. But it better be careful and not interfere with his private life. If it does, he's apt to make a phone call to God and cancel the order."[33] Yet those on the periphery of the culture are viewed as unwelcome strangers or potential threats. While it might have been an era in which it was common to talk about a "shine killing", Chandler's description of a section of LA's Central Avenue as one of the blocks "that are not yet all Negro"[34] implies transgressing into a foreign territory at a time when it was not uncommon for whites to frequent the area. Likewise, one wonders what Chandler was saying about an era in which the streets are "dark with something other than night". Because the private eye novel is a genre in which artifice and reality are interconnected, such comments are used by less observant writers or those whose reasons or political intent are obvious. To heighten reality, the likes of Jonathan Latimer and James Ross litter their work with racial epithets. But Chandler's powers of description and deconstruction turn all such minutiae into objects of scrutiny.

The product of an English public school, Chandler would always remain an outsider in the pulp culture era. With only a tenuous connection to state power, his narratives explore places of wealth, sleaze and crime:

> We curved through the bright smile or two of the Strip, past the antique shops with famous screen names on them . . . past the gleaming new night clubs with famous chefs and equally famous gambling rooms . . . past the handsome modernistic buildings in which the Hollywood flesh-peddlers never stop talking money . . . down a wide smooth curve to . . . Beverly Hills . . . and up into the twisting foothill boulevard and the sudden cool dusk and the drift of wind from the sea.[35]

But Los Angeles is more than a geographical setting for Chandler's narratives. Through Marlowe's eyes, LA generates a narrative in which Marlowe and the reader are accomplices in a passive investigation of objects, commodities, gestures and personalities of a culture so on edge that crime and dementia are subject to whim and weather patterns:

> There was a desert wind blowing that night. It was one of those hot dry Santa Anas that come down through the mountain passes and curl your hair and make your nerves jump and your skin itch. On nights like that every booze party ends in a fight. Meek little wives feel the edge of the carving knife and study their husbands' necks. Anything can happen.[36]

Seeing their world collapse, those employing Marlowe often impede the progress of his investigation. For Marlowe will deliver more than his clients bargain for, implicating them in the crimes they've hired him to investigate. Appearing out of nowhere, Marlowe's prospective clients simply enter his office with cash in hand. Unable to receive the attention from the police that their bank accounts demand, those who hire Marlowe illustrate how money can make and break the law. Oblivious to the incomprehensible narrative awaiting them, they plead with Marlowe to take their case. That he must step into a Hammett-like world to find the thread of his narrative indicates how much

Marlowe depends on the monied class to personalize his investigation. With an embittered marginalia, a belief that proof is relative, and an ambiguous relationship with his employers, Marlowe is not only precariously employed but lucky to be working at all.

Tolerating no outside interference, Marlowe internalizes both plot and prose; his musings, sarcasm, cryptomania, moralisms, cynicism and humour become a facade behind which he conducts his investigation. With a remark for every occasion, Marlowe is told by Hemingway – the cop in *Farewell, My Lovely* who is an advocate of a "moral rearmament" programme, one of the few instances in which Chandler recognizes a cultural movement – "You could get so smart you couldn't think about anything but bein' smart."[37] Which, for Chandler, is a pretty good description of Marlowe, whose wit hides the fact that he's not the dissillusioned romantic he pretends to be, but a sentimentalist dressed in cynic's clothing. A post-war Marlowe in *The Long Goodbye* says to Terry Lennox, "I'm supposed to be a tough guy but there was something about the guy that got to me."[38] Yet, out of place in the culture, Marlowe is condemned to live by wit alone.

Constantly impinged upon, Marlowe, a loner, ends up "adapting to corruption: not just material, but also moral corruption, as a supporter of McCarthyism."[39] Having turned to writing at the age of forty-five, Chandler, with his business background, is indicative of those whose politics do not allow them to see the benefits of social organization, who are afraid of committing themselves, but whose materialism gives death a resounding finality. Just as individuals during the Cold War were unable to influence the historical drift of the nation, so Chandler's convoluted narratives appeared to be beyond his control. Working on half-sheets of paper to sharpen his focus, Chandler was less interested in putting together a coherent plot than in noting details about people and places. His need to react to cultural details and be driven by the culture accounts for his lack of narrative control. As Knight maintains, "[H]e was writing *personalized adventures of a hero*, not plots which created a sharply focused problem or a pattern of a social reality."[40]

For Marlowe, everyone is a potential adversary. Consequently, he is not so much pulped into a state of matrimonial bliss as eventually ground down by an era of increased uncertainty. Yet Chandler remains tolerant of those who retain their moral certitude. As Hemingway says to Marlowe in *Farewell, My Lovely*, "Cops don't go crooked for money ... They got caught in the system." At least Hemingway knows where power resides: "[T]he guy that sits back there in the nice big corner office ... he ain't giving the orders either ... You know what's the matter with this country, baby? ... A guy can't stay honest if he wants to ... You gotta play the game dirty or you don't eat."[41] With pulp culture corruption more widespread than he was willing to acknowledge, Chandler's propensity for moral certitude, deconstructive description and witty ripostes soon began to look strained, irrelevant and a poor substitute for political analysis.

As the pulp culture era progresses, Chandler's writing becomes less complex and self-conscious. Curtailing his sarcasm and pithy description, Chandler begins to exert greater control over his narrative. Yet what is notable about his earlier work is his stylistic self-consciousness and lack of narrative control. Had Chandler burnt himself out, or become a victim of an era demanding simpler and more commodified narratives? Whichever, Chandler's narrative is inextricably linked to his sense of composition, exemplified by the splicing together of *Farewell, My Lovely* from three unrelated short stories. The less abstract his composition, the more Chandler strains to control his narrative.

Meanwhile, Chandler's post-1950 descriptions of LA sound as though they could be voiceovers for one of the era's TV cop programmes. Looking at the city, a more complacent Marlowe says:

Twenty-four hours a day somebody is running, somebody else is trying to catch him. Out there in the night of a thousand crimes people were dying, being maimed, cut by flying glass crushed against steering wheels or under heavy car tyres. People were being beaten, robbed, strangled, raped, and murdered. People were hungry, sick, bored, desperate with loneliness or remorse or fear . . . A city . . . rich and vigorous and full of pride, a city lost and beaten and full of emptiness. It all depends on where you sit and what your own private score is. I didn't have one. I didn't care.[42]

Likewise, the more Chandler attempts to exert control over his narrative, the more conventional and garrulous it becomes. With his descriptions of women reaching greater heights of cliché and misogyny, a single sentence might once have expressed the following:

All blondes have their points, except . . . the metallic ones who are as blonde as a Zulu under the bleach and have a disposition as soft as a sidewalk. There is the small . . . blonde who cheeps and twitters, and the big statuesque blonde who straight-arms you with an ice-blue glare. There is the blonde who gives you the up-from-under look and smells lovely . . . and hangs on your arm and is always . . . tired when you take her home . . . There is the soft and willing . . . alcoholic blonde who doesn't care what she wears as long as it is mink or where she goes as long as it is the Starlight Roof . . . There is the small perky blonde who is a little pale and wants to pay her own way and is full of sunshine and common sense and knows judo . . . There is the pale . . . blonde with anaemia of some non-fatal but incurable type . . . And . . . there is the gorgeous show piece who will outlast three kingpin racketeers and . . . marry a couple of millionaires . . .[43]

Yet Marlowe continues to mythologize himself, to bridge the gap between self-deprecation and self-centredness, and to assure the reader of his testiness:

I'm a lone wolf, unmarried, getting middle-aged, and not rich.
I've been in jail more than once and I don't do divorce
business . . . The cops don't like me too well, but I know a
couple I get along with . . . and when I get knocked off in a
dark alley sometime, if it happens, as it could to anyone in my
business . . . nobody will feel that the bottom has dropped out
of his or her life.[44]

Though still acerbic about the police, Marlowe begins to drive
his sentences by cliché rather than venom: "[A]n honest cop
with a bad conscience always acts tough. So does a dishonest
cop. So does almost anyone, including me."[45] Having parodied
the genre, he can now only parody himself, such as saying that
Captain Gregarious is "a type of copper that . . . solves crimes
with the bright light, the soft sap, the kick to the kidneys, the
knee to the groin, the fist to the solar plexus, the night stick to
the base of the spine".[46] Though still identifying with law
enforcers, Marlowe recognizes that everyone is a potential law
breaker: "The most unlikely people commit the most unlikely
crimes." For Marlowe, this is indicative of the fact that "[w]e
know damn little about what makes even our best friends tick".[47]

While nothing can keep Marlowe from his investigation, he
becomes less reliant on humour than on cultural identification.
Passing a building in Hollywood, Marlowe comments that those
inhabiting it make substantial amounts of money from various
illicit businesses. He goes on to make a short inventory:

Shyster lawyers who are partners in a bail bond racket on the
side . . . Abortionists posing as anything you like that explains
their furnishings. Dope pushers posing as urologists,
dermatologists, or any branch of medicine in which the
treatment can be frequent, and the regular use of local
anaesthetics is normal.[48]

Yet a span of fourteen years between the publication of *The
Big Sleep* and *The Long Goodbye* is a considerable period of time
for anyone to remain on the job, much less conduct private

investigations. Consequently, Marlowe, still working out of his office at the Cahuenga Building, continues to ruminate on the life of a private eye:

> You don't get rich, you don't often have much fun. Sometimes you get beaten up or shot at or tossed into the jailhouse ... Every other month you decide to give it up and find some sensible occupation ... Then the door buzzer rings and you open the inner door to the waiting-room and there stands a new face with a new problem ... and a small piece of money.[49]

So problematical were his pulp culture years, one wonders if Chandler's description of Roger Wade, the embittered alcoholic writer in *The Long Goodbye*, might have been self-referential:

> I've written twelve best-sellers ... And not a damn one of them worth the powder to blow it to hell. I have a lovely home in a highly restricted residential neighborhood that belongs to a highly respected multimillionaire. I have a lovely wife who loves me and a lovely publisher who loves me and I love me the best of all. I'm an egotistical son of a bitch, a literary prostitute or pimp – choose your own word – and an all-round heel.[50]

Not surprisingly, Chandler's work – its point of view disguised in a perceptual frame that denies the existence of a point of view – would find a new readership in the post-Viet Nam era. For Chandler's writing plays on one's sense of nostalgia, and is well suited for eras whose secrets demand investigation. This was true in the 1970s with the decoding of cultural narratives surrounding events such as Watergate and the traumas of war. With his own investigatory process having reached a cul de sac by the end of the 1940s, Chandler was neither comfortable in, nor in touch with, the 1950s. Yet, when it comes to post-modern investigation, Chandler remains a primary reference point, indicating the degree to which past readings of the culture contribute to new investigations and narratives.

A Lifetime Ain't No Crime

"I'm a detective. A kind of poor-man's sociologist." (Ross Macdonald)[51]

Ross Macdonald's Lew Archer is arguably pulp culture's most humane, if not realistic, private detective. Along with Chester Himes and Charles Willeford, Macdonald brought private investigation safely through the pulp culture era and into the 1960s. In the process he was astute enough to make his own investigation of the genre: "I tried to work out my own version of the 'hard-boiled' style, to develop both imagery and structure in the direction of psychological and symbolic meaning."[52]

Publishing his first four novels under his real name, Kenneth Millar, Macdonald turned to detective fiction in 1949. Not wanting to be confused with his wife, Margaret Millar, also an excellent writer of detective fiction, he wrote his first Lew Archer novels under the name John Macdonald. To avoid confusion with John D. MacDonald, he adopted Ross as his middle name, eventually dropping his first name to become Ross Macdonald. With a career extending beyond the pulp culture era, Macdonald's writing strives for realism and literary quality, while centring on two themes: the search for lost fathers and how the sins of parents are visited upon their children.

Describing his work as an extension and critique of Chandler, Macdonald writes:

> Chandler . . . wrote like a slumming angel, and invested the sun-blinded streets of Los Angeles with a romantic presence. While trying to preserve the fantastic lights and shadows of . . . Los Angeles, I gradually siphoned off the aura of romance and made room for a completer social realism. . . . Archer is not so much a knight of romance as an observer, a socially mobile man who knows all the levels of Southern California life and takes . . . pleasure in exploring its secret passages. Archer tends to live through other people, as a novelist lives through his characters.[53]

Born in Canada, Macdonald, like Raymond Chandler, observed America as a cultural outsider. Linguistically less self-conscious than Chandler, his Lew Archer may be more prosaic than Chandler's Marlowe, but he's also more plausible. Lacking the latter's inclination for mythologizing himself, Archer – named after Sam Spade's murdered partner in Dashiell Hammett's *The Maltese Falcon* – is more a cultural conduit whose passive behaviour reifies the investigative process. For, like most ex-cops, Archer knows investigations consist of waiting, listening and watching. Once a petty hoodlum in Oakland and then a Long Beach policeman, Archer's conscience has pushed him on to the streets: "The money wasn't the main thing. I couldn't stand podex osculation. And I didn't like dirty politics. Anyway, I didn't quit, I was fired."[54] But it is only when his wife leaves that Archer, his world collapsing around him, ceases to be a tough guy and becomes a thinking person's private eye, thoughtful enough to use a term like podex osculation rather than ass kissing to parody the investigator's need to control language.

Responding to the final days of pulp culture, Macdonald's fiction switched gear in 1958 after he moved to San Francisco and became interested in psychotherapy. Though an unusual pursuit for a pulp culture crime writer, psychotherapy enabled Macdonald to extend further his investigation into the realms of private detection. According to Macdonald, *The Doomsters*, published in 1958, is his first book to make "a fairly clean break with the Chandler tradition . . . and freed me to make my own approach to the crimes and sorrows of life".[55] While the following year saw the publication of *The Dalton Case* – "a story roughly shaped on my own life, transformed and simplified into a kind of legend"[56], and the first of a series of novels about fathers, sons and families.

As Macdonald's fiction came increasingly to investigate family life and how it contributes to the creation of crime, so his protagonist was often portrayed in a "home" setting. Archer's domesticity, combined with a certain street credibility, means he can combine Marlowe's deconstructive sensibility with the adversarial approach of traditional private investigators. But because his narratives veer towards the domestic, and are rarely as artificial as those created by Chandler, Macdonald could survive an era which witnessed the decline of the private eye and a plethora of Cold War investigations, and continue writing through the 1970s. Moreover, Macdonald's intelligence constantly struggles against the constrictions of the genre and the conditions in which private investigation take place:

> The murder story . . . offers the mind some knowledge and control, but tends to return that knowledge to the physical, the scientific, the social, the merely commensurable. The center of man is . . . avoided as if there were a darkness there, beyond the reach of understanding. . . [I]n the works of Hammett and Chandler there is a . . . division between the hunter and the hunted, the knower and the known . . .
> The detective . . . is invulnerable, perhaps miserable. He deals in death but is untouched by it . . . he represents our lingering fear of death, and our . . . inability to submit ourselves or our imaginations to tragic life. We live in the illusion of the hunter even while we are being hunted.[57]

Regarding the public's attitude towards the detective, Macdonald, in his 1950 *The Drowning Pool*, says, "Everybody hates detectives and dentists. We hate them back."[58] For investigators, like dentists, often touch a raw nerve. Yet as an understanding liberal, Macdonald avoids the unnecessary adoption of a tough-guy stance. Though sometimes, of course, it's unavoidable. When someone says, "You're a hard man", Archer answers, "I hope so. It's the soft ones, the self-pity boys like you, that give me bad dreams."[59] Likewise, he reserves the right to make the occasional cynical remark: "Here we go again, I said to myself. True confession morning, featuring Archer the unfrocked priest."[60] Perhaps it's his cynicism that allows him, unlike other detectives, to dirty his hands by doing divorce work. Despite its unsavoury quality, it's an expanding market, prompting Archer to say, "I am rhinoceros-skinned and iron-hearted. I've been doing divorce work in LA for ten years."[61] For Archer neither glamorizes nor denigrates his work: "I've done a good deal of work in and about Hollywood . . . Peeping on fleabag hotel rooms, untying marital knots, blackmailing blackmailers out of business. Dirty, heavy, hot work on occasion."[62]

In contrast to Marlowe, Archer is constantly tolerant. Yet, sensing an impending cultural tragedy – whether the result of McCarthyism, the bomb or an expanding middle class – he knows when to keep his head down. Told that the "great hordes of low-class people, Mexicans and dirty oil crews, came in from gosh knows where, and simply blighted the town. We can't let it happen here", Archer, ever the liberal, simply agrees with "a phoniness she had no ear to catch".[63] Although his clients are invariably white, Archer has no problem sharing space with others who comprise California's cultural ménage, nor in recognizing their contributions to the economy: "The Mexicans lived off the land when the canneries were closed. The rest of the townspeople lived off the Mexicans."[64] After stopping "in front of an overgrown cigar store that sold guns, magazines, fishing tackle, draught beer, stationery, baseball gloves, contraceptives, and cigars", Archer spots "[t]wo dozen Mexican boys with grease-slicked duck-tail haircuts [who] were swarming in and out of the store, drawn two ways by the pinball machines in the back and the girls on the street". Unlike Marlowe, Archer is neither alarmed at their presence, nor afraid to ask two *pachucos* for assistance. Noting that, despite their social status, the two boys show unusual politeness – "I thanked them. They bowed and smiled and nodded as if I had done them a favour"[65] – Archer fails to consider that, given the era, they might believe it in their interests to be deferential, particularly when caught in someone else's investigation.

Hardly a booster of southern California culture, Archer comments: "There was nothing wrong with Southern California

that a rise in the ocean level wouldn't cure."[66] But as an ecologist
in an era that had yet to recognize a need for the term, Archer
says, "They had jerrybuilt the beaches ... bull-dozed super-
highways through the mountains, cut down a thousand years of
redwood growth, and built an urban wilderness in the desert.
They couldn't touch the ocean. They poured sewage into it, but
it couldn't be tainted."[67] Without grinding it into grist for a post-
modernist's mill, Archer's depiction of southern California,
particularly its suburbs, never succumbs to the bathos that typifies
Marlowe's *noir* romanticism:

> The oil wells from which the sulphur gas rose crowded the
> slopes on both sides of the town. ... [T]he town had grown ...
> like a tumor. It had thrust out shoots in all directions: blocks of
> match-box houses in raw new housing developments and the
> real estate shacks to go with them, a half-mile gauntlet of one-
> story buildings along the highway ... The people were
> different and there were too many of them.[68]

Capable of a sharp turn of phrase, Archer neither hides behind
witticisms nor denies the intellectual component of private
detection. When Olivia Slocum, referring to her home – as yet
untouched by the suburban sprawl – says, in *The Drowning Pool*,
"They've ruined the town and desecrated the rest of the valley,
but they shan't touch my mesa", Archer, claiming to understand
her sentiments, lobs an intellectual hand grenade her way: "A
friend of mine who lectured in economics at UCLA would call it
the *mystique* of property. What I failed to understand was the
power of her obsession."[69] Not something Marlowe, even with
his college degree, would have been caught dead saying. And
though he's fond of quoting philosophers and poets, Archer has
little time for intellectual pretension. Describing an evening with
a group of theatre people, Archer says:

> Existentialism, they said. Henry Miller and Truman Capote
> and Henry Moore. André Gide and Anais Nin and Djuna

Barnes. And sex – hard-boiled, poached, coddled, shirred, and
fried easy over in sweet, fresh creamery butter. Sex solo, in
duet, trio, quartet; for all-male chorus; for choir and
symphony; and played on the harpsichord in three-fourths
time. And Albert Schweitzer and the dignity of everything that
lives.[70]

When it comes to women, Archer is hardly an extremist in pursuit
of vice or virtue: "I stole a look at the woman, to confirm my
first impression. Her atmosphere was like pure oxygen; if you
breathed it deep it could make you dizzy and gay, or poison
you."[71] For Archer is "the introverted kind"[72] of detective who
lives "in a five-room bungalow on a middle-class residential street
between Hollywood and Los Angeles. The house and the
mortgage on it were mementos of my one and only marriage.
Since the divorce I never went home till sleep was overdue."[73]
 Although Archer, despite his solitude, refrains from portraying
women as objects, the objects he does portray constitute an
entirely different matrix of signification:

 I picked my way through the debris that littered the threadbare
 carpet. Old photographs and newspaper clippings and black-
 edged funeral announcements, used condoms and love letters
 tied with pink ribbon, ashes and cigarette butts brown and
 white, empty whisky bottles, dried sickness and dried blood,
 cold half-eaten meals on greasy plates. Behind the numbered
 doors there were shrieks and groans and giggles, and howls of
 ecstasy and howls of pain. I looked straight ahead, hoping
 none of the doors would open.[74]

With a "certain darkness in himself",[75] and a thin line separating
detective from potential killer, Archer knows he has no licence
to kill and is critical of those who do: "The fictional detectives
who revel in killing don't belong to the real world. They inhabit
a sado-masochistic dream world where no license is required,
either for the detective or the wild dreamer at the typewriter."[76]
 A liberal, Archer rarely takes an overt political position.

Though some might have believed him sufficiently left wing to be politically suspect, Archer was cagey enough to work throughout the McCarthy era. Given the political climate, Macdonald's belief that "the typical detective hero . . . speaks for our common humanity . . . has an impatience with special privilege, a sense of interdependence among men, and a certain modesty"[77] could mean anything. But Macdonald does not hesitate in claiming the private eye as a modern hero, "one of the central figures of fiction in which the shift from aristocracy to democracy has visibly occurred, decade by decade".[78]

At the same time, Macdonald often places politics at the core of his narrative. In *The Galton Case* Archer is told by Cassie Hildreth that Tony Galton "disapproved of expatriates. He always said he wanted to get *closer* to America. This was in the depression, remember. He was very strong for the rights of the working class." Archer says, "Radical?" and is told, "I guess you'd call him that. But he wasn't a Communist, if that's what you mean. He did feel that having money cut him off from life. Tony hated social snobbery . . . He often said he wanted to live like ordinary people, lose himself in the mass."[79]

Though Archer harbors an addiction to the dangers inherent in being a private eye, he prefers "[t]ame danger, controlled by me. It gives me a sense of power, I guess, to take my life in my hands and know damn' well I'm not going to lose it." Recognizing that the world is more complex than he once imagined it to be, and that many factors contribute to the creation of a given criminal act, Archer's fieldwork is essentially that of a social scientist:

> I used to think the world was divided into good . . . and bad
> people, that you could pin responsibility for evil on certain . . .
> people and punish the guilty . . . When I went into police
> work . . . I believed that evil was a quality some people were
> born with . . . But evil isn't so simple. Everybody has it in him,
> and whether it comes out in his actions depends on a number
> of things. Environment, opportunity, economic pressure, a

piece of bad luck, a wrong friend . . . But most of my work is watching people, and judging them.[80]

In a genre dominated by hard cases and private dicks, one must admire a detective writer who notes family and environment as factors contributing to crime. Or who takes their influence seriously enough to draw comparisons between crime writing and sociology. Of course, taking the genre too seriously can be as much of a literary crime as not taking it seriously enough. Despite what Macdonald says about moral ambiguity, Archer is yet another example of the invulnerable private eye. Nevertheless, Macdonald was successful in moving the genre beyond Chandler, and, in adapting his writing for the 1950s, is one of the few writers unafraid and untarnished enough to go down those not so much mean as meaningless suburban streets. Though Macdonald implicates both hunter and hunted, he leaves Archer outside that particular investigation. Finally, Macdonald's insistence that he is replicating reality is, in the end, no more believable than Chandler's cavalier attitude towards the world. Though he may lack personal perspective, Macdonald's honesty, intelligence and sense of reality have done much to legitimize detective fiction.

Sunglasses After Dark

Harold Browne's Paul Pine is another fictional private eye influenced by Raymond Chandler. Using the pseudonym John Evans – Chandler's detective in "No Crime In The Mountains" – Browne published the first of his Paul Pine novels, *Halo In Blood*, in 1946. It was followed in 1948 by *Halo for Satan*, and in 1949 by *Halo in Brass*. Another eight years would pass before Browne, under his own name, would publish *The Taste of Ashes*.

Describing himself, Pine says: "I'm thirty-one, five feet eleven, one hundred and seventy pounds. The dent in the bridge of my nose came from high-school football. I was an investigator in the State Attorney's office until a change in administration gave me a new boss. He had a nephew who needed a job."[81] An independently minded Chicago private eye, Pine dislikes the popular image of his profession, for which Chandler is, to a large extent, responsible, saying: "If there was a place for private detectives . . . Siberia was it and I would contribute modestly to a fund for that purpose."[82] Less cynical but no less impervious than Chandler, Pine – named after a Chicago skip tracer – is as irreverent as his mentor.

Browne's ability to generate suspense through the construction of comprehensible plots, and his lackadaisical attitude regarding cultural clues, make him more traditional than Chandler in his approach to the genre. Nor is he as introspective as Lew Archer. But Pine can also be self-deprecating. Explaining that he works "for my clients and my conscience", he acknowledges that his work is often tedious. All that was required was that you "sat and listened or you stood and listened. And when the calluses got thick enough so you didn't have to fidget, then you could be a private detective."[83]

Like Chandler and Ross Macdonald, Browne writes in the first person, giving him the opportunity to make any number of terse observations: "Chicago's Loop is a few acres of skyscrapers encircled by elevated trains like an iron wedding ring on the upthrust hand of a giant. A place of big business and little people, of smoke and noise and confusion beyond Babel, where there is satisfaction for every appetite and a cure for every disease."[84] Likewise, when it comes to description Pine can be razor-sharp: "His mouth was about the size of the quarter slot in a juke box",[85] or "I've seen wider smiles on a cue ball".[86]

Browne can also extend his descriptions, as in his portrait of John Sandmark, a Chicago millionaire who in *Halo in Blood* hires Pine to break up the relationship between Leona, his step-daughter, and Marlin, a local hoodlum:

Even sitting down he was a big man . . . with a head like a

lion . . . His face was square, heavy in a massive way that had
nothing to do with soft living. His eyes were dark blue and they
looked at you without apology. His nose would have been at
home on an Indian chief and the large mouth under it wasn't
much more than a straight line. You could have hung a lantern
on his chin but not without his permission. He could have been
forty and he could have been sixty.[87]

Like Archer and Marlowe, Pine tries to be choosy about those
who employ him and the work he does. When Sandmark tells
Pine he's too independent for a working man, Pine says, "There's
no point in getting mad at me . . . I make my living by working
at a business that has more bad smells to it than most."[88]

Yet Pine, like many fictional private eyes, avoids investigating
the politics of crime, preferring to chase petty criminals rather
than corporate scum. Following in Marlowe's footsteps, Pine's
investigative skills are so probing that he invariably discovers
crimes within crimes, the motivations for which are to be found
in human foible rather than corporate greed. In *Halo in Blood*,
Pine begins by working for Sandmark. After Marlin is murdered,
Pine is hired to deliver some ransom money. Before he can do
so, he is beaten up, saved by the intervention of Marlin's old
gang. To repay them, Pine agrees to find Marlin's killer for them.
Eventually, the crimes interconnect, leading Pine back to
Sandmark. Though the latter appears "more the bank president
type . . . the kind who'd use a mortgage instead of a blackjack",[89]
it's Leona who is responsible for three murders, revealing her
guilt by a slip of the tongue rather than through Pine's
investigatory skills – not an uncommon means for pulp culture
detectives to solve a crime. After sending for the cops, Pine
excuses himself, saying, "I don't want it noised around that I do
the cops' work for them. It could hurt my business."[90]

While Macdonald prides himself on being influenced by poets,
it's Browne who comes up with the most poetic lines: "Something
made a noise behind me. It wasn't much of a noise. About as
loud as a cigarette ash falling on a snowdrift."[91] His concern

with language, thought and style is reflected in what he reads. In *Halo in Blood*, Marx's *Das Kapital* sits next to P.G. Wodehouse's *Leave It to Psmith* on Pine's bookshelf. The fact that Wodehouse attended the same public school as Chandler possibly reflects Browne's deference to Wodehouse. But, despite his interest in Marx, Pine believes that "theories don't mean a thing".[92] Consequently he opts for a well-formed plot rather than a long-winded analysis.

Likewise Pine, as a skilled private dick, avoids using firearms unnecessarily. When he sees Marlin shot down in the street, Pine chooses not to intervene: "I was packing about as much heat as you'd find in an icicle, and without a gun I tackle no killers. Nor with a gun, if I can help it."[93] As though a critique of the tough-guy school, Pine confesses that "[t]here are times to get tough and there are times when being tough doesn't get you anything".[94]

Typical of the era are Pine's remarks regarding women: "She had two excellent reasons for wearing a sweater and her legs were probably good for walking too."[95] Though, after meeting Leona, he is more subtle, though no less physiological, in his judgement: "She wasn't an unspanked brat from the idle rich any more. She was a nice firm round young woman, with bowels and a complexion and a sense of humor."[96] Meanwhile, Browne's women are always willing to engage in verbal combat. As Leona says to Pine, "I bet it would be fun to take you apart . . . I mean in an analytical sense, of course."[97] Though made to toe the male pulp culture line when it comes to analysing what women find attractive in men, Leona proceeds with her dissection. She begins with Pine's "hard finish":

> Perhaps . . . you've seen too much of the wrong side of people. You go in for crisp speech and a complete lack of emotion. In a way you're playing a part . . . and it's not always an attractive part. Yet there's plenty of strength to you, and a kind of hard-bitten code of ethics. A woman could find a lot of things in

you that no other man could give her . . . Besides, you're rather good-looking in the lean, battered sort of way that all sensible women find so attractive in a man . . . We should investigate each other.[98]

Later Leona says, "Detectives are all alike, aren't they? Even private detectives . . . All they really want is information."[99]
Yet information does not come cheaply. And when it comes to the job of gathering it, Pine is ambivalent. The strain of working as a private eye, at some point, takes its toll: "Five minutes under the shower would have been like two weeks in the mountains. But I was a workingman."[100] Yet, as a working man, his hours are not all that conducive to reading Wodehouse: "Two-twenty-three. All the grocery clerks and necktie salesmen were home in bed. But I had to be a private detective."[101] Or Marx. For Pine wonders why he's a private eye, on his own, and, regarding working conditions, unrepresented: "I looked down at the gun in my right hand. I wondered if I couldn't join a union and go on strike and sleep through the negotiations."[102]
When Leona tells Pine he's hard and embittered, Pine claims his experience as a detective has lowered his expectations:

> I get wet-eyed in the movies once in a while, and I think kids are wonderful. Maybe I give the impression . . . because my work makes me see people as they actually are . . . I thought people, even the shoddy ones, would give a straight deal if they got one themselves . . . But after a few years of being lied to and cheated and double-crossed – well, I quit handing out halos. Too many of them were turning out to be tarnished instead of glowing; red instead of gold . . . halos in blood.[103]

Of course, Pine has to be hard. Especially when he realizes Leona has committed a capital offence: "I closed the books a little too early, baby. You see, one more will have to die. That will happen the day they you in the electric chair and throw the switch."[104]
Then comes the moral and Pine's dubious personal stamp:

Murder is a matter between you and the State, baby. But when you try to lock the door permanently by running a love affair with me . . . that is where it becomes a personal matter – a matter between you and me.[105]

Does Pine turn Leona in because she is a murderer or because she uses him? In either case, Pine, having grasped the rudiments of Marxism, feels no obligation to Leona and her social class. Likewise, having read his Wodehouse and been a Jeeves for the upper class, Pine knows their willingness to use anyone they consider socially inferior. Even though Leona's exploitation of Pine is no different from the way the upper class traditionally exploits private eyes, Pine, realizing Leona's criminal behaviour, will not allow love to get in his way. After all, Pine must protect his reputation and his tenuous connection to the state. At least Leona does the decent thing, killing herself after being detected by the man she loves – a case of one more *femme fatale* biting the dust. Hearing the shot, Pine, in typical tough-guy fashion, says, "I got into the cage and rode down to the first floor and went out into the hot clean light of a new day."[106]

For all their concern about locale, there's little indication that Browne's narratives belong in the post-war rather than in the pre-war era. One would have thought from reading Browne that private investigation was still in its heyday. Working for the wealthy as well as the crooked, Pine's investigations illustrate the extent only of local crime. Pine clings to the belief that it was nepotism, and not politics, that caused him to leave the state attorney's office. And it's for the same reason that Pine is more interested in a good turn of phrase than in the cultural signifiers surrounding him. Without reading the culture, Pine relies on Wodehouse and Marx – the latter more as an intellectual trophy than a text that supplies meaning – to clue him into the genre and the culture.

Though well planned, Browne's narratives signify a comprehensible world where history moves in linear fashion and corruption is the result of personal foible rather than political manipulation. While Pine believes that crime creates crime, he sees no contradiction in his cordial but sometimes strained relationship with the state. As a pragmatist, Pine is aware that tough-guy tactics are often impractical, but, indicative of the era, he believes that women are attracted not to the pursuit of cultural clues and marginality but to a "battered leanness" which comes from tough guys living in a tough world.

No wonder Pine is disillusioned with people and society. Having realized the world does not become a better place because another crook has been arrested, Pine, having substituted autonomy for social organization and change, is on his own. Nevertheless, with his conscience as his guide, Pine is democratic enough to be intolerant of the "bad smells" which accompany private investigation. Unfortunately, even with Marx at hand, Pine never questions the politics of crime, nor his relationship to it. And, since his narratives might have taken place at any time from the 1920s onwards, Pine gives no sense of the historical era in which he's writing. Which, for a writer of hardboiled fiction, might be the biggest crime of all.

Kill, Kill, Kill

With little of Lew Archer's humanity, Paul Pine's wit or Philip Marlowe's skill at decoding the culture, Mickey Spillane's Mike Hammer is an invulnerable and primeval detective who inhabits a nightmare world of law and disorder. Like the other three writers, Spillane's narratives are in the first person, but, unlike the others, his narrative viewpoint does not so much create a sense of intimacy between writer and reader as demand the reader's collusion in his attempt to gain a degree of narrative order and control a world he cannot understand. Embellishing his work with lashings of sadism, Spillane's narratives are fanciful, perverse and psychotic. Yet, or because of this, Spillane remains one of the most popular crime writers in the world, who, by the early 1980s, had sold over 150 million books.[107] Indicative of pulp culture paranoia, confusion and fear, Spillane's writing, if one isn't offended by its pathology, can often be perversely humorous.

Few crime writers have been as universally disliked as Spillane. Raymond Chandler commented: "Pulp writing at its worst was never as bad as this stuff", while noted writer and critic Anthony Boucher maintained that *I, The Jury* should be "required reading in a Gestapo training school".[108] Apparently only Ayn Rand, confusing objectivism with objective realism, was perverse enough to remark that "Spillane gives me the feeling of hearing a military band in a public park".[109]

Though a product of the post-war era, Spillane's work recalls the worst aspects of *Black Mask* writing. Sanctioned by the state, and by J. Edgar Hoover-type politics, Spillane makes no effort to hide either his politics or his mode of operation. Says Hammer:

> I lived to kill so that others could live. I lived to kill because my soul was a hardened thing that revelled in the thought of taking the blood of the bastards who make murder their business – I was the evil that opposed other evil, leaving the good and the meek in the middle to live and inherit the earth.[110]

Hardly introspective, Hammer fights everything he considers evil and, with such a heavy burden, has little time for subtleties or perspective. With an appropriately named protagonist, Spillane hammers away at the narrative and the culture contained within it. With comic-book intensity (Spillane began his career writing for comic books such as *Captain Marvel* and *Captain America*), he exploits the genre for all its worth, making use of tough-guy action, invective and oversimplification. For this is pure pulp, to be discarded after, or before, it's read. And as pulp, such writing qualifies as grist for the Cold War mill.

Hammer prides himself on his charisma. Are not all pulp protagonists supposedly charismatic? But Hammer is so charismatic women are unable to keep their hands off him. Understandable since, according to Hammer, women find sadists irresistible. It doesn't take much insight to realize that Hammer hates women almost as much as he hates "commies" and organized crime. So passionate about those who threaten him, neither is it surprising that Hammer's only friends are policemen, one of whom has the temerity to say:

> Facts are one thing but there's still that crazy mind of yours. You make the same facts come out different answers somehow . . . you're cooperative and all that jazz. You lay it on the line like you are requested to do . . . But all the time you're following a strange line of reasoning nobody who looks at the facts would take.[111]

Despite his relationship with the police Hammer, like a vigilante in heat, recognizes no law other than his own. For Hammer occupies the centre of his fictional world, from which he administers justice. There's no point in retching over the thought of Hammer's utopia. For, lacking imagination or ability to see beyond his own primeval interests, Hammer most likely would opt for the very world Spillane creates for him. Try as he may to convey the notion that violence is a means to an end, it's obvious that violence, for Hammer, is an end in itself: "I don't underrate the cops . . . But cops can't break a guy's arm to make him talk, and they can't shove his teeth in with a muzzle of a .45 to remind him that you aren't fooling."[112] A one-man vigilante, Hammer isn't interested in convictions so much as retribution. Police, judge and jury rolled into one, Hammer says: "I am not letting the killer go through the tedious process of the law . . . The dead can't speak for themselves . . . Nobody in the box would know how it felt to be dying . . . The law is fine, but this time, I'm the law and I'm not going to be cold and impartial."[113]

With blatantly right-wing politics, Hammer's fight for justice and democracy is conducted on behalf of those who also hate "commies", crime and women, but are too weak to do anything about it, or are too young or stupid to realize what's at stake. Likewise, Hammer makes no attempt to hide his belief that some don't deserve the benefits of democracy. Explaining his simplistic theory of law and order, he says:

> Go after the big boys. Oh, don't arrest them, don't treat them to the democratic process of courts and law . . . do the same thing to them that they'd do to you! Treat 'em to the unglorious taste of sudden death . . . Kill 'em left and right, show 'em that we aren't so soft after all. Kill, kill, kill, kill.[114]

Not quite your typical laid-back detective. But life, for Hammer, is straightforward. Disregarding nuance, he explains the reasons for committing murder: "First classify all murders: There are only a few. War – Passion – Self-protection – Insanity – Profit and Mercy."[115]

However, the likes of Ernest Mandel inflate Spillane's value in claiming Hammer to be a bridge between "Holmes and Poirot on the one hand and Bond and Quiller on the other, just as Carnegie's US Steel Corporation or Krupp were a bridge between the free-enterprise industrial firms of the 1850s and the true multinational corporations of the 1950s".[116] With none of the cerebral investigatory techniques of Holmes and Poirot, Hammer has more in common with Race Williams – "I used to say that's the kind of story I'm going to write"[117] – and the blood-and-guts school of pre-war pulp writing. As a sledgehammer for late capitalism, Hammer is more like a bridge between dime novels and Chandler. Appearing to be a by-product of J. Edgar Hoover's distorted imagination, Hammer is less a signifier for late capitalism than that which it signifies.

When it comes to being a protagonist, it's difficult to say if Hammer is a more fanciful creation than Marlowe, or if he contradicts Chandler's dictum that the fictional private eye is "an exaggeration – a fantasy, but at least . . . an exaggeration of the possible".[118] For the Cold War era virtually sanctioned

Spillane's morbid fantasies, which, according to one critic,[119] saw within his first five books the violent deaths of forty-eight people, thirty-four of whom would have lived had not Hammer intervened. Not all that much different from US foreign policy ventures. For Hammer, like the US, is unconcerned about the consequences of his actions, or the quality of his work. Describing himself as the "chewing gum of American literature", Spillane hammered out *I, The Jury* in six days.

Although Hammer, a keyhole cop, has few paying clients, he is seldom short of work. Spending his time seething with rage, he makes no effort to hide his tendencies: he smashes together the heads of two men who comment as he walks by with a woman at his side; he flips a lighted cigarette into the eye of a man who puts his arm around the woman he is with; he stuffs money into the mouth of an elevator operator who's provided him with some information; he strips the clothes off and whips a woman who is a communist. In fact, Hammer's sex life consists of masturbatory fantasies in which women are submissive and always available. Except for Hammer's secretary, Velda. Though she longs to get him into bed, Hammer thinks too much of her to turn her into another fallen woman.

For Hammer represents the dark side of America, whose symbol for detection is a keyhole through which the combatant male attempts to penetrate the culture. Hammer is a deeply disturbed person who inhabits a world comprised of other equally disturbed people. Stuck in the mire of adolescent rage and sexual desire, he despises difference as much as he hates communism. Fortunately, in 1952, Spillane became a Jehovah's Witness and retired from writing for the next ten years. But not before leaving behind a legacy of revenge, execution, penetration and destruction. At the same time, Spillane can be read as a barometer of the culture, expressing what more literary writers would ignore or place on the periphery of their texts. Hardly civilized, Hammer, in contrast to private eyes who try to maintain a semblance of humanity, represents US business and political interests and the ethics of the Cold War at their most primitive. At the same time, like Pine, Archer and Marlowe, he maintains a dubious relationship with the world of crime. Regardless of his attitude and style of detection, he cannot help but perpetuate crime. At the same time, like the other writers, he fails to recognize the public service provided by criminals. In the words of Paul Pine's co-favourite author:

> The criminal breaks the monotony and everyday security of bourgeois life. In this way he keeps it from stagnation, and gives rise to that uneasy tension and agility without which even the spur of competition would get blunted. Thus he gives a stimulus to the productive forces. While crime takes a part of the superfluous population of the labour market and thus reduces competition among the labourers – up to a certain point preventing wages from falling below the minimum – the struggle against crime absorbs another part of this population.[120]

The Wages of Detection

As intermediaries between the proletariat culture and those wealthy enough to hire them, pulp culture private eyes, while protecting those with money, do their best to remain honest. In fact, ethics and street credibility are all they possess as they face the perennial working-class dilemma: how to maintain one's principles while selling one's labour. Though self-employed, private eyes rarely refuse work. For remuneration is as necessary as making sense of the historical process in which the narrative takes place. So a private eye's pay is established – by haggling or fixed rate – in the opening pages of the text. This, in turn, becomes an essential and unrepeatable stage of any private eye narrative. Investigating these pages shows that private eyes were neither as marginal nor impoverished, as their mythic reputations suggest.

In *The Big Sleep*, Philip Marlowe bemoans the fact that he's had no business in a month,[121] only to receive $100 merely for taking Marriott's money to a designated spot where he's to exchange it for some precious stones. Further into the narrative, Marlowe maintains he makes $25 a day including expenses "when I'm lucky", though he later insists his $25 per day does not include expenses.[122] At other times, Marlowe doesn't say, or doesn't know, what he charges, but relies on clients to pay him amounts that obviously exceed his worth or rate.

Despite his confusion, Marlowe's rate of $25 per day was not a bad wage in 1939, when *The Big Sleep* was published. And by 1953, with the publication of *The Long Goodbye*, Marlowe admits making $750 a month "tops", or approximately $35 per day. Yet Mrs Wade in *The Long Goodbye* offers Marlowe a check for $500 to look after her alcoholic husband. This means that, after working fourteen years as a private eye, Marlowe's wage has increased by $10 a day, which demonstrates the era's inflation rate or, as good money is thrown after bad, Marlowe's personal economics.

On the other hand, private eye Paul Pine charges $30 per day including expenses in 1946. Four years later, Lew Archer asks $50 a day *and* expenses.[123] Though seemingly expensive for 1950, Archer's fee remains virtually unchanged throughout the pulp culture era, charging $50 in 1951 in *The Way Some People Die*, and the same amount in *The Ivory Grin* (1952) and *The Galton Case* (1959). Though this could be a sign of the country's economic stability, it's more likely an indication that, with a proliferation of private eyes, supply has exceeded demand. Unless the otherwise diligent Archer is, in fact, economically slack.

In theory, private eye rates are negotiable, subject to ability to pay and the economic climate. In *The Moving Target*, published in 1949, Archer says to Graves, a lawyer and friend, "You're not prosecuting any more". Graves replies, "I couldn't afford to". Archer says, "Married?" Graves answers, "Not yet. *Inflation*". Archer says, "How much is she good for?" Graves: "Whatever you say. Fifty a day and expenses?" Archer: "Make it seventy-five. I don't like imponderables in this case." Graves: "Sixty-five . . . I've got to protect my client."[124]

At $65 a day, one wonders if Archer, otherwise fair in his negotiations with women, is about to overcharge his friend's client. Or perhaps he has an unconscious desire to price himself out of the market? Though the cost of a private eye hardly increases – indeed in Archer's case it decreases – inflation remained a permanent feature of the post-war era.[125] Meanwhile, one wonders if there is a kind of logic to Archer's rates. Though there are times when Macdonald's detective appears to sell himself wholesale, he often notes the prevailing economic conditions and the culture's tendency to overinflate the capability of the private eye to solve what are often political problems.

Nor was it unusual for ethical private eyes to tell clients to take their case to Missing Persons, saying it "would be a waste of money to hire me",[126] or: "You might do better with one of the big organizations."[127] For private investigators were apparently less concerned about overcharging or providing an adequate service than hinting that once hired, the case would become the private property of the investigator who could offer no guarantees regarding where the investigation might lead.

If $25 was not a bad wage in 1939, neither was $35 per day in 1953. Despite the danger, the days without work or the possibility of hospitalization, $35 per day – $175 per week which, allowing two weeks unpaid vacation, amounts to approximately $8,750 a year – was a better wage than that received by firemen and policemen who, as of 1959, were the highest paid workers in the service sector.[128] Yet real private detectives were, from 1970, unable to match the wages of their fictional counterparts, with male private eyes receiving an average income of $6,989, and female private eyes receiving $3,588. Even though wealth was unequally distributed, fictional private eyes, if employed, were hardly poor.[129] This despite the fact that private eyes were rarely seduced by luxury items, even preferring – with the exception of Archer, whose divorce left him sole occupant of his house – rented accommodation to home ownership.

Though no longer part of the working class, private eyes used their working-class links to their advantage, particularly when gathering information or offering their point of view. Self-employed and with no family to support, private eyes could be choosy about clients, dirtying their hands only when the price was right. Estranged from the working class and the class that employed them, they could afford to speak their minds. But, with their rates doubling from Marlowe's 1939 rate of $25 per day to Archer's 1959 rate of $50 per day, they were subject to inflation and the economics of supply and demand. Which raises a series of questions, some metaphorical and some literal. Were fictional private eyes supplying or demanding a service? To what extent did the monied class need private eyes? Did the privatization of the investigative process result from a need to maintain the status quo or from fears of public investigation? And, if cleaning up after those with money is such a thankless task, was it economic or ego inflation that stopped embittered private eyes from becoming politically involved?

To those clinging to the free market, inflation might well be considered criminal – the economic equivalent to the Red Menace and organized crime. In fact, communism and crime were doubtless cited by some economists writing during the era of pulp culture as factors causing inflation. Meanwhile, Keynesians have argued that a low but permanent inflation rate is an economic stimulant which, in countering mass unemployment, prevents crime. If the free market tends to offer fictional private eyes greater employment possibilities, it suggests that it might not have been only McCarthyism that prompted private eyes to keep their heads down and their mouths closed. On the other hand, interventionism, particularly at street level, has been the stock in trade of private eyes whatever their politics. With little choice, private eyes took work where they could get it. Consequently their investigations centred on small-time crooks and minor abuses of wealth and power. Rarely did a private eye investigate in detail how wealth and power are acquired or follow crime to its source.

Nevertheless, fictional private eyes, particularly in the early days of pulp culture, appeared to have limitless employment possibilities. Was it purely the economics of the era, or had it something to do with the paranoia and needs of those holding the money? For this was a time when defence spending was able to stave off economic crises, acting as a more potent stimulant than J. Edgar Hoover's belief that he could crime-bust the country to economic growth and police-led stability. Though the Korean War brought America out of the 1949 recession, taxes were unable to cover military spending and inflation became a permanent feature of the economy. However, excess purchasing power also meant that luxury items – including the exploits of fictional private eyes – were thrown on to the market.

Of course, inflation does not affect everyone equally. More interested in crime than economics, fictional private eyes might well have profited from permanent inflation. Unfortunately, those with the financial ability to initiate private investigations were unable to appreciate having their lives interrupted and their narratives read into. Meanwhile, private eyes like Lew Archer, having glimpsed comfort, lived through an era of public intervention, were reluctant to go flat out against the interests of their former social class. Though engaging, this was not the most economically prudent path for them to follow.

Yet fictional private eyes were also victims of their own individuality. While the likes of Paul Pine bemoaned not being unionized, no private eye would have allowed himself to be represented, much less organized. As inhabitants of rundown offices and flea-pit hotels, private eyes would work only for themselves, conducting their lives in states of near chaos. Meanwhile, their rates for detection, sometimes seemingly arbitrary, were subject less to market forces than to the price fixing of those whose profit margins allowed them to dominate the market. Had private detectives not worked on a cash basis and refused to be cultural middlemen, they might have been able to create demand *through* supply rather than simply supply *on* demand. Unfortunately, fictional private eyes were unable to read the economic clues that indicated they were about to not so much price themselves out of the market as succumb to the class that employed them. Facing political devaluation, private eyes opted for the path of least resistance, pursuing petty criminals, front men, easy marks and the obviously culpable. How different the genre would have been had they, instead, reflated and redirected the investigatory process, taking it to its logical conclusion.

4

FEMME FATALITY

The portrayal of women in pulp culture fiction; women hardboiled writers; Leigh Brackett's *The Tiger Among Us*, Dolores Hitchens's *Sleep With Strangers* and Dorothy B. Hughes's *In a Lonely Place* as tacit critiques of a male-oriented genre

> "Was this his woman – or an alien life form?" (Jack Finney, *The Body Snatchers*)
>
> "What Strange Desires Drove This Woman?" (Vera Caspary, *The Weeping and the Laughter*)[1]

Private Dicks in Public Places

Bad women. Good women. Dead women. Crazy women. Beautiful women. However they were described, women in pulp culture fiction were objects of male fantasy and obsession, their representation a reflection of their position in society. Moreover, pulp culture women, like Jim Thompson's fictional psychos, were, for most pulp culture men, unfathomable. Unlike Thompson's warped protagonists, women portrayed in pulp culture fiction are often one dimensional, depicted as dangerous *femmes fatales* or sugar-coated housewives; sexually promiscuous or frigid; murderous or boring.

Revelling in misunderstanding, pulp culture literature nudged the prevailing attitude regarding women to an extreme. Whether re-enforcing or occasionally subverting the prevailing attitude, the titles of pulp culture paperbacks depict the era and tell the story: *Four Boys, A Girl and a Gun, Behold This Woman, The Devil's Daughter, Swamp Sister, Savage Bride, Sinful Woman, A Dame Called*

Murder, Dormitory Women. Either *femmes fatales* or *femmes* fatalities, women in the work of writers like Cornell Woolrich and David Goodis are, for the most part, portrayed as potentially pathological, manipulative and marginal, while men are simply victims of a hostile world. James M. Cain's pre-pulp culture *femmes fatales* like the notorious Mildred Pierce or Cora in *The Postman Always Rings Twice* go to great lengths to gain their independence. While Horace McCoy, politically more in tune with a pre-pulp culture era, populated his work with women whose sexual promiscuity has as much to do with political radicalism as the licence derived from personal wealth or from personal immorality. Yet McCoy's extremism in pursuit of vice occasionally went too far. As previously mentioned, his NAL editor saw fit to change Myra, in *No Pockets for a Shroud*, from a communist to a sexual pervert, making her more marginal to the narrative, though certainly no less extreme.

As in William McGivern's *The Big Heat*, women in pulp culture literature, whether housewives or *femmes fatales* could look forward to a violent death. For a woman's outward beauty often indicated an inner ugliness, as in Gil Brewer's *13 French Street*, where Petra, wife of Verne, gives the impression she's a domesticated housewife, but fools everyone and turns into a deceased *femme fatale*. Looking at Petra's body, Verne says, "She was truly beautiful", to which Alex answers, "But only on the outside. On the inside she was evil."[2]

Femme fatales can be viewed either as products of the hardboiled imagination, or as popular images derived from paranoid fantasies of independent and, therefore, threatening women. Whether considering Goodis's *Cassidy's Girl*, Homes's *Build My Gallows High*, or Woolrich's *The Bride Wore Black, femmes fatales* are integral to pulp culture literature. However, their greatest cultural impact has come via *film noir*. The likes of Barbara Stanwyck (*The File on Thelma Jordan, The Strange Love of Martha Ivers, Double Indemnity*), Joan Crawford (*Mildred Pierce, Possessed*), Jane Greer (*Out of the Past*) and Gloria Grahame (*In a*

Lonely Place, The Big Heat) portray women who are invariably the property of a criminal boss. Tough talking, *femmes fatales* have two sides to them: objects as well as subjects; materialists as well as sentimentalists; intelligent as well as stupid; vulnerable as well as coldhearted. In pursuing them, hardboiled heroes venture into forbidden territory, endangering the lives of all concerned.

If women, so dangerous and treacherous, were not what they seemed, why couldn't men fathom them? Did men live such surface existences that they weren't interested? Or were they paranoid about what might lurk under the surface? Whatever, male introspection in pulp culture fiction rarely went beyond blood, sweat and the smegmatics of male bonding. But then men were paid to work, not to think, while women worked for no pay, with few caring what they thought.

Likewise, redomesticating post-war women was essential to the success of the Cold War. Returning from overseas, men could live out their wartime fantasies, while women were confined to the home, de-skilled, de-educated and de-politicized. Needing political and economic scapegoats, the Cold War had little time for dissidents. Perhaps this was why female pulp culture writers like Patricia Highsmith or former communist, feminist and author of *The Blue Gardenia* and *Laura*, Vera Caspary, picked up stakes and moved to Europe.

For the political neutralization of both sexes depended on women performing unpaid tasks at home while men worked for wages on the wheel of production.[3] Only at home could men, as breadwinners, hope to exercise what little power they had. Which accounts for the temperature of *The Big Heat*'s domestic as well as criminal discourse, as Bannion, drink in hand, patronizes his wife as she prepares dinner: " 'How you squeeze steaks out of my salary is a source of wonder to me,' he said. 'At work they don't believe it. They insist you've got a private income, or something.' "[4]

Should they fail to provide home comfort and sympathy,

women were easier to blame and rail against than a political system that crushed dissent. But for extremists like Jim Thompson, who had no problem gouging out and chopping off offending members, the "private eye" as metaphor and protagonist was beyond redemption. Thompson's women are as paranoid and pathological as his male characters: Ruthie, in *Savage Night*, reduces Bigger to a blood-drenched torso; Helen, in *Hell of a Woman*, castrates Dolly; Lilly in *The Grifters* outsmarts her son. But Thompson could be subversive because he, like a handful of pulp culture writers, remained outside the private eye tradition, and was politically astute enough to investigate the culture rather than merely try to solve the crime.

As the culture became immersed in the Cold War, private eyes became increasingly known as private dicks, their egoistic voyeurism having permutated into something more onanistic but no less misogynistic. As Chandlerite Howard Browne, aka John Evans, said in his 1957 *The Taste of Ashes*:

> Private dicks had no business being married. Private dicks should live with nothing except for a few books and a bottle or two on the pantry shelf and a small but select list of phone numbers for ready reference when the glands start acting up. Private dicks should be proud and lonely men who can say no when the hour is late and their feet hurt.[5]

With a proliferation of private dicks, Richard Matheson's 1956 *The Shrinking Man* underpinned male pulp culture paranoia regarding women. No need to speculate on what's shrinking, as the Gold Medal cover shows a minute Scott Carey, needle in hand, fighting for his manhood. Fearing death, inversion or neuterization, Carey, like many males in an era before small was considered beautiful, is convinced size matters: "He thought of them up there, the woman and the little girl. Were they still that to him? Or had the element of size removed him from their sphere?"[6] That the nuclear male member should shrink is a disaster with a sizeable fallout. And naturally, the perfect suburban housewife is "beside herself" when her once-perfect suburban husband breaks the news:

> "*Shrinking?*" The word was spoken in a trembling whisper.
> "Yes" was all he could manage to say.
> "But that's – " . . .
> "Honey, it's what's *happening*," he said. "He showed me the X-rays – the ones he took four days ago and the ones he took today. It's true. I'm shrinking." He spoke as though he'd been kicked in the stomach, half dazed, half breathless with shock.
> "No!" This time she sounded more frightened than resolute. "We'll go to a specialist," she said.[7]

A specialist? In shrinkage? One wonders if the narrator is as obsessed as the protagonist – "He touched himself . . . How much had he shrunk in the night?"[8] Having been outgrown by his wife, Scott eventually comes to terms with his disability, and finds advantages in being small, such as an ability to extend American foreign policy into places hitherto unknown:

> He shook his head in confusion. How could he be less than nothing. The idea came. Last night he'd looked up at the universe without. Then there must be a universe within, too. Maybe universes . . . Yet he'd never made the obvious connection. He'd always thought in terms of man's old world and man's own limited dimensions. He had presumed upon nature. For the inch was man's concept, not nature's. To a man, zero inches means nothing. But to nature there was no zero . . . Then he thought. If nature existed on endless levels, so also might intelligence. He might not have to be alone.[9]

With much of the era's male paranoia deriving from sexual anxiety regarding women or homosexuality, it's appropriate that the cover of Matheson's Gold Medal paperback should show the "little man" of the house fending off a black widow spider. Confronting this mate-consuming arachnid while lamenting his increasing dependence, Carey's fear of women becomes a subtext straining to emerge from its psychic bunker. Rejecting insanity,

Carey's nightmare becomes a new, though disembodied, way of life. Regarding Carey's sex life little is known. Whether this is a blessing in disguise is uncertain. Because, in this instance, it's not technology or McCarthyism that's responsible for shrinking pulp culture man, it's women. Less than a household object, Carey, not unlike pulp culture women, must take refuge in a doll's house from where he fends off a large and hostile world and awaits his eventual reduction to a single cell swimming blissfully in an amniotic sea of unconsciousness.

The Shrinking Man illustrates how men, lacking the confidence to engage the government, viewed domesticity. At the same time, there's little indication that men were overly concerned about how much the world of women had been miniaturized. Without the time or mobility to find other modes of organization, women watched their earning power diminish in direct proportion to their desire to consume.[10] Which, in turn, ensured that a large proportion of the population would be in debt and inextricably screwed into the system.

Women were to be looked after, watched and guarded. While the pulp culture line was one of "no wife of mine is going to work", working men, to cover family expenses, were meant to overproduce. It was easier, according to Betty Friedan, for women to think about domestic matters than about communism, McCarthyism and the bomb, easier to look for Freudian sexual roots in human behaviour, ideas and wars than to "look critically at . . . society and act constructively to right its wrongs".[11] Likewise, women's magazines began to work from the premiss that women were not interested in politics.[12] Stressing the creation of a self-enclosed nuclear unit, magazines set an agenda that corresponded with the interests of the Cold War. Without an extended family, nuclear parents like the Bannions had only the era's approved books to rely upon:

> "Seriously, the book says to be patient but firm . . ."
> "The book, the book," Kate said. "It's scientific and calm,

but it doesn't work . . . The baby books never heard about
Brigid, that's the trouble."
   "The thing is, she's madly in love with me," Bannion said.
"The Oedipus business, you know. Naturally she's jealous of
you, as any sensible woman would be, and that's why there's
conflict. Reasonable?"
   "Yes, but I don't believe it," Kate said.
   "Well, it's a little too pat, I guess . . . It's like circumstantial
evidence. If everything fits too well, look out . . ."[13]

Though pulp culture paperbacks constitute a male-oriented genre
which reflects prevailing attitudes,[14] a number of women made
major contributions to the genre. Even *Black Mask* which, under
Joseph Shaw (editor from 1926 to 1936), called itself "The He-
Man's Magazine", employed its first woman writer and heroine
– Katherine Brocklebanks's "Tex of the Border Service" – as
early as 1928. Over the next two decades some thirty women
were published in *Black Mask*, though the majority of their work
would be closer to romantic fiction than hardboiled crime.
Moreover, in 1936, F. Ellsworth, a woman, took over as editor of
Black Mask, bringing with her Steven Fisher, Cornell Woolrich
and Frank Gruber. Not that such genre bending would affect
the likes of Carroll John Daly, whose character Florence
Drummond, aka The Flame, was illustrative of how women
supposedly influenced, and even controlled, the world of pulp
culture: "Oh, I've used men . . . My mind guided me – that
criminal mind . . . There's never been a man who held me in his
arms and kissed me who hasn't come back and back and back.
Moths! . . . And now, Race, I can offer you . . . power."[15]
   Yet *Black Mask*-influenced fiction, much of which consisted
of little more than urban adventure stories, has long appealed to
men obsessed by juvenilia and caught within a cycle of narrative
repetition. Breaking free of that cycle and expanding one's
narrative horizons requires the ability to distance oneself from
one's obsessions. Not even Ernest Hemingway could accomplish
this, though, in legitimizing this particular strand of pulp culture

fiction, he managed to rescue it from becoming the male equivalent of romantic fiction. But equally important is the influence of proletariat writers like Jack London, Tom Kromer, Edward Anderson, Michael Gold and Jack Conroy, whose texts, though still male oriented, are accompanied by a political analysis which permits readers to see themselves as habitual offenders caught within a repeating narrative.

Readers of *Black Mask* were even told how to read the genre: "You cannot get the full force of these stories if you spoil your own pleasure by reading them the wrong end first."[16] Besides the fact that such advice is based on the assumption that detection is necessarily a logical progression rather than a process involving intuition, deconstruction or paranoid fantasy, fiction should be read in any way that elicits meaning, especially when investigating those misrepresented or missing from the narrative. Consequently any enquiry into how women are represented in the genre should be coupled with an investigation of specific women pulp culture writers. In doing this one glimpses how women represented themselves and whether they were able to subvert the genre's overtly masculine, if not misogynist, tendencies.

Leigh Brackett

Initially, there is little to indicate that the author of *No Good From a Corpse* and *The Tiger Among Us* is a woman. Her hardboiled writing can be both elegant and humorous. Never considering she might be female, director Howard Hawks was so taken with *No Good From a Corpse* that he hired Brackett to work alongside William Faulkner and Jules Furthman on *The Big Sleep*. Born in Los Angeles in 1915, Brackett, who began her career writing for science-fiction pulp magazines, soon became one of Hawk's favourite scriptwriters, working for him on such macho classics as *Rio Bravo*, *Hatari*, *El Dorado* and *Rio Lobo*. In 1973 she scripted Robert Altman's *noir nouveau* classic *The Long Goodbye* and, later in the decade, wrote the screenplay for *The Empire Strikes Back*. Significantly, her scripts and stories take place in a male world in which there is no shortage of violence. Brackett, best remembered for her fourteen volumes of science fiction, died in 1978.

Published in 1957 – a year which saw the death of Joseph McCarthy, the publication of Jack Kerouac's *On The Road*, the final issue of *Woman's Home Companion* and the Supreme Court's "Red Monday"[17] – Brackett's *The Tiger Among Us*, as well as being a hardboiled thriller, is part of that strand of pulp culture fiction which, in the last half of the 1950s, examines the theme of juvenile delinquency.[18] To give the book a harder edge, the narrator, suburban hero Walter Sherris, issues the following disclaimer:

> They were "boys" only by arbitrary definition, and they were "juvenile delinquents" only by accident. Their urges had nothing to do with overcrowded slums or broken homes, or submerged minorities. Those are social problems, but the thing that drove these boys is older than society, as old and as deep as the roots of the human race. Theirs was the problem of the tiger that is always among us, the immemorial tiger whose first given name was Cain.[19]

While the reference is biblical, Cain could just as well have referred to James M. or Paul, for *The Tiger Among Us* strains for hard-core status. However, its wafer-thin social awareness makes this a half-hearted throwback to liberal narratives like Thomas B. Dewey's 1954 *Mean Streets*. With Sherris's hunger for revenge revealing the weakness of his politics, Brackett indemnifies herself in an era when liberalism was suspect.

The Tiger Among Us, published in a period of suburban expansion,[20] also illustrates the extent to which suburban man will go to protect himself and his home. For suburban growth was accompanied by an ideology based on an obsession with the value of property. Because blacks were, for the most part, excluded from suburbia, racism in these middle-class utopias would become rife. With anti-social behaviour a supposed threat to suburban peace and property, homeowners kept an ever-open eye on interventionists and recalcitrant teenagers. Meanwhile, with suburban life supposedly the norm, women were expected to be housewives.

Thus the scene is set as archetypal suburban man, Walter Sherris, is attacked and badly beaten by a gang of teenage hoodlums while out for a walk. How could Sherris not have known that in suburbia – in a "I drive therefore I am" culture[21] – anyone without a car is a potential victim? But Brackett's book isn't so much about the dangers of pedestrianism as about how being a victim affects one's life, endangers one's family and threatens the fabric of suburban life itself.

Aware of her place in suburbia or sensing the portentousness of the narrative, Sherris's wife, Tracey, seeing her husband laid up in hospital, fabricates a story about receiving a threatening letter from the hoodlums, and, with kids in hand, makes a hasty exit. With the possibility that his wife has scarpered merely to gain possession of the family car, Sherris is left in an awkward position. For, in pulp culture suburbia, a man not only in traction but with neither car nor wife is hardly a man at all.

At the same time, *The Tiger Among Us* focuses on male violence, caused, says Sherris, "partly because of our laissez-faire attitude toward the young. Or perhaps it is only because the population is bigger and so there are numerically more of these violent children who grow up to be violent men."[22] While the consensus is that young people need guidance and discipline, Brackett might also have been issuing a warning about male sexual violence towards women when, after being hit, Sherris says:

> You feel degraded to be afraid of them but you are afraid. You feel outraged because they have laid hands on you for no reason except that they just felt like it. You feel that they're protected by all sorts of laws and customs and that it is somehow not right to fight them, even in self-defense . . .

You want to kill them. This is a feeling you do not ask for or plan on having. It just comes.

Several people have said that what happened then was my fault.[23]

With women once again homemakers, their places on the production line taken by husbands, many of whom bore the psychological scars of war, conditions were rife for domestic violence. This situation might well have given Brackett an added degree of empathy regarding victims of violence and their families. For Brackett, writing for a specific market, gives no quarter to the hoodlums who populate her novel. Yet they can't be all bad, not when their goal is to deconstruct suburban life and patriarchs like Walter Sherris. Using Sherris's dull existence to remind his cohorts of what suburbia offers, Chuck, the gang leader, might have been applying for future membership of Class War, saying, "Yes, sir, no, sir, and cut the lawn every Sunday . . . That's what your mammas want you to grow up to be."[24]

As far as Sherris is concerned, when the going gets tough the tough turn to vigilantism: but for the fact that he's not into exterminating tramps, this makes Sherris no different from the thugs he's chasing. Though Sherris is irked by the fact that the hoodlums are middle class, he has enough of a social conscience to turn one cowardly gang member into an indentured servant, making the not-so-tough kid perform menial tasks in his backyard. This "tough love" extends to Tracey who, over the phone, is told to come home and look after Sherris – "I'm afraid that's your job, Tracey. You're my wife."[25] Burdened with this biological destiny, Tracey, a natural product of pulp culture, is expected to be "pretty and gay and a lot of fun . . .[which] didn't give Tracey much scope for her particular talents".[26] Though she's not without possibilities, Tracey has apparently read enough magazines to know her best bet for survival is to traipse back to the suburbs and tend Walter's wounds.

That the thugs mistake Sherris for a tramp rather than a sober and upright member of the middle class is an example of an error commonly made by sociopaths in pulp culture fiction; namely, an inability to distinguish social classes.[27] The insistence that class difference is irrelevant has long been the engine driving haves and have nots to violence. Had the hoodlums thrashed only tramps, no one would have cared. Though that would have been Sherris's loss for, despite his injuries, pursuing the "hoods" – with a "bitter stimulating taste of vengeance" – is an obsession. As for the thugs, their lack of vision exposes some unwholesome attitudes.

Because suburbia shall be tarnished neither by "commies" nor criminals, Sherris believes he's performing a public service in cleansing his turf of sadists and bullies. At least Tracey is shrewd enough to put forth a class-based analysis: "[T]hey haven't anything to lose, and we do. They don't care what they do to people, but we care what's done to us. It makes you wonder if they really are human like us, or if they're – I don't know. Throwbacks. Just animals."[28]

With neighbouring non-suburbanites supporting Sherris, this is a cosy picture of America coalescing to fight the "enemy within". Even the local black population – none of whom are likely, whatever their aspirations, to live next to Sherris – who've had their own problems with the hoodlums, realize Sherris has good intentions. Enlisting the bartender of the neighbourhood dive to help infiltrate tramp culture, Sherris is given the lumpen line on how to keep one's kids from becoming juvenile delinquents – show them how sordid the real world is and don't be afraid to hit them however much the wife screams. When Sherris and the barkeep get to the local strip mine and find the body of a tramp, the cops are called. When they arrive, one cop looks at the body and decides this is "big city stuff", while another – an advocate of scratch and claw capitalism – says, "I don't think this has anything to do with towns or cities [or] juvenile delinquency. This is a matter of the individual."[29]

When the hoodlums are within range, Sherris's individualism turns ugly: "I lusted to kill them . . . I wanted it beyond justice or reason or self-preservation. The tiger stripes were showing on my own hide." For, given a legitimate enemy, everyone is a potential killer. When it's over, Sherris points out the therapeutic value of vigilantism, saying, "My wife and I have a finer relationship based on what we went through together."[30] Though *The Tiger Among Us* is supposedly about the arbitrariness of crime, Sherris appears to advocate either the metaphysics of despair or the benefits of genetic engineering: "Sooner or later we'll have to find the answer. Because we all live closer together now, more interdependent and intertwined than ever before, and the tiger is flourishing among us." Though her thoughts remain hidden, Tracey, for the moment, appears content. Once having had the sense to run, she is now determined to stick it out in the suburbs with a man who is a danger to society. Here suburbia is portrayed as a refuge for the middle class, and Sherris, though a loose cannon, is only being vigilant. In fact, *The Tiger Among Us* should be required reading for anyone investigating post-war middle-class values, the revised role of women and obsessions regarding the enemy within.

What makes Brackett's portrayal of suburban life different is her willingness, however strained, to empathize with victims of violence, and her exploration of the domestic tensions inherent in suburbia. According to Brackett, those tranquil suburban streets can be, if one is not vigilant, as dangerous as the mean streets one normally associates with pulp culture fiction. For paranoia regarding possible invasion – be it by communists, blacks, Jews, the poor, juvenile delinquents or uninvited dinner guests – exists everywhere. Obviously, suburbs can be spooky places. Who knows what dangers – insanity, domestic violence, incest – lurk behind its doors? Stuck at home, women were ideally placed to read the culture, recount the dynamics of suburban life and, given the opportunity, explore its intricacies in domestic pulp fiction.

In fact, *The Tiger Among Us* differs considerably from novels such as William McGivern's *The Big Heat*, which denote the transition between urban and suburban life. For defence of the suburbs is the sole subject of Brackett's novel. Without a trace of revisionism, here there are no reconnaissance missions to the city where an otherwise wholesome man refortifies himself on the pleasures of a world embedded in *noir* urbanity. Nor are there any fanciful forays to flush out mob bosses and corrupt police chiefs. Walter and Tracey, unlike the misguided couple in Lionel White's *The Big Caper*, are dedicated law-abiding suburbanites. Defending a barbecue version of the new frontier, Walter can forgive repenting invaders, at least so long as they do his power mowing. But, more interesting is Brackett's depiction of Walter and Tracey's relationship. Either Brackett's portrayal of Walter as a patronizing piece of pulp fiction and Tracey as a frightened but dedicated suburban pioneer is tongue in cheek, or she is attempting to outdo men at their own genre. If the former, *The Tiger Among Us* becomes a brilliant satire of suburban culture; if the latter, it stands as a blatant condemnation of the era's sexual political and consumerist obsessions.

Dolores Hitchens

Born in Texas in 1907, Dolores Hitchens worked as a nurse and a teacher before turning to writing in the late 1930s. Over the years she wrote some forty-eight novels, sometimes collaborating with her husband, while at other times disguising her sex behind such pseudonyms as Dolan Birkley, Noel Burke and D. B. Olsen. In 1964 the director Jean-Luc Godard based his *Bande à part* on her novel *Fool's Gold*. Hitchens died in 1973.

Written under her own name, *Sleep With Strangers* was published in 1956 and features Jim Sader, an ageing, ex-alcoholic, Chandler-influenced private eye. Set in the relatively unromantic and slightly sleaze-ridden California town of Long Beach in the

1950s, Sader is hired by Kay Wanderley to investigate the disappearance of her wealthy mother. At first glance, *Sleep With Strangers*, like Leigh Brackett's *The Tiger Among Us*, gives little indication that its author is female. Yet discerning readers might point to the novel's attention to detail, depiction of relationships, wry humour, and portrayal of women, particularly when it comes to undercutting the role of the *femme fatale*, as qualities that differentiate Hitchens's work from her male pulp culture counterparts.[31] With oil literally holding the plot together – creating wealth, relationships and animosities – Hitchens's novel, lighter and less self-conscious than *The Tiger Among Us*, walks a thin line between the macho hardboiled detective novel and the more feminine drawing-room mystery.

With a cinematic eye, Hitchens is particularly observant when it comes to women:

> They looked at each other across the space between Sader's chair and her rose-velvet couch. The rhinestone earrings she wore glittered in the cloudy light let in by the windows. Between the earrings was a face that interested Sader; it had character as well as beauty . . . Her make-up had been applied lightly and skilfully.[32]

Likewise, Hitchens, with her acute sense of irony, does not flinch in her portrayals of men talking about women. Says the eccentric Ott: "[Mrs Ajoukian] fed anybody she figured was hungry, providing Ajoukian wasn't there to keep her from giving food away. . . . She was too ignorant to know about banks. Too dumb to know her rights."[33]

When Sader says to Kay Cole, a friend of the missing Felicia Wanderley and in the process of divorcing her husband, that perhaps Felicia thought Cole's attorney wasn't doing right by her, Cole simply says: "My attorney is a woman."[34] End of discussion. Cole then warns Sader about how private eyes, unlike women, are guilty of overinterpretation:

[P]erhaps in your work you've learned to examine other people
with an X-ray eye. Perhaps you discover all sorts of meanings in
their casual social behaviour. You see guilt, and anger, and
terror, and evil intentions under their outward appearances.
But I don't. When I glanced in and saw Felicia talking to Mr.
Ajoukian, I thought only that they might have found a topic of
common interest. Or at most, that she was being pleasant to an
old and rather unattractive man.[35]

Though no one needs X-ray eyes to understand the California
property boom and the machinations of Sunshine Capitalism:
"You know how real estate people are – afraid you and the buyer
might get together without them."[36]

Concentrating on money, real estate, oil and women, *Sleep
With Strangers* delves into a world of unholy alliances and misconceptions. For Kay and the young Ajoukian have misconceptions
about themselves and are misconceived by others. Says Kay
Wanderley regarding her missing mother:

It was when she began to drink that I began to notice she no
longer craved the company of men. I'm not going to apologize
to you for my mother's behaviour . . . A couple of mild attachments she formed with men turned out badly. She took up
selling real estate, mostly to pass the time, and she saw a new
side to life, trickery and knavery and sharp dealing. She grew
impatient and quick tempered. She – she started to drink.[37]

For Sader, "Kay's loyalty to her mother would blind her to the
woman's obvious coldness, self-interest and vanity".[38] On the
other hand, Tina Griffin, a bar-hopping friend of Felicia
Wanderley, who "not only loved to mystify but to end the mystery
with a clash of cymbals",[39] says, regarding herself and Felicia,
"most widows sleep alone – too long".[40] No wonder she takes a
liking to Sader. For the book, with its mother fixations and older
men lusting after young women, takes the reader along a path
of desire in which sleeping with strangers becomes a euphemism
not only for sex without companionship, but also for silent

business partners, and the oil sump grave where two strangers – the young Ajoukian and the forty-seven year old Felicia Wanderley – end up.

Hitchens's women, whether Felicia Wanderley or Annie the maid – "under that soft politeness was a whim of steel and a rigid sense of propriety"[41] – are complex individuals. Even their clothes have significance. The book-keeper at the oil rig tells Sader a woman wearing a fur coat over a pair of slacks looks "crappy as hell". Mrs Griffin identifies Ajoukian by his clothes, while the taxi driver mentions the clothes Mrs Wanderley wears when riding in his cab.

As for Sader, he has an eye for detail and a severe case of empathy: "She was fifty, or nearly, and to someone like Kay Wanderley, in spite of her denials, fifty was doddering and sexless and past all thought of romance. Let Kay live, Sader thought; she'll learn it isn't so."[42] Though priding himself on being a gentleman, Sader catches himself staring at the young Ajoukian's wife after he notices how little emotion she shows upon hearing about her husband's death. Assessing her, Sader says:

> In that moment she was the most beautiful woman he'd ever seen. There wasn't a flaw in the soft face, the silver curls, the slim figure dressed in red wool. Almost too perfect . . . to be real. A doll that had learned to talk, to move, to understand. A doll with a steel spring instead of a heart.[43]

When he asks about the possibility of her husband having another woman, old man Ajoukian cuts in, saying, "Can't you get women out of your head for a minute? My son had money! He didn't have to worry over women!"[44] Of course, Sader takes an instant dislike to Ajoukian's materialist lifestyle which leads to his son's death. Says Hitchens, when it comes to Sader's reaction: "He hated this old man who stank of greed, of corrupting avarice."[45]

After a glib start amidst the mansions of Long Beach, *Sleep With Strangers* moves into familiar pulp culture territory – amusement arcades, pig concessions, oil sumps and a variety of eccentrics – accompanied by such bizarre moments as when Ott grabs at Sader's groin, saying: "[Y]ou won't be a private dick no more. Not if I can help it." Or, while pig-sitting at the Pike, Sader goes through the comic book collection of Felicia Wanderley's cousin, Milton:

> He decided that Milton liked stories about space men with antennae on their head who were thwarted by earth heroes. He noted the presence, in these yarns, of lovely young ladies in danger of being carried off to set up housekeeping on Mars. This could mean that Milton had a subconscious compulsion about being a hero. It could even mean . . . that Milton had shot young Ajoukian because in the heat of the argument he thought Ajoukian was threatening Mrs Wanderley. This was interesting.[46]

It is in its final chapters that *Sleep With Strangers* generates the paranoia associated with pulp culture fiction. Sader's partner, Dan, has realized who's responsible for the murders but, having phoned Sader to tell him the news, is shot as he says something about "weak ankles". With Dan in hospital, Sader, unable to figure if he's a private eye or private dick, goes off the deep end. Convinced Kay is the culprit, he heads off to Las Vegas with her, certain he's found the *femme fatale*. Sader tells Kay he'll marry her. Kay tells him he must be crazy. "Didn't it occur to you that I might not want to marry you because there was somebody else?"[47] At which point one expects Kay, if only to disentangle herself from the attentions of a lunatic, to confess her love for Annie the maid.[48] Coming to his senses, Sader realizes that Kay could not have committed the crimes, and that he's fled with the wrong *femme fatale*. After speaking to Dan, Sader learns that "weak ankles" refers to Mrs Ajoukian who – if she exists – is the real *femme fatale*. But before Sader can turn her in, old Ajoukian kills her. Lying there, she whispers "I didn't like that part – putting them in the oil",[49] indicating that she either has scruples or does not like getting her hands dirty. The book ends with Sader, having dropped Kay, about to dive off the wagon with the wicked Tina Griffin.

What is noteworthy about *Sleeping With Strangers* is Hitchens's refusal to aim her writing at the lowest common denominator, while creating believable characters, particularly when it comes to women. For one knows more about Felicia Wanderley, though dead from the opening page, than one ever learns about the women who inhabit the work of Raymond Chandler. Moreover, Sader's inability to find the *femme fatale*, his falling off the wagon with Tina Griffin, or Dan's penchant for women's ankles rather than breasts – the more usual anatomical interest in pulp culture literature – illustrate Hitchens's willingness to confound expectations.

At home and observant within the confines of the middle class, Hitchens gives the culture only a surface reading, and is unable to supply a subtext of any substance. Lacking Leigh Brackett's market-oriented politics, the closest Hitchens comes to addressing real desires and discontents is when Sader takes Kay to Las Vegas, when he examines Milton's comic book collection, or when he walks out of the Wanderley home, saying: "I'm getting to feel at home in a crazy kind of way. I'm beginning to get the idea that you could sit in one of these piles surrounded by your stuff, and feel as miserable as if you were broke."[50]

Dorothy B. Hughes

After writing a series of brilliant pulp culture novels, Dorothy B. Hughes's career was cut short by a demanding domestic life. Writing without the aid of a pseudonym, her best-known work – aside from her 1942 anti-fascist thriller *The Fallen Sparrow* – is *In a Lonely Place*. Published in 1947, it would be freely adapted for the screen in 1950 by Nicholas Ray. While Ray's film is about Dix Steel, a charming though violent screenwriter, Hughes's novel is about Dix Steel, serial killer. Whereas Ray's film can be viewed as a critique of Hollywood blacklisting, Hughes's book is a blatant attack on patriarchy, misogyny and male violence.

It is typical of the era that Nicholas Ray – briefly a member of the Communist Party during the 1930s – was unable to recreate Hughes's novel; that Hollywood would allow a veiled attack on political witch hunting within its ranks, yet not entertain a plot in which a middle-class, well-educated man just out of the service kills women. Though Dix might appear normal – calm, confident and in control of himself – nothing could be further from the truth. For Dix spends his time stalking women in the night, killing them when he can.

Unable to stop killing, Dix is told by Brub, his wartime friend, now a police detective investigating the killings, that "a murderer is a murderer as . . . an actor is an actor. He can stop acting professionally but he's still an actor."[51] Regarding the murderer's state of mind, Brub informs Dix that the insane are more careful and clever than the sane: "It's normal for them to be sly and secretive. That's part of the mania."[52] All of which Dix takes as a challenge, particularly when hearing that murderers give themselves away by the repetition of a pattern. Like pulp culture fiction, killers are also caught in a cycle of narrative repetition.

Finding himself "in a lonely place", Dix continues to kill. Perhaps Brub already suspects something is wrong. When he and his partner, Lochner, insist that dust – "We've got dust from the drive-in. We're got dust from her clothes and her shoes. There'll be some of that same dust in his car."[53] – will eventually lead the police to the culprit, Dix feels a tremor of panic. As he holds a metaphorical mask to his face, Dix is told that the dust will remain in the air for years; every action and narrative repetition will only increase the amount of residue. Dust is everything, and all that separates innocence from guilt, life from death, chaos from order, and Dix from Brub.

Moreover, there's a homosexual bond between killer and cop that goes back to when they were stationed in London and both in love with Dix's first victim, Brucie. It's Dix who renews their friendship, unaware that Brub's become a cop. When he finds out, Dix enjoys being able to get hold of Brub whenever he wants. In fact it is, for Dix, "more exciting than anything that had happened in a long time. The hunter and the hunted arm in arm."[54]

War has had a strange effect on Brub and Dix. Describing those whose wartime alienation has been exacerbated by the Cold War, like themselves, Brub says: "We're a casual generation." So casual neither sees beyond the surface. Brub's wife, Sylvia, however, might be talking about the murders, or the reader's place in the narrative, when she says, regarding her husband's reasons for becoming a policeman: "He hasn't found the underlying motive yet . . . He's full fathoms deep in detecting."[55] While Brub's detection is paltry, it's Sylvia, college educated and perceptive despite the stupefying effect of the Cold War, who ensnares Dix and emerges as the real detective. As a potential victim, Sylvia, a housewife subservient to her husband, does not hide her fear; while Brub, who has little reason to be afraid, reminds us of how dangerous a war mentality can be in a time of peace, saying to Dix, "I'm the one who's scared; I've infected her."[56] Though Dix dominates the narrative, it's Sylvia with whom one identifies. Even following Dix's every move and thought does not make him understandable, for, as Dix says, there are "some things a man kept secret".[57]

As an excuse for inhabiting an apartment that does not belong to him, his lack of gainful employment and his interest in murder, Dix tells Sylvia and Brub he's writing a detective novel. When Sylvia maintains she knew something was wrong the moment Dix walked into her home, she might have said that Dix's claim to be fabricating a story without text or narrative has made her suspicious. While Hughes implies that writing – including the letters Dix writes to his wealthy uncle requesting money – is a form of sublimated murder, Dix, regarding his non-existent book but frighteningly real narrative, says to Brub: "I'll dedicate the book to the *dick* who brought me lunch."[58]

As we hear Dix complain about a "squawk-voiced woman at the bar", the "drab woman" on the bus, or Sylvia as "probably a wonderful woman to bed with",[59] Dix's hatred of women is obvious, its perversity in keeping with the era. With such remarks socially acceptable, Sylvia, when she first meets Dix, comments that the murderer could be any man, for any man is free to express such views, and only dust separates thought and action.

But Dix is so warped that, when out of sorts, he can regain his equilibrium only by killing women. Priding himself on his audacity, it's women who threaten to reveal his secret: "Women were snoopy. He hated women. Dix would be snoopy too; he was a detective." Dix might proclaim himself a detective but, unlike Sylvia, he's accountable to no one. Naturally, Sylvia suspects Dix. For, as well as having a perverse, if professional, interest in murder and breaking down when hearing about Brucie's murder, Dix, the commodity fetishist, has kept himself outside post-war attempts to forge a safe, bourgeois, nuclear society.

As the police close in on him, the suspense is generated by Dix's paranoia and one's willingness to empathize with the women – most of whom are victims – in the book. Though Dix, enclosed in his own paranoid world, is incapable of empathy: "[Dix] didn't want to get comfortable; he wanted something lively. Something amusing and stimulating and male."[60] When Dix meets Laurel he's certain he's found his soul mate, and sees her in feminine detail: "[T]he outfit wasn't shades of moonlight blue but pale yellow, the pullover deeper yellow; the jacket, loose over her shoulders, was white. And her hair wasn't red, it was burnt sienna with a shimmer of gold dusting in it."[61] But Dix is also attracted by Laurel's dubious inner qualities: "She was greedy and callous and a bitch, but she was fire and a man needed fire."[62] Dix has her figured out: "She was brittle only on the surface. Underneath she too was seeking." And apparently it is true: Laurel is not only after money, but hates men as much as Dix hates women: "There's nothing wrong with money. It's what goes with it . . . Bastards . . . Rich men. And women. They believe the earth was created for them."[63]

Though paranoid, Dix, when first meeting Laurel, is

stimulated by her lack of caution: "She rested herself carelessly against the seat of the car, her left knee half-turned toward his thigh."[64] But what really turns Dix on is Laurel blaming the murdered women for being victims: "Someday those dopes will learn not to pick up strange men."[65] Momentarily wondering if Laurel should be added to his list, Dix says: "You've picked me up." But Laurel senses Dix's barbed edginess and replies wisely: "You picked me up, Princeton."[66]

Dix is as obsessed with Laurel as he is with murder, and it's through his love for her that his hidden self surfaces: "He wanted to surprise her . . . Only by whetting her interest would she remain with him long enough to become entangled with him. Because she was spoiled and wise and suspicious."[67] But Dix's jealousy means he is unable to translate his obsession into his possession. Seeing her in his apartment, Dix realizes she knows her way around: "Had she been here before? . . . [H]e knew she had been touched by other men; there was no innocence in her."[68]

What is interesting is how Hughes has taken the pulp culture cliché of contrasting women – housewife and *femme fatale* – and turned their traditionally adversarial relationship into an alliance whose target is Dix. For Dix is certain that Laurel and Sylvia will hate each other. And though this appears to be the case when they first meet, Laurel moves away from Dix and closer to Sylvia as she grows more fearful of Dix's maniacal behaviour. Perhaps Laurel and Sylvia's rivalry exists only in Dix's mind: "They were eyeing each other in the faint patronizing manner of all women to women."[69] In any case, Dix's assumption that the two women are competing for his affection proves fatal: "She didn't think any more of Sylvia than Sylvia of her. She was more open about it, that was the way of her . . . Yet she had a fear of Sylvia that had no echo in Brub's wife. She was harder than Sylvia could ever be but she wasn't steel; she couldn't be broken."[70] For Dix believes that Laurel and Sylvia represent two different views of the world, two social classes, not realizing that, when threatened with male violence, Laurel and Sylvia are ideological twins.

Dix commits a further error when, thinking she has money, he mistakes Sylvia's social class. As in Leigh Brackett's *The Tiger Among Us*, this misconception, based on the belief that one class has the right to exercise power over another, proves damaging. Likewise, Dix thinks Laurel believes he has money. Desperate, Laurel makes it clear that she was never fooled by Dix, and knew from the moment they met that Dix, like herself, was out for whatever he could get. And Dix is certain that Laurel has shocked a wealthy Sylvia when, referring to patriarchal power and that something odd might be going on, she says: " '[Dix] says Brub Nicolai's the smartest young dick in the department.' He felt Sylvia cringe at Laurel's use of the word *dick* for detective."[71] Not only does Dix misinterpret Sylvia's social class, he also misinterprets her intelligence.

But Dix has more nerve than brains, and revisits the scene of the crime in the company of the police, secretly laughing at the thought that they believe a murderer returns to the scene of the crime. Unfortunately, the police are convinced that the murderer is more intelligent than he actually is. After all, if the murderer isn't intelligent, why take so long apprehending him?

But, as in *The Tiger Among Us*, a misreading of LA car culture leads to a turn in the plot. Coming from the east coast, it doesn't occur to Dix that a person with a car would be unlikely to walk into a drive-in restaurant, particularly with a woman they're about to murder. Like pedestrians, drivers ignorant of local customs are easy prey. Which is why, when Dix reacts irrationally to her mentioning "the drive-in", Laurel knows something is wrong. Her suspicions are confirmed when, while pouring a drink – "Only one drop spilled"[72] – Dix becomes unusually if not dangerously calm.

Dix loses himself and his nerve as the net closes, and the tension of the novel grows as the reader becomes enclosed within the confines of Dix's paranoia. It is here that one becomes aware of the book's narrative ambiguity. Though written in the third person, Dix controls the book's velocity, driven by a tension between his emotional state and the voice of the author. Reading the author reading Dix, one enters the text by way of a voice twice removed. While the crimes Dix commits are described from his point of view, they are filtered through Hughes's writing. But this means that those women who survive are able, though narrative objects, to break out of a male-oriented narrative, take Dix's abuse, solve the crime and entrap the killer. Perhaps Dix really has written a detective novel and we're reading it? Why else would Hughes accept Dix's view of the world, allowing only Laurel to regard him as an object as she looks him over slowly, "[t]he way a man looked over a woman".[73] Or when interrupting a conversation about the latest murder: "He hid his annoyance. Just like a woman, interfering, imposing her whims on the party."[74]

Unlike Leigh Brackett's and Dolores Hitchens's work, *In A Lonely Place* is imbued with paranoia, part of which results from its narrative ambiguity. Yet, though the narrative is constructed as a vehicle for Dix, it is hardly possible to identify with him. While Dix fantasizes about marrying the Banning girl and seducing Sylvia, whose intelligence he cannot acknowledge, one views Dix as though he were an image reflected in the eyes of his victims. Dix might want Sylvia's body, but it's her mind that he fears. Particularly when, regarding the difference between her way of looking at the world and Brub's, Sylvia says openly: "[Brub] just looks at the envelope. Now I'm a psychologist. I find out what's inside."[75]

In the end, it's Dix's delusions, rather than his crimes, that are interesting. Having moved inside the mind of a murderer, Hughes makes it clear that Dix could be any man. For what separates Dix's obsessions from Brub's obsessive determination to crack the case? Though the reader knows little about Dix's life, one can speculate on why Dix kills women. But what connects that speculation to male obsession is illustrated in the position of women in the pulp culture era.

*

*

Writing in a male-dominated society, female pulp culture writers were able to represent women only in relationship to men. For women to write about women was for them to write about women *and* men, which in itself was a radical departure. Moreover, to get their work published these writers had to be adept at their craft and aware of the genre. This means that texts are often self-conscious and tread a thin line between pulp culture reality and pastiche.

That the likes of Leigh Brackett, Dolores Hitchens and Dorothy B. Hughes were able effectively to convey pulp culture paranoia can be attributed both to their writing ability and to the fact that being female in the pulp culture era was itself cause for paranoia. All three writers were able to undermine traditional notions of the *femme fatale*, and though they often portray women as victims, they refrain from portraying them as helpless objects. Furthermore, they frequently turn an adversarial relationship between women into an alliance with a common enemy.

Despite a tendency to give unrealistic renderings of male culture, Brackett's, Hitchens's and Hughes's portrayal of men – private eyes, private dicks or public misogynists – is invariably convincing. Meanwhile, their critiques contribute to the "pulping" of male pulp culture protagonists. This physical, psychological and narrative deconstruction was, in an era of male domination, an essential, if at times unconscious, feature of these three writers. Not that male pulp culture writers did not also indulge in the process, nor were any less severe in its application; they merely approached it from a different perspective.[76] Nevertheless, the most significant aspect about the work of Brackett, Hitchens and Hughes *is* their work, and how each author creates a space in which women are represented as complex individuals within a culture intent on rendering them powerless. In that sense, women writing pulp culture fiction could not help but subvert the genre and the prevailing attitudes on which such fictions are based.

5

PROFITS OF CRIME

The crime novel as social critique: William McGivern's _Odds Against Tomorrow_ and _Death Runs Faster_; Gil Brewer's _3 French Street_; Lionel White's _The Killing_ and _The Big Caper_

> "[N]eighborhood" should often be read _Gangland_. Social organization: _protection_. Society: _racket_. Culture: _conditioning_. Leisure activity: _protected crime_. Education: _premeditation_.
> (Atilla Kotányi, "Gangland and Philosophy")[1]

The Origin of Crime

Following the deflation of the private eye, crime fiction, with its implied hostility to the state, became the dominant strand of pulp culture literature. Having fought corruption, fictional private eyes had revealed themselves culpable and often criminal in their relationship to those employing them. Out of step with the era, peddling inadequate investigative techniques, private eyes had convinced themselves of their social usefulness and invulnerability. Unable to rid society of corruption, many ended up using their skills to criminalize their former class.[2] As their employers laughed their way to the bank and positions of power, private eyes, unable to solve society's problems, were left to wallow in states of drunken investigation.

The origins of pulp culture crime fiction can be found not so much in the private eye novel as in pre-war gangster fiction. Investigating the unexamined world of crime, earlier _objective realists_ like Armitage Trail (_Scarface_), WR Burnett (_Little Caesar,_

High Sierra), Paul Cain (*Seven Slayers, Fast One*), Edward Knight
(*You Play The Red and The Black Comes Up*), Jack Black (*You Can't
Win*), James Ross (*They Don't Dance Much*), Edward Anderson
(*Thieves Like Us*) and James M. Cain had, for the most part,
focused on criminals seeking retribution in a hostile or
indifferent society. In pulp culture crime fiction, criminal and
victim are often indistinguishable. Still pursuing a mass
readership, these writers took gangster fiction a step further.
Crime, for these post-war writers, was no longer the exclusive
province of localized corruption, but an essential component of
a more affluent and universally corrupt Cold War culture.

Often representing the viewpoint of the criminal or person
implicated in crime, pre-war and post-war crime fiction is rooted
in a period when urgent action – whether New Deal state
intervention or criminal activity perpetrated by proletariat crooks
– was necessary if personal and national catastrophes were to be
avoided. Consequently, post-Depression crime writing is
preoccupied with the social and psychological factors which
create crime. While early crime writers, including contributors
to *Black Mask*, hint at something more than the relationship
between crime and the desire for economic security, later writers
– like William Gresham (*Nightmare Alley*), Horace McCoy (*Kiss
Tomorrow Goodbye*), David Grubb (*Night of the Hunter*), Kenneth
Fearing (*The Big Clock*), Jo Pagano (*The Condemned,* aka *Die
Screaming*), Robert Finnegan (*Many A Monster*), Geoffrey Homes
(*Build My Gallows High*), Cornell Woolrich, William McGivern,
David Goodis, Lionel White, Gil Brewer, Jim Thompson, Charles
Williams and Charles Willeford – extend their investigations to
include the desire for autonomy, crime and the pursuit of power.

Few pulp culture writers portray political corruption and the
misuse of power as effectively as WR Burnett, whose literary
career begins in 1929, at the time of the stock market crash,
with the publication of *Little Caesar*, and continues through the
McCarthy era and the publication of *Vanity Row* in 1952: "The
ethical side of the business he pushed completely into the

background. It was not a question of innocence or guilt. To the Administration this was a complete irrelevancy... Staying in office was the main, in fact, the *only* point."[3]

Likewise, few explore the dark crevices of the human mind as convincingly as Horace McCoy, from the opening sentence of *Kiss Tomorrow Goodbye* with its Proust-like preoccupations, in which a criminal is born –

> This is how it is when you wake up in the morning of the morning you have waited a lifetime for; there is no waking state. You are all at once wide awake, so wide awake that it seems you have slipped all the opiatic degrees of waking, that you have had none of the sense-impressions as your soul again returns to your body from wherever it has been; you open your eyes and you are completely awake, as if you had not been asleep at all.[4]

– to its ending, with its psychological preoccupations, in which the death of a criminal implies the birth of a criminal culture:

> I could see nothing and could feel nothing, but I had a vestige of awareness left that made me know that I was pulling knees up and pushing my chin down to meet them, and that ... I was safe and secure in the blackness of the womb from which I had never emerged.[5]

McCoy, in narrating from inception to disintegration the psychological life of a criminal, pre-dated pulp culture's critique of state crime. Producing most of his work prior to the pulp culture era, he found it necessary, in common with other pulp culture writers, to sustain his literary output at the expense of literary quality. Having worked as a professional picketer during the Depression he ended his career not only in poor health and needing money, but also in search of a narrative that would allow him to step off Hollywood's treadmill and its cycle of exploitation. Unfortunately, McCoy's escape came in the form of *Scalpel*, his worst yet most profitable novel. At the same time, other pulp culture authors would attempt to beat the system by turning private investigation into state detection, as their protagonists – no longer private eyes but *de facto* public cops – began to pursue criminals rather than investigate the politics of crime.

Whatever their attitude, crime writers tended to follow the dictates of the genre. But anyone worth their pulp culture reputation must have stumbled upon the metaphorical question of whether crime narratives were, in themselves, criminal. However, crime writers rarely pilfered from other genres. Nor did they commit bodily harm on the dominant narrative. In fact, pulp culture writers seldom strayed from mainstream narratives to suggest an alternative voice, format or political position. With publication dependent on a fluctuating market, most writers fell back on the state's moral arguments and its manner of investigation, which made narrative non-interventionism a radical departure. Likewise, the genre's emphasis on reportage rather than editorial was easily negotiated by such pulp culture writers as McCoy, Burnett, Jonathan, Latimer, Donald Tracy, Daniel Mainwaring (aka Geoffrey Homes, whose "radical" politics made him, despite his many screenplays, *persona non grata* at RKO in Hollywood) James M. Cain, Jim Thompson and Bruno Fisher (once editor of the *Socialist Call*, the official newspaper of the Socialist Party), all of whom had come to the genre after serving time as working journalists.

But not all crime writers needed a background in journalism to turn "hack" on its head. Amongst early crime writers, Paul Cain – real name George Sims – was adept at squeezing poetry from crime and violence. Born in Iowa in 1902 – where, before going to Hollywood, he wrote the screenplay for Edgar Ulmer's *The Black Cat* under the name Peter Ruric – Cain, in one novel and a series of stories, minimalized his writing to the point of cinematic precision:

> There was a man sitting on one of the benches at one side of the narrow breakfast table. The table was set lengthwise into a

niche, with a bench at each side, and the man on one of the
benches was sitting with his back in the corner of the niche, his
knees drawn up, his feet on the outside end of the bench. His
head was back against the wall and his eyes and mouth were
open. There was a thin knife handle sticking out of one side of
his throat.[6]

Ex-journalist James M. Cain, author of *Mildred Pierce*, *Double
Indemnity* and *The Postman Always Rings Twice*, had a more twisted
view of the world. More concerned with mental than physical
cruelty, Cain "created a world immense with freedom, women
hellish and infantile . . . , money, power, the tantalizing promise
of adventure".[7]

I'm getting up tight now, and I've been thinking about Cora.
Do you think she knows I didn't do it? After what we said in
the water, you would think she would know it. But that's the
awful part when you monkey with murder. Maybe it went
through her head, when the car hit, that I did it anyhow.[8]

Clearly Cain was Chandler's opposite, prompting the latter
to say of him, "He is every kind of writer I detest, a faux naif, a
Proust in greasy overalls, a dirty little boy with a piece of chalk
and a board fence and nobody looking. Such people are the
offal of literature, not because they write about dirty things, but
because they do it in a dirty way."[9] Never claiming to be a
hardboiled writer, Cain was neither as controlled as Chandler
nor as interested in commenting on the culture. Cain, for
instance, could never had said, as Chandler does in *The Long
Goodbye*, "That's the difference between crime and business. For
business you gotta have capital. Sometimes I think it's the only
difference."[10] After all, Cain, in portraying a culture based on
desire, is less concerned with politics than the suffocating and
destructive effect of uncontrolled passion.

The proliferation of state and individual crimes turned
everyone into a potential criminal, which at least guaranteed a

readership for pulp culture fiction. Though for most criminals crime does not pay, or does not pay well enough, the gulf separating state crime from individual crime mirrors the difference between state narratives and individual narratives.[11] For the state invariably imposes its storyline on the culture, affecting perpetrators, victims and anyone who has been indicted or implicated by the state.[12]

Consequently, alternative narratives – plots, alibis, confessions, half-truths – are needed to locate the real story. Charley Bower, the lawyer-turned-murderer in Harry Whittington's 1958 *Web of Murder*, provides a narrative which should serve as a warning to all slaves of the free market:

> Maybe you never think about murder until you're pushed to the brink . . . I hadn't stopped working for a minute in the last sixteen years. College and law school had depleted me . . . Maybe even in the ten years of practice I had begun by looking at things in a slanted, cockeyed way. All the ideals learned in school were quickly beaten out of me, and I fought back with every trick I knew. I saw innocent men convicted and criminals escape justice. I'd begun thinking I represented forces of law and order. I found the courts are places of lawlessness, where intelligent jurors are not wanted, where procedure is so gimmicked that witnesses are restrained from telling important facts and tricked into admitting untruths, half-truths. It had become a racket to me, and the prize went to the smartest racketeer.[13]

For surviving the state's enquiries and infringements undermines the state's narrative, logic, line of attack, interrogation methods and notions of guilt.[14] Like Jim Thompson's Lou Ford or Charles Williams's John Harlan in *The Big Bite*, it's often judicious to feign collusion until the enemy and reader can be taken by surprise. Jack MacDonald in James Ross's *They Don't Dance Much* keeps his cards close to his chest: "I opened my mouth and listened . . . Twenty thousand bucks! I began digging it up in my mind. Then I started spending it."[15] But paranoia awaits those who act recklessly or, self-deceived, do not act at all. Unable to maintain sufficient perspective, Cornell Woolrich would be haunted by his own narratives, from *Rear Window* to *Waltz Into Darkness*, and the notion that urban life – "I think of it as a personal enemy . . ."[16] – had become a nightmare: "[H]e could feel hands fumbling around him, lots of hands. They weren't actually touching him; they were touching things that touched him."[17]

But Woolrich's personal crimes – paranoia, self-neglect, alcoholism – were only against himself. State crimes, in comparison, had become so apparent that even President Eisenhower was forced to focus publicly on one particularly blatant example, the military-industrial complex.[18] The contradiction between law-abiding citizens and a criminal state became all too clear. In such an environment, and with America's outlaw tradition, the definition of crime and criminality was called into question. What constitutes being a criminal? Is one a criminal merely for the duration of that crime? Or is one a criminal only if convicted? Can one be a criminal without ever committing a crime? This crisis of definition was double-edged: while normalizing crime, it allowed law enforcement agencies to criminalize particular social groups. This widened the canvas on which pulp culture writers could overlay their narratives, and allowed them to question whether crime fiction is simply a narrative in which a crime occurs, or if every fiction might not constitute a crime.

Nor was there particular agreement on what constitutes psychopathic behaviour.[19] With their solutions entangled in a complicated relativism, writers were best able to investigate the politics of crime simply by portraying its existence. Though to some Cold War critics this itself might have constituted a criminal act, it caused others to renegotiate their notions of objective realism. With literary style and ideology inextricably linked, most crime writers were objective only in regard to their dispassionate depiction of violence and the criminal act.[20]

Influenced by cinematic montage, writers like Paul Cain and Horace McCoy maintain highly subjective viewpoints. With objectivity a relative concept, writers could choose either to side with the state, and its definition of criminality – which, at its most objective, would lead to police procedural fiction such as that written by Ed McBain – or identify with the criminal element whose narratives suggest the breakdown of society. Whichever, eliminating the detective as moral arbiter allowed crime narratives to pursue an extended range of subject matter and narrative voice. Likewise, with the search for the culprit reversed, writers could investigate crime's inherent anti-authoritarianism.[21]

Because crime was so apparent and guilt universal, no one could remain untarnished or unafraid. Consequently, his profession consistent with his point of view, Mickey Spillane became a more accurate representation of the era than either Lew Archer or Philip Marlowe. But so long as it retained an adversarial edge, pulp culture crime fiction was able to investigate the culture and its relationship to crime, wealth, power, desire and autonomy. While the desire for autonomy is, for many, indistinguishable from the desire for wealth and power, the search for autonomy often necessitates committing a crime. With the state scapegoating criminal and political dissidents, the chances of achieving autonomy were then, as now, remote. But for those with nothing to lose, it was a chance worth taking. And if apprehended, but lucky enough to escape death,[22] prison was simply a more brutal site of narrative resistance. However, in a world where paranoia is endemic, escaping prosecution was not easy. Backed into a corner where he watches time run its course, George Stroud, in Kenneth Fearing's *The Big Clock*, sums up the era's sense of paranoia, criminality and impending disaster:

> The big, silent, invisible clock was moving along as usual. But it had forgotten all about me. Tonight it was looking for someone else. Its arms and levers and steel springs were wound up and poised in search of some other person in the same

blind, impersonal way it had been reaching for me the night
before. And it had missed me, somehow . . . But I had no
doubt it would get around to me again. Inevitably. Soon.[23]

For pulp culture's obsession with crime and autonomy can be
seen as a desire to move beyond the political, economic and
social constraints imposed by the state. Likewise, it is
understandable that those burdened by dreams might believe
autonomy can be gained through crime. Yet it is ironic that,
despite the variety of fictional crimes and criminals, the private
eye should remain a cultural icon. Neither autonomous nor
capable of solving crime, private eyes were rarely as arresting as
those they pursued: the unfathomable, deranged, simple-minded,
psychotic, over the edge and out of control. It was the over-dilation
of the private eye that allowed pulp culture fiction to transgress
forbidden territory and, in representing the necessity and
universality of crime, investigate what separates the individual
from the state, and the extent to which the culture is based upon
and permeated with crime, violence and corruption.

William McGivern

There is no pulp culture writer more professional or versatile
than William McGivern (1922–82). Having published numerous
titles with companies like Dell and Pocket Books, McGivern
remains best known for his classic novels, *The Big Heat* and *Odds
Against Tomorrow*. The latter is a gripping narrative about a group
of men who arrive from out of state to rob a small town bank.
Published in 1957 – the year *Sputnik* was launched by the USSR
– it is also a flawed investigation of racial and class tensions in
an era of Cold War uniformity and civil rights activity. Filmed
by Robert Wise in 1959, the novel centres on Earl Slater, a white
Texan, and John Ingram, a northern black. Both have a history
of being exploited: as soldiers, civilians and now as accomplices
in a robbery.

Like Bannion in *The Big Heat*, the sheriff in *Odds Against Tomorrow* is a widower. But, unlike Bannion, the sheriff in this book remains within the law. Though the community he presides over is riddled by Southern racism and class division, it numbers, amongst its population, a handful of upstanding liberal-minded citizens. Yet, despite some powerful clichés, *Odds Against Tomorrow* is a fascinating artefact of the era, particularly when it comes to Slater, whose economic and social circumstances have turned him into a racist constantly on the verge of going out of control.

Ingram, played in Wise's film by Harry Belafonte – the future *bête noire* of black militants – is too perfect not to be an object of hatred. Here niceness becomes a racial, and even a criminal, trait. Yet Ingram takes his revisionist traits on a working holiday, travelling from the relative freedom of the north – tinged with the bigotry of fellow-criminals – to smalltown America where racism is rife and the robbery is to take place.

> Ingram . . . was a realistic man and he had heard and seen enough in life to convince him that hatred was as tangible a thing as the hard city sidewalks under his feet. But he had lived in the North all his life, in the colored neighborhoods of large cities, and he had kept out of trouble by sticking with his own people and minding his own business. He had no patience with Negroes who made an issue out of being served in white restaurants and bars; why get stared at or pushed around over a sandwich or a glass of beer?[24]

Published three years after Malcolm X arrived in Harlem, and the same year in which Arkansas Governor Faubus defied a court order to desegregate Little Rock schools, *Odds Against Tomorrow* is as much about McGivern's attitude towards the era's racism as it is about the era itself. Moreover it suggests a bleak future for a country in which crime and racism flourish: "Earl . . . removed the gun from the pocket of his overcoat. 'You see this?' he said . . . 'It means you don't have any rights at all. Get this straight now; we aren't partners . . . We don't vote on things. You got a chance just as long as you jump when I tell you. You got that, Sambo?'"[25]

With his politics warped by circumstance, Ingram is absurdly tolerant. Instead of wanting to snuff out the racist Slater, Ingram "wanted to help the man; that was the fact of it, the senseless, pointless fact of it".[26] Was this McGivern's paean to passive resistance, or a way of canonizing any Uncle Tom who crossed the page? So uncertian are his politics that Ingram, given the gun culture in which he finds himself, cannot understand why the doctor, with a "peacemaker" pointed at him, refuses to be bullied into visiting Slater:

> Ingram resisted a crazy impulse to laugh. The man with a gun called the turns; it was practically an American institution. Everybody knew that. The gunman didn't wheedle or whine for people to do what he wanted; he just waved his gun and they jumped. Ingram wondered fleetingly how many gunmen had watched this myth explode in their faces.[27]

Or could it be that the doctor cannot comprehend why a black man would point a gun, much less shoot someone who has taken their oath – whether Hippocratic or loyalty – seriously.

At least Ingram has a rudimentary understanding of capitalism's contradictions. When Slater mentions how he was befriended by two property developers, Ingram, insisting that free enterprise exists only for those free enough to be enterprising, says:

> You got some funny ideas about the business world. You think smart guys go around saying, 'Let's cut this youngster in for a piece, and let's give a chunk to the happy kid behind the bar.' It just doesn't work that way . . . just being around money doesn't mean anything. Rich folks aren't giving anything away.[28]

Not that Ingram's insight is of much help; for Slater and Ingram are debilitated by wounds – caused by gunshots, debt, racism,

poverty – which have yet to heal. With little chance of scaling
the economic ladder, they tend to view the war with nostalgia.
" 'I'll check the news,' says Earl. 'Maybe Russia declared war or
something, and they've forgotten all about us.' 'Well, our
draftboards would be after us then,' says Ingram. 'We just can't
win for losing, man.' "[29]

It is Slater's girlfriend, Lorraine, who proves to be the most
vehement racist. With Slater buddying up to Ingram – who, as a
fellow veteran, is the only person in whom Slater can confide –
Lorraine, so understanding at first, turns into a *femme fatale* whose
bigotry leads to his death. While this might be due to Lorraine's
inability to tolerate Slater's newly emerging class solidarity, it is
also an example of how women are habitually forced to the
periphery of pulp culture narratives. An embittered Slater says,
"That's what we were fighting for. Democracy. Community crap
houses." Meanwhile, Ingram tells a story about a man in London
who showed him the sights and quoted Disraeli – "The good
things in life are for the few – the very few."[30] At which point
Slater comes clean:

> "I'm put together with bargain-basement junk . . . Sometimes
> I'd look at my hands and think about it. I'd see the skin and
> the veins and the hair, and I'd realize that none of it was any
> good." . . . They were both in the same mess . . . They were
> alive and they were alone.[31]

"Alive and alone", like drunks in a bar who must confide in one
another. Even the sheriff, when within whispering range of Kelly,
the FBI agent investigating the case, admits he doesn't
understand his daughter. But his daughter is a grown woman
who, once jilted, has become the sheriff's surrogate wife. In the
tradition of lawmen–philosophers who've travelled through the
digestive system of American frontier literature, Kelly tells the
sheriff he won't be the last man to say he can't understand a
woman. Though capable of cracking the case, the sheriff remains
oblivious to its Oedipal overtones. As for Kelly, he might well be

putting forward a critique of "new age dicks":

> Kelly retreated . . . into the protective cliché. He distrusted too-
> tidy explanations of emotional conflicts. And he distrusted
> people with quick solutions for them. Loose talk about
> Oedipus complexes and sibling jealousies made him uneasy.
> The amateur analyst might be right; that was the hell of it . . .
> You could even hit a hornet with buckshot but that was no way
> to stop a swarm of them.[32]

Returning to rescue Ingram, Slater is killed in a police ambush, indicating that, despite his racism, he wasn't all bad. For McGivern, a glimmer of class consciousness is a definite antidote to racism. But only for males who, like single-cell creatures, must first bond with one another.

Having written about detectives, police corruption, psychopaths and spies, McGivern's 1948 novel, *But Death Runs Faster,* calls on his knowledge of pulp culture publishing to construct an excellent thriller aimed at a middle-class readership. Here pulp writer and detective magazine editor Steve Blake must extricate himself from a self-created narrative to avoid being a suspect in the murder of his assistant editor, Byron Crofield.

Set in Chicago, *But Death Runs Faster* sees McGivern squeezing the genre for all its worth. Likewise, Blake exploits writers to the tune of two to five cents a word: Blake maintains these are "very fancy prices to pay for pulp material. With that to dangle in front of writers I knew damn well I could get the best stuff being done in the detective and mystery field."[33] Taking his rates into account, and the fact that payment for such writing would fall as inflation increased, one realizes that such writing would become increasingly devalued. There is, of course, an inherent contradiction in a genre that prides itself on conciseness yet pays by the word.[34] Blake's rates may have been above average, but pulp culture writing is ill suited to the gentrification Blake envisages. Not surprisingly, the manuscripts he receives vary in quality: some are about the war which "dated them completely",[35] while others "had an insidiously evil mood that would make a reader sweat if he read it in an empty house around midnight".[36] Concerned with how, as well as what, writers are paid, Blake, unlike finance department head Gail, believes it fairer and encourages a higher standard of work if fiction writers are paid upon acceptance rather than upon publication. Ironically, it's Blake's liberal attitude to payment that allows money to be embezzled from the company.

Imagining an up-market *Black Mask*, Blake misunderstands the politics and class orientation of the genre. Fighting a recalcitrant employer whose requirements for a story – conflict, strong motivation, action, colour and suspense – clash with his own knowledge of the genre, Blake says, "There are various types of action and conflict and suspense doesn't necessarily mean the Hollywood thriller variety, which consists of forcing the audience to watch the slowly burning fuse attached to a stick of dynamite on which the unfortunate heroine is lying."[37] And, in rejecting a cover showing two gangsters firing tommy guns at each other in front of a bank as a provocatively dressed blonde woman with blood coming from a wound in her temple lies in the gutter, Blake maintains that the person who buys a detective story magazine is no moron, but rather someone who likes the stories and "takes the cover because it goes with the book. Pulp editors must assume that their readers are fools or half-wits because they've been giving them these gory, sadistic covers for years."[38] In fact, Blake would prefer to depoliticize the genre, to disassociate it from its mass readership.

When Crofield states his qualifications and lands the job of assistant editor, one is struck by how easy it is for an unconventional cad to find work. Yet Blake, like any pulp cultist, is intrigued by Crofield's past:

> When I was nineteen I left college after two years . . . I
> believed that education was for those who needed it and I felt
> sure I didn't. I began to write then, the usual crap that young

intellectuals have to get out of their system. I wrote a defense
of Communism, a defense of Oscar Wilde and a few confused
monographs proving that organized religion was invented by
Wall Street to justify marginal stock trading. None of this
made much sense and it certainly made no money. So I began
writing pulp fiction to pay the rent.[39]

An interesting resumé for a crook, though Crofield's spiel says
less about McGivern's politics and more about pulp culture
attitudes towards dissidents and con men. It's possible that Blake
hires this wastrel simply to protect his own reputation as a
dedicated writer. For, though Blake claims to be working on a
novel about the war, McGivern never depicts him doing any actual
writing. Despite the subject of his purported book, Blake
questions the legitimacy of narratives about the war. Waiting
for his secretary, Carol, to arrive at his apartment, Blake picks
up a book by a friend about readjusting to civilian life and to a
country that "violated in practice the principles for which it had
fought a costly, terrible war".[40] Though his friend cites racial
inequality and the venality of politicians as examples of such
violations, Blake believes the author is a bitter man with no faith:
"[H]e didn't believe that fighting was a worthwhile end in itself,
regardless of the outcome. And when a man can't see the value
of fighting for what he believes in, he might as well turn around
and walk toward death with his hands at his side."[41] Does this
mean that men should believe in fighting for its own sake? Not
quite. But, in saying that one must be prepared to fight for a
cause regardless of the outcome, Blake expresses a maniacal belief
that only he possesses the line on war. detection, investigation
and narration.[42]

Consistent with his position as an editor of fictional narratives,
Blake keeps the truth to himself. Meeting Alexis, a wealthy victim
of Crofield's philandering, Blake criticizes the way those with
money use the truth as a bludgeon: "More harm is done by people
acting in what they think to be a 'frank' and 'fair' fashion than
in most wars. Some things are just better left unsaid."[43] Another

one of Blake's interesting remarks. No wonder Martin, the police detective, is unconcerned that Blake might be withholding information or twisting the truth. Believing he has given him just enough rope, Martin is fascinated by Blake, and allows the editor to lead him not only to the killer but to a good tailor. Sharing the same sartorial and social values, a thin line separates editor and cop.

Not that the pulp writers who gather around Blake hoping for a handout have much in common with the forces of law and order. Says hack writer Max Ringold, "Good God, what do you have to do to get a little security in this business? I've sold over three hundred stories and I haven't got a nickel in the bank. And *Dynamic Publications* is selling foreign rights to all my stuff and not kicking back a penny." To which another writer responds: "Let's not discuss the rape of the American writer right now."[44] Drunk most of the time, the writers are friends as well as rivals. Ostensibly subversive, their politics have been neutralized by the degree to which their exploitation has driven them to drink, cynicism and resignation. State ignorance and paranoia about writers surface when the police question Blake. Asking about the writers, one cop says, "They sound like a bunch of communists to me."[45] Even Blake, as a writer, is not beyond suspicion of being a subversive if not a murderer. Justifying the presence of a wealthy woman at Crofield's party, a policeman says to Blake, "You sound like the *Daily Worker* now."[46] For communists and fiction writers and criminals are all supposedly adept at distorting reality.

As a crime writer, Blake is wary of state authority, realizing, when he returns to Crofield's apartment with Carol, that he should call the police. But Blake knows they will deconstruct a narrative he has yet to edit: "Would the police believe Carol's story? Possibly, but first they would take her to jail and hammer away at her with questions . . .; then the reporters would get to work on her."[47] For Blake knows the police have to construct their own narratives and exclude any extenuating circumstances, what Martin refers to as "Freudian" explanations:

> See why I don't like Freud? Get him into a case and right away
> you've got a headache. Everything a guy does gets explained
> away because he didn't make his high school track team, or
> because he dreamed about snakes when he was two. Nothing is
> good or bad, right or wrong, it's just an inevitable reaction to
> pressure. Thank God we don't have to worry about anything
> but whether or not a guy did a certain thing at a certain time.[48]

About Carol's false and "Freudian" confession, Martin, offering
another critique of middle-class investigative literature, says,
"[S]he's confessed to it. That's good enough for me . . . See how
it is with a real detective? . . . We just hang around and wait for
the breaks."[49]

Lacking imagination or clues about public taste, Martin knows
enough to let Blake "poke around and maybe stir things up . . .
like a private eye in the book".[50] When Blake finds him at his
desk reading a manuscript, Martin, realizing that fiction and
reality sometimes merge, says, "[T]he cop in the story is quite a
jerk . . . This private eye makes a fool out of him every time they
get together . . . I never met one of these characters, but that's
probably because I've only been a cop about fourteen years."[51]
But Martin, dealing with professional storytellers and the wealthy,
is out of his depth. "Maybe I was trying to be smart like a story-
book detective. But the people in this case are a little smarter
about some things than most of the people I handle."[52] Here the
middle-class orientation of the book regarding characterization
and plot becomes apparent. In keeping with the era, Martin,
like an upstanding Cold War cop, openly admits to Blake that
he's been checking into everyone's background: "I been doing
all the dull routine work, but I was hoping you'd be playing it
like one of the characters you write about."[53]

When the police release Carol, Blake reconsiders the narrative
and the arbitrariness of murder:

I realized the potential motivations for murder were too obscure and numerous to consider. Why should one man kill another? As easily decide why one leaf falls today and another tomorrow. A man might murder for ten dollars; or because he wanted to make the world safe for organized anarchy; or because he didn't like the way another man parted his hair. Or for any better reason. The motivation might be more apparently significant, but deep within each human being were wells of hatred that could be churned to violence by the softest touch, the lightest word.[54]

In a conclusion that recalls the tradition of the drawing-room mystery, Blake assembles the suspects and solves the crime as his friends and the police, admiring his detecting and narrative skills, look on. Not only does Blake pad the story but, as judge, jury and law enforcer, he usurps the power of the state. *Death Runs Faster*, like *Odds Against Tomorrow*, illustrates how crime fiction often retreats into the safety of solutions provided by the state. With neither crime nor pulp fiction paying adequately, a single individual is forced to solve the crime and edit the periodical. Meanwhile, readers rest comfortably in the knowledge that, given the right investigator, crime can be defined and explained.

Gil Brewer

With its reputation for corruption, racism, poverty, backwardness and primitive sexuality, the South is an ideal setting for pulp culture crime fiction. Consequently, the likes of Gil Brewer, Charles Williams, Jim Thompson, John D. MacDonald, Day Keene and Harry Whittington set many of their criminal narratives in small Southern towns whose citizens have, for the most part, no access to, or influence upon, the centres of economic and political power. With their straightforward narratives and lack of literary artifice, the above writers share neither the urbanity of their northern counterparts like William

McGivern, nor the thematic canvas belonging to more acceptable Southern writers like William Faulkner, Thomas Wolfe and Carson McCullers. Manipulating specific clichés, Southern pulp culture crime writers aimed their work at a different readership and, as working writers, were unafraid to exploit the popular conception of a primitive, if not polymorphously perverse, South. Moreover, their marginal literary status enabled them to counter inflationary notions of literature and attack the centralization of political power.

Not that Southern pulp culture writers would openly criticize state crimes. While racism was treated as a by-product of ignorance, little comment was made regarding such crimes as US "police action" in Korea. Yet by placing individual crimes alongside state crimes, writers like Brewer could investigate the culture and the effect of state crimes on the local population, as well as noting the effect of the locale on those arriving to commit crimes, seek refuge or mix with the locals.

Though he set his stories in the South, Gil Brewer was, in fact, born in New York in 1922, the same year as William McGivern, and died in 1983, one year after McGivern. Self-educated and from a poor background, he served overseas during the war, after which he worked in a gas station, a canning factory and a warehouse. Also known as Eric Fitzgerald, Bailey Morgan and Elaine Evans, Brewer was fortunate to have as a literary agent a former editor of *Black Mask*, Joseph Shaw, who, over the years, placed some five hundred of Brewer's stories. Publishing his first novel in 1950, Brewer went on to write over fifty novels, including war and gothic novels. But it is his crime writing for which he is known, particularly *13 French Street*, *The Red Scarf* and *Wild to Possess*. From 1951 to 1960 Brewer published thirteen paperback titles with Gold Medal, including three in 1951 – *13 French Street*, *So Rich, So Dear* and *Satan Is A Woman*.

In *13 French Street*, Alex Bland, an archaeologist and museum keeper, visits his old army buddy, Verne Lawrence. Though they've corresponded, Verne and Alex haven't seen each other since the war's conclusion. Verne is now married to Petra, who is established as a *femme fatale* in the book's opening pages: a "bold, beautiful woman",[55] she "leaned back against the door, one hand resting on the doorknob, the other fussing with the bottom of the long V neckline of her black dress".[56]

Not only does Alex learn that Petra is the author of the letters he's been receiving, but also he discovers that Verne must make a business trip, leaving Alex alone with her. This makes Alex anxious, having "been born with a deadly conscience; something I detested, but something I couldn't override".[57] But his conscience begins to dissolve when Petra tells him – the sexual overtones understood even by Alex – that Verne has "shot his bolt",[58] having "spent" himself on business rather than the marriage bed. According to Petra, Verne "believed in elbowing the other guy out of the way. A little judicious lying got a fellow places . . . Sock the other guy out of the way. Everything was business with Verne. There are millions of Vernes, and they don't honestly mean to hurt anyone."[59]

13 French Street takes place on the eve of the Korean War, at a time when the work ethic was severe and society at its most uniform. This could not help but affect a person like Verne, in whom Alex sees a "beast . . . gnawing at the already frayed edges of his being",[60] who "looked like an old oil painting that someone had carelessly spilled a small amount of acid on".[61] As an archaeologist, Alex is situated outside the cultural mainstream, digging up answers to historical rather than immediate questions of survival. Yet, forced to investigate the domestic situation in which he finds himself, Alex would have to be an idiot not to have noticed the rotting state of Verne and Petra's marriage. Though Verne might be spent, Petra, believing Verne's senile mother is spying on her, has seemingly hocked her sanity. Whenever the old woman and Verne are out of sight, Petra, like any normal Southern belle under house arrest, makes a play for the first available man. When Alex rejects her, Petra accuses him of being too feeble to entertain this most modest form of criminality. This offends Alex who, like any pulp culture male under attack, responds by slapping Petra.

In a claustrophobic setting and on the verge of violence, Alex receives a letter from his girlfriend, Madge, consisting of two blank pages and a note telling him to fill them "with all the things you'd like to have me say".[62] Ironic that Alex is asked to create a narrative for Madge when he has neither the space nor the imagination to create a narrative for himself. With Verne conducting business in the wrong places, Petra's fantasy narrative regarding Alex has progressed from letters to demands that Alex collude with her. But it's Alex who, as an impassive protagonist, is something of a blank page on which women impose their narrative. Unable to say what he wants because he doesn't know what he wants, he manages to write a letter which, with its lack of specificity and hidden meanings, he hopes will satisfy Madge. No longer knowing what his feelings towards Petra and Madge are, Alex's reason for not returning home is his fear that Petra might read Madge's letters. Like Dix Steel in Dorothy B. Hughes's *In A Lonely Place*, Alex is paranoid that the women in his life will communicate with one another, discover his real personality, and conspire against him. "You want to go but you want to stay", says Alex to himself.[63] He wonders if Verne might have been serious when he had said, during the war, that when they married they should share their wives, as a tribute to their friendship. Perhaps Alex's problems regarding Petra and Madge are based on something more than a desire to "shoot the breeze" with Verne.

Sneaking into Alex's bedroom one night, Petra says, "There's nothing wrong with me, only I'm too much for him . . . He couldn't keep me happy. Now he doesn't even try . . . He's sapped. He's a dead weight."[64] Petra is beginning to frighten Alex – "I thought of tales of the succubus"[65] as he realizes that, if he remains, he will eventually submit to Petra's advances. When Alex does eventually acquiesce, he becomes Petra's prisoner – at which point Petra fends him off, using the proximity of Verne's mother as an excuse.

In keeping with the era, and his precarious mental state, Alex again turns to violence as his sexual frustration grows: "Once I tore Petra's blouse off. Once I fastened my fingers in her hair and told her I wouldn't let her get away",[66] and "I wanted to hit her, smash her. But I knew I wouldn't."[67] Grabbing her, he "ripped the halter away from her breasts".[68] When Verne's mother enters the room after this incident a struggle ensues, and Petra throws her mother-in-law out of the window to her death, saying that, if he tells Verne, she will assert that it was Alex who killed the old woman when she found him trying to rape her daughter-in-law. Aware of how deranged Petra actually is, Alex says, "I was filled with the insidious sickness of her and the only doctor was time."[69]

To clear the house of witnesses and any semblance of sanity, Petra fires Jenny, the housekeeper. With no one now to exploit, Verne asks Alex to bring her back. But Jenny, too sensible to return, says to Alex, "She's got you, hasn't she? . . . You're stuck like a fly in the glue."[70]

Recalling *The Postman Always Rings Twice* and *Web of Murder*, Verne, in town to pick out a headstone for his mother, has a heart attack. Learning of it, Petra tells Alex they can make sure Verne's heart attack will kill him. When Alex hesitates, Petra says, "You can't stand hearing me tell what's true; what's in your own mind."[71] Alex knows she's right, and feels guilty only because he doesn't love her: "If there had only been love . . . then it would have been all right. I could have killed then, maybe. No, not killed. That wouldn't have happened . . . Because it would have been all right then. We would have gone to Verne and told him."[72] Believing love justifies homicide, Alex, sensing the flames rising around him, hits the bottle.

> Without the whisky to hold me up, it was hell . . . I was living in a fire and she was the one kept hurling gasoline on the flame. Being with her had been a kind of hellish heaven. It was maybe like trying to drown yourself in pleasure, hoping to God that you would drown, but hoping that the pleasure would continue and in the back of your mind hating every second of it.[73]

The incident involving Petra and Verne's mother has been witnessed by a voyeuristic farmhand who wants to blackmail Alex and Petra, but can't decide if it's Petra's body or hard cash that he wants. On the verge of cracking up, Alex pays the farmhand and goes into town. Finding Jenny in a bar with a man, Alex drags her to the lake and rapes her. He excuses his behaviour by convincing himself that Jenny reminds him of Madge. Having been offered the freedom of a blank page, and with his emotional growth stunted by the war and a repressive era, Alex maintains his right to desecrate anything reminding him of his girlfriend. At the same time, his decision to drag Jenny from the bar might have been because, for him, Jenny – a woman who refused to do someone else's housework – is the only sane member of the community. Because she reminds him of Madge, Alex seeks to usurp Jenny's sanity and desecrate her perfect image. But their relationship is pulped before it starts, as Alex, now impulsive rather than passive, demonstrates how dangerous a permanently enflamed pulp culture man can be. But it's only after "spending himself" on Jenny that Alex can commodify his brief liaison and pull his twisted thoughts together:

> The mental torture was something I would never have believed possible. To be any kind of criminal one had to be conscienceless. The ones who had a conscience . . . were those who did the screwy things. . . . [I]t would be a pleasure to kill her. Not with a gun – not even with a knife. With my bare hands.[74]

The next step for *homo erectus* is to locate the farmhand. Beating him to a pulp, Alex returns to Petra and tears the front of her pyjamas from her. Overspent after his encounter with Jenny, Alex realizes that sadistically attacking Petra no longer arouses him, and that their warped relationship has ground to a halt. But Petra insists that everything has gone according to plan, including the incident with Verne's mother. Alex, realizing he's been Petra's pawn, leaves to search for Verne so he can make a full confession. But the farmhand, smarting from Alex's beating, has already nobbled Verne. Confronting Verne and Alex, Petra tells them that it was her idea to have Alex visit – "Didn't take me long to break you down, did it?"[75] With both male culprits cowering in her presence, she tells them she intends to kill them both, and rid herself of a money-loving capitalist and a dangerous rapist, both of whom, as returning soldiers, are responsible for Petra's domestic demotion. Though Verne may be spent, he still has his army "equalizer" and, like a good soldier, kills Petra. Verne turns to Alex and orders him to leave. As Alex walks away, with the tragedy – not so much Petra's death as the fact that he will never be able to swap army stories with Verne – weighing heavily on him, he hears another shot and knows that Verne, without having had a chance to hire another housekeeper, has done the decent thing.

Never fully enveloping the reader in paranoia, Brewer's fiction conveys repression, irrationality, temptation and desire, all of which surface when his male protagonists are confronted with the two great temptations – money and women. Due to their circumstances – economic, social or domestic – Brewer's protagonists are faced with crimes they cannot refuse to commit. As ordinary citizens of smalltown Southern culture, they would like nothing better than to confess their misdeeds but, because of their crimes, they are alienated from those to whom they should be closest. Unable not to look a gift horse in the mouth, Brewer's passive protagonists choose a world of crime. But as the plot thickens, and external forces affect their personal narratives, they recognize their predicament. At the same time, their passivity and irrationality mirror the passivity and irrationality of a population faced with state crimes of violence committed in their names on a national or international scale. Taking only the area of defence, the crimes were manifold. Within three years of *13 French Street*'s publication, for example, the Far Eastern Air Force would make its first unseen kill in Korean aerial warfare, the Boeing B-52 would begin flight tests, the first supersonic fighter plane would be produced, the navy would launch the first nuclear-powered submarine, the Lockheed X-7 ramjet would be tested and become the basis of the company's new Missile Systems Division, the Eniwetok hydrogen device, built for the Defense Department by Du Pont, would be exploded and the US Air Force's long-range rocket study group would be charged with investigating the feasibility of an intercontinental ballistic missile.[76]

Lionel White

Born in 1905, Lionel White worked as a police reporter in the 1920s. By the 1940s he was writing for, and then editing, true-crime magazines like *Underworld Detective*, *Detective* and *Homicide Detective*. Turning to fiction in the 1950s, White's work is underpinned with a sense of impending violence, fear and desire. Rooted in the Depression, White's narratives, in novels such as *The Killing*, *The Big Caper* and *Death Takes A Bus*, are constructed around the planning and execution of large-scale robberies. But he also depicts the ease with which desperate and dissimilar individuals can be thrown into a world of crime, and the power relationships that occur. For White's work examines the dialectic between the individual and the group, co-operatives and dictatorships, criminality and honesty. Here crime – which, for White, is just an extra-legal form of venture capitalism – goes awry due to human error, chance, foible and the division of labour. Likewise, those wishing to improve their lives through crime are invariably thwarted by events beyond their control, which upset the best-laid plans and turn crimes intended against property into crimes against people.[77]

Published in 1955, and in the tradition of crime novels like WR Burnett's *The Asphalt Jungle*, White's book *Clean Break* would soon become known as *The Killing* after Stanley Kubrick's 1956 film adaption with a screenplay by Jim Thompson. This co-option is indicative not only of the throwaway aspect of pulp culture fiction, but of a narrative which, with its overlapping scenes and objective mode, is already cinematic in structure.[78]

Johnny Clay, a smart working-class hoodlum recently released from prison, is *The Killing*'s central character. Planning to rob the local racetrack, Johnny recruits seven men – five to carry out the robbery and two to create diversions, which include killing a horse in mid race. Because each gang member desires a "clean break", not only with their share of the money, but from their past and the hand society has dealt them, White details each person's motive for taking part in the robbery. Meticulous, secretive and uninterested in racing, Unger, a court stenographer, wants to make a killing that will set him up for life. Mike, a bartender at the racetrack, is married with a wayward daughter. An inveterate gambler, he sees no reason why a fraction of the money taken each day from ordinary people should not be his. George, a cashier at the track, wants money to placate his wife who constantly belittles his inability to provide for her. Keenan, a cop, plays the horses, chases women and owes money to gangsters. Regarding the amateur status of the gang, Johnny, also looking for one big score, says, "I'm avoiding the one mistake most thieves make. They always tie up with other thieves. These men . . . all have jobs, they all live seemingly decent, normal lives. But they all have money problems and they all have larceny in them."[79]

Meeting in Unger's seedy apartment, the gang members have little in common and no great liking for one another. When Unger says he has reservations about Mike the bartender, Johnny replies, "I didn't pick them because they're tough . . . I picked them because they hold strategic jobs. This kind of a deal, you don't need strong arm mugs. You need brains." After Unger asks, "If they have brains what are they doing . . .", Johnny cuts him off: "They're doing the same thing you are . . . Earning peanuts."[80]

These are intelligent men, under-appreciated, if not ignored, by society. Additionally, as victims of circumstance, each merely wants to lead a comfortable life. According to Johnny, their need for money makes them reliable:

> There isn't a professional criminal who isn't a rat . . . They'd turn in their best friend for a pack of butts – if they needed a cigarette . . . That's the main reason I think this caper has a good chance of working. Everybody involved, with the exception of myself, is a working stiff without a record and a fairly good rep . . . Anyone of us crosses us up, he's in just as deep as the rest of us. It won't be a case of the testimony of a bunch of criminals which will involve him; it'll be the testimony of honest working stiffs.[81]

Because they require money to salvage their wrecked lives, they believe the ends justify the means.

Though the execution of the robbery goes without a snag, the heist fails due to an unforeseen intrusion: after George's wife, Sherry, tells her hoodlum boyfriend about the robbery, he and his associates attempt to rob the robbers. Likewise, the robbery fails because those involved cannot, as criminals or workers, adapt to Johnny's "Taylorist" tendencies. (With its division of labour – there is someone to finance the operation, another to collect the money at the track, someone to open the door to let Johnny into the office, another to divert attention by starting a fight, someone to make sure no one follows Johnny into the office, another to shoot the horse, and someone to drive the car – only Johnny knows the overall plan and all those involved in the robbery).[82] George, for instance, cannot separate his working and domestic life, which results in Sherry's boyfriend and his friends bursting into Unger's apartment. Unable to find the money, a shootout ensues and everyone is killed except George who, though wounded, escapes, and Johnny, who arrives as the police enter the building. Realizing something has gone wrong, Johnny takes the money to the airport followed by an irrational George who is certain that Johnny is escaping with the money *and* his wife. At the airport George shoots Johnny, and the money falls from Johnny's case, ensuring the randomness of its redistribution.

The Killing could be interpreted as being less about the morality of crime than the effects of hierarchical organization on an alienated labour force, the rise of white collar crime, and, with the introduction of automation, demands on workers to increase production and eliminate human error. Not such a far-fetched reading when one considers how each person's role in the robbery creates dissension and paranoia, how an organized system of wealth accumulation defeats the best-laid plans by petty criminals, and how easily dehumanisation can result from the pursuit of perfection.

Also published in 1955, *The Big Caper* concerns a group of crooks who plan to rob a bank in a small Florida town. As in *The Killing*, the labour force in *The Big Caper* is divided – there's a safe blower, an arsonist, a killer, a driver, among others. They've been brought together by Flood, the head of the syndicate. A dictator, Flood plans to throw the town into chaos to divert attention from their robbery. Using the ideology of capitalism and its production methods to redistribute wealth to a small band of crooks, *The Big Caper* not only illustrates the limitations of capitalism but also juxtaposes the rise of suburbia with the failure to tackle poverty and inequality.

But *The Big Caper* focuses principally on Kay and Frank. Caught between crime and a bourgeois existence, they owe their lives to Flood, who has sent them to Florida to pose as a happily married couple and set up house for the bank robbers. Reiterating the era's paranoia regarding the presence of communists and criminals, Kay and Frank, living off the profits of crime, become indistinguishable from other upstanding members of the community. While Frank takes over the running of a gas station, Kay becomes a perfect housewife. Surrounded by kitchen gadgets, gas guzzling cars[83] and a good-neighbour policy, they are quickly seduced by the attractions of suburbia:

> She ... awakened very slowly, gradually becoming aware of where she was and who she was ... Quickly she discovered that [working in the kitchen] was something that she liked to do. What had started out as a chore had soon become a pleasure and something she looked forward to each day ... Frank had been a perfect partner in the game of make-believe domesticity ... And so they played the game, and before long it was no longer a game, but had become a part of their fabric of life together ... She couldn't have tried harder or been more deadly serious if they had actually been married and starting out in a real home of their own.[84]

Like Johnny in *The Killing*, Flood assembles a bizarre group of criminals. With the exception of Kay and Frank, each is a confirmed psychopath. Rather than human error, anti-social behaviour ensures failure and keeps those involved from investigating the renegotiation of surplus value. Which is why, enamoured with each other and their new life, Kay and Frank prepare to relinquish their share of the money and end their life of crime. As ordinary people pretending to be criminals pretending to be ordinary people, Kay and Frank are apparently no different from most suburbanites, their criminal peccadilloes having been the result of circumstances beyond their control. Consequently, as though converted on the road to the supermarket, Kay rejects the past and embraces ordinariness: "What in the name of God, she thought, are Frank and I doing here? Frank is no criminal, no bank robber. Neither am I. Perhaps we have done some unconventional things, perhaps we have even done things that are not legal. But neither of us is a criminal."[85]

Realizing something is wrong, Flood's sense of retribution alternates between fatalism and biodegradability as he makes plans to kill everyone except the most dangerous psychos, who will be left to self-destruct or multiply. As the psychos fight amongst themselves, Kay and Frank, spending a pleasant evening playing cards with the neighbours, decide to quit their life of crime. Now upstanding citizens, it is their duty to stop the pyromaniac, Kosta, from torching the school auditorium. Not that Kay and Frank openly object to destroying institutions for, despite a severe case of commodity fetishism, crimes against property are fair game. It's just that the robbery will coincide with the school play. Though some criminally-minded readers might feel that school plays deserve no less, it's ironic that Frank should remain loyal to Flood and the notion that the play, as well as the robbery, must go on. For when Frank tells Flood that they run the risk of barbecuing both thespians and audience, Flood, aware that Frank has stolen his property, feigns sympathy and assures him the kids will be safe, and the City Hall torched instead. Unwilling to report Flood to the police, Frank accompanies Kosta, who knocks him unconscious – though some might believe he has been in that state since being converted to barbecue culture. Though Kosta sets the City Hall alight, he retains, perhaps due to an early theatrical trauma, his perverse interest in the school auditorium. Fortunately, Frank regains consciousness in time to stop him.

When Frank's worker at the gas station – a black man who appreciates Frank's running of the garage and his sense of equality – runs to Frank and Kay's home to inform them of the fire, he's shot by Flood. At the bank, there is a shootout between Frank and the crooks. Though Frank is wounded and two crooks die, Flood and the girlfriend of one of the dead psychos get away. Chased by the police, their car runs smack into a truck, prompting someone to say, "It was . . . so bad that when we finally pulled them from the burned wreckage, there was no chance of ever identifying them. Not him or the girl. It's strange that the only thing that didn't burn was the money."[86]

Like Gil Brewer, Lionel White has little faith in the state. Portraying the way people act when faced with a cash shortage, White doesn't convey paranoia so much as how those living in the shadow of state power rebel in manners of their own invention. Libertarian in his approach, White focuses on crime as a means of moving outside state control. Swallowing the state line, Kay and Frank mistake consumerism for autonomy. However, White's criminals mirror the organization and hierarchy of the state and the existence of corporate and criminal Keynesianism. Though White implies that crime might pay if properly organized, the correlative is that if society were equally well organized, there would be no need for organized or unorganized crime. But the reality is that ordinary people – whether criminal, suspect, witness or victim – have little chance for autonomy or financial security. Unable to give their side of the story, they are left reading a state narrative in which they occupy a peripheral position.

Amidst the luggage, letters, scarves, guns, tight dresses, gambling sessions, venture capitalism and theft, pulp culture crime fiction is, at its most thrilling, infused with paranoia, but is more often merely saturated in suspense and suspicion. Representing the difference between investigating the criminal mind and the criminal act, one reads the crime and culture from the inside, noting its paginal effect and signification, as cultural objects and pulped material are obsessively thrown across the reader's path. For commodity worship would itself become an occasion for criminal activity, sponsored by the state and President Eisenhower's declaration that "[t]o save the economy, we must buy, buy anything".[87]

With commodity fetishism dependent on climbing the economic ladder, the employment prospects of criminals like those portrayed in Lionel White's assembly-line robberies were no better than average. Though criminal skills would continue to be in demand, criminals, like workers everywhere, would be affected by automation. With the workforce becoming increasingly de-skilled and inactive, it appeared that only criminals possessed the skills around which a personal code and ethical position might be constructed. And, with the possibility that soon it would be a crime merely to possess a skill, criminals, like their counterparts in craft unions, guarded their knowledge. As Peter Rabe writes in *Kill The Boss Goodbye*, "A hit was a secret and personal craft, done alone, with no one around."[88]

Though the criminal act is never plotless, pulp culture crime narratives generate interest in so far as they reflect state crime – consumerism, militarization, economic and social inequality, the centralization of power – which, in turn, demands investigation and alternative narratives. In the end, for commercial and political reasons, most pulp culture crime writers returned to the cliché of the state – that crime does not pay, or does not pay well enough, or pays for some criminals but not for others. But a few writers, like Jim Thompson, David Goodis, Chester Himes, did move to the edge and, whether consciously or not, begin to chip away at the dominant narrative. Unfortunately, the likes of Gil Brewer, Lionel White and William McGivern could never transgress the accepted format to break the laws of fiction. But even though they did not take their narratives to their criminal conclusion, their popularity demonstrates the search for alternative narratives and the need for cultural critiques.

6

BEATEN TO A PULP

The end of an era, reflected in Charles Williams's *The Big Bite* and Charles Willeford's *Pick-Up* and *The Woman Chaser*

"I warn you that what you're starting to read is full of loose ends and unanswered questions. It will not be neatly tied up at the end, everything resolved and satisfactorily explained. Not by me it won't, anyway. Because I can't say I really know exactly what happened, or why, or just how it began, how it ended, or if it has ended; and I've been right in the thick of it. Now if you don't like that kind of story, I'm sorry, and you'd better not read it. All I can do is say what I know."

(Jack Finney, *The Body Snatchers*)[1]

Separating Pulp from Pop

The year 1960 – in which The Shirelles sang *Will You Still Love Me Tomorrow?*, John F. Kennedy campaigned for the presidency, and pulp culture novels like Charles Williams's *The Sailcloth Shroud*, Charles Willeford's *The Woman Chaser* and Walter Tevis's *The Hustler* were published – marked the beginning of the end for pulp culture. As apathy turned to false optimism, the grainy reality of an era obsessed with guns, low necklines and shadows would be overtaken by the sharp textures, public icons, blatant sexuality and sophisticated war technology of popular culture. Though hardboilers with adaptable narratives would continue to be published throughout the decade, the genre had reached saturation point, its vitality sapped by more immediate forms of popular literature – spy fiction, science fiction, soft-core pornography and writing associated with an emerging counter-culture. Meanwhile, the "new frontier" would extend the external borders of the United States to Southeast Asia and outer space, while its internal borders would be defined by events in Dallas's Dealy Plaza in November 1963 – an event that might be tastelessly termed the "pulping" of a president.

But by the time JFK had assumed office, the pulping of other nations was already in full swing.[2] And those who, belonging to what had been known as a non-generation,[3] were suddenly transformed into idealistic adventurers exploring the new frontier. Naturally, would-be pulp culture readers were not going to be so interested in narratives – whether smalltown capers or psycho-romances – that reflected the insularity of the preceding decade.

For this was a period when a competitive spirit was deemed essential if one sought success, power and autonomy. It was the era of the new frontiersman, ready and willing to find new markets and marks. Says Sarah to Eddie in Tevis's *The Hustler* – a novel in which the spirit of capitalism and individualism are localized and pushed to an extreme – "You're a great man, Eddie . . . You know how to beat the system."[4] For pool-playing Eddie, inhabiting the margins of the culture, "the need to win was everywhere in life, in every act, in every conversation, in every encounter between people. And the idea had become for him a kind of touchstone – or a key to the meaning of experience in the world."[5] But as a synonym for Manifest Destiny, the new frontier had more to do with expansionism than exploration, and corresponded with pulp culture fiction's interest in commodities, while the paranoia of change became the subtext of narratives concerning the invasion of smalltown America by organized crime.

Because pulp culture fiction was more concerned with objects, human foible, moral ambiguity and regionalism than consumerism, its decline would coincide with the increasing importance of the "spectacle" in American life, significant manifestations of which was the "manufacturing" of JFK as president[6] and US forays into Cuba. Suddenly pulp culture fiction, with its micro-revisionism, appeared uncultured, barely literate and out of date. With proletariat leanings and an emphasis on moral ambiguity, pulp culture crime fiction could not compete with, or resist, such a calculated historical movement. Nor could it surpass the perverse narrative produced by the spectacle.[7]

But it would not be until JFK's assassination that Americans, living on an atomic precipice, would become unnaturally, but understandably, obsessed by conspiracy theories and doom-laden visions. Significantly, few pulp culture writers had the ability to make the appropriate investigations into the machinations of state power or the politics of the spectacle. Some – Jim Thompson, Ross Macdonald, Chester Himes, Tevis, Williams and Willeford – preoccupied by state power and the demands made by capitalism, were able to adapt to the new fragmentation and formulate cultural critiques allowed their work to extend pulp culture's sell-by date.

However, in the hiatus between pulp and pop culture, the crimes of obstreperous hardboiled protagonists were rarely going unpunished, while the increased presence of state-oriented protagonists indicated that, in an era of economic growth, discontent might be bought off through wages that would eliminate, or at least fracture, the working class.[8] Accordingly, economic growth contributed to the decline of pulp culture hardboiled writing.[9] Though the American working class did not suddenly disappear, those with economic aspirations might have begun to regard pulp culture literature as overly brazen in its critique of the state. Moreover, reading time would be severely curtailed by increased television viewing. With the demise of a mass readership, pulp culture fiction, with its tendency to look to the past, would soon move from critique to pastiche.

Furthermore, the likes of Charles Williams and Charles

Willeford portrayed a nation in which personal and political infringement was rampant, an atmosphere created by the Cold War. The paranoia caused by the possibility of such infringement was eloquently, if facetiously, expressed by Williams in his 1958 novel, *Operator*:

> I suppose everybody has that same sinking feeling in the first fraction of a second, wondering what crime he's committed . . . Then it's gone . . . as soon as you realize it's just a routine security check. Your old friend Julius Bananas has applied for a job balancing a teacup for the State Department and they want to know if he was ever a Communist and how he stood on some of the fundamental issues like girls. I grinned at him. "Don't tell me I made the list."[10]

For the crude methods of McCarthy were no longer necessary. Citizens now appeared to fear any type of investigation. Ruminating on how a trained investigator can engender terror, Godwin, in *Operator*, notes the era's suspicion when confronted with passivity meets technology:

> [A] man who listens to the answers to his questions can scare you. The tip-off is the complete . . . lack of any response . . . There's no use trying to tell him something else six months later because he knows what you said the first time . . . [I]f you're guilty of something, he kills you with simple mathematics. It's easy to make two answers jibe. Try ten thousand. Then, I reflected, a tape-recorder should have the same effect . . . Not necessarily . . . In the twentieth century we accepted the miraculous as commonplace in the Machine, but we still expected Man to talk more than he listened. When he didn't, it was unnerving.[11]

Not that the encouragement of entrepreneurism was the Cold War's sole impropriety. For it allowed the likes of Russell Haxby in Charles Willeford's *High Priest of California* to spread a rumour that his girlfriend's syphilitic husband was once a communist. When asked if he has any proof, Haxby, pretending to represent a veteran's group, replies, "We piece this bit of information together, another little bit, and so on, but when it comes to getting . . . definite proof – we run into a stone wall. Our laws . . . are designed to protect the innocent. But they also protect the guilty."[12]

Williams and Willeford offer interesting critiques of late 1950s car culture, at a time when it was about to turn into a monster.[13] To both writers, the automobile is a primary cultural signifier and the car salesman the ultimate scam artist. Here purchasing a car is, for Williams, a two-sided negotiation, as buyer and seller confront each other through double talk, lies and sexual imagery: "The salesmen . . . assured me if things were different they would adopt me and let me . . . lie naked among Lincoln Capris."[14] Meanwhile, sex and power is associated with speed and technology: "[T]hey'd just refurbished the frammistan and put new whirtles in the springerwarp, and I said . . . maybe his sister was diseased. Very young, he said; first time piece, she don't catch nothing from sailors."[15] To Willeford, it's a sucker's game as successful used-car scamsters earmark potential customers, ascertain their weaknesses, and assess how much they can be taken for:

> [H]is credit rating is examined, and his gullibility is tested on the spot. If it is possible to add the line in the next higher column of the insurance table without the buyer being aware of it, this is done in front of his eyes. The extra dollar or so is added to the monthly payment and is kicked back, of course, to the dealer.[16]

Having grown up during the Depression, Charles Williams and Charles Willeford produced work indicative of their antipathy to state power, state crimes and the creation of social conditions leading to criminal activity. Relying on wit, humour and ingenious plotting, Williams's characters constantly attempt to outwit the system. Willeford, a less polished writer but more chameleon in his approach to the genre, concentrates on creating characters who inhabit the margins of American culture. As libertarians, both writers focus on alienated and flawed individuals. With post-war heroes somewhat tarnished, if not corrupted, Williams and Willeford equate the pulping of the era with the pulping of their protagonists who, as perpetrators, victims, suspects and investigators, fail in their fight against authority. While both note the attitudes of the era regarding sexual politics, class, work and alienation, Willeford, the more class conscious, creates characters who search for autonomy but settle for survival. While Williams's embittered protagonists succeed or fail according to their greed and intelligence.

Concentrating on regionalism, Williams and Willeford rely on popular notions about an already pulped region to upset expectations and subvert values. Williams was particularly adept at exploiting the paradox of Southern pulp, and the belief that its inhabitants are uncultured if not backward:

> [T]his weird and goofy set of values people seem to have, we can't discuss the possibility Mrs Redfield might have a lover, or have had one, because it's simply not done. But there's no social law says we can't speculate as to whether or not she's guilty of some relatively minor thing like murder.[17]

Whereas Willeford, concerned with the effect of capitalism on the individual, never abandons his class perspective. Creating characters who are trampled by the culture or who trample the culture, he views survival as an individual matter – "One man alone, without responsibilities, has got a fighting chance in this world."[18] But Williams is more fatalistic:

> This world is a rough place to live in, unless you lived in it one day at a time and never thought of what was gone or what could happen. You used up Today, threw it back over your shoulder, put your hand around a blind corner, and a little man put another one in it. Some fine morning you'd shove your hand around the corner and there'd be no little man. Just a seagull with a sense of humor. You couldn't

buck a system like that; you joined it.[19]

Yet the last days of pulp culture would necessitate a further pulping of text and nation before its narrative could be read with clarity. Inevitably, pulp culture fiction had become a victim of its own success. Because it was a marginal literary pursuit, it was allowed the freedom to identify state crimes. But its very ability to identify the era's crimes and conditions contributed to its marginalization and eventual demise as both a political and a literary pursuit. For an increasingly homogenous society, in which television was already undermining a mass readership, class-based critiques and gritty subject matter were rarely appreciated.

Charles Williams

So prolific and accomplished a writer was Charles Williams that he single-handedly made many subsequent pulp culture novels seem like little more than parodies. Born in Texas in 1909, Williams served with the US Merchant Marines as a radio operator from 1929 to 1939, after which he found employment in shipyards, as well as the radio and electronics industry. Turning to writing in the early 1950s, Williams set many of his narratives in the country bayous of the South. Moreover, his narratives invariably feature seemingly amoral *femmes fatales* who motivate male protagonists to crime. Desiring money, women and freedom, Williams's protagonists investigate crime with a ruthless selfishness. Because "the attrition of honesty varies inversely with the square of the distance and directly with the mass of the temptation",[20] Williams's protagonists find they must extricate themselves from the very crimes they seek to investigate.

Relying on suspense rather than paranoia, irony rather than cliché, Williams, appropriating elements of James M. Cain and Erskine Caldwell, averaged a novel a year until 1975 when he committed suicide by drowning off his boat. Within that period,

Williams not only created his own subgenre of pulp culture fiction, but helped pave the way for future Southern-based writers like Carl Hiassen, James Hall and Harry Crews. Neither as perverse as Jim Thompson, nor as romantic as David Goodis, Williams, in reworking standard pulp culture themes – the battle of the sexes, the individual's relationship to the state, attitudes to work and the desire for autonomy – could be simultaneously subversive and, by reflecting the attitudes of the era, conservative. This political ambiguity, and his intricate plotting, made Williams a favourite of film-makers like François Truffaut, whose *The Long Saturday Night* was adapted from *Finally Sunday*, Phillip Noyce, whose *Dead Calm* recycled a script that Orson Welles had once intended to use, and Dennis Hopper, whose *Hot Spot* was taken from a 1961 script based on *Hell Hath No Fury*.

Published in 1957 and typical of Williams's work, *The Big Bite* is set in the vicinity of Galveston, Texas and centres on John Harlan who, following a road accident, is forced to retire from professional football. Harlan receives a modest sum of money from Julia Cannon, whose husband dies after running him off the road. He learns from Purvis, a private investigator who once worked on the case for the insurance company, that the accident occurred because Harlan had been mistaken for Julia Cannon's lover. Purvis convinces Harlan that, since Cannon and her boyfriend, Tallant, stand to make a large sum of money from the insurance company, some of it should go to him. But at Purvis's apartment, the two men fight and Harlan is knocked out. As he regains consciousness, Purvis is murdered, leaving the ex-footballer to collect $100,000 of Julia Cannon's money on his own.

From investigating how pulp culture men and women relate to one another, Williams proceeds to examine crime, class and even the process of writing. After visiting Julia Cannon, Harlan composes a blackmail note. Realizing money can be made from writing, Harlan believes his note must constitute one of the highest-priced pieces of prose ever written. Already showing signs of becoming a pulp culture hack, Harlan states that to be a successful writer all one needs is a guaranteed audience: "Hitler had proved that."[21] Like other Williams narratives, the plot of *The Big Bite* hinges on deception. At their first meeting, Harlan believes Cannon takes him for a "simple muscle-head", whereas she, in tight-fitting bullfighter pants, is "a construction job from the ground up".[22]

Of course, Harlan underestimates Cannon; and, from the moment they meet, their exchanges are filled with innuendo, as they attempt to extract information from each other. But it's only after she sleeps with Harlan that Julia Cannon emerges as a formidable opponent. When Harlan tells her not to be an "egg-head . . . [you're] stacked in all the wrong places", and takes a cigarette from her without asking, Julia responds by saying: "An entire philosophy in one gesture."[23] Yet Harlan is no more bothered by his gesture than he is by the moral implications of blackmail: "I'm a bastard. I admit it . . . Look it's a jungle out there. They throw you into it naked and sixty years later they carry you off in a box. You just do the best you can." Cannon is quick to respond: "The beginnings of thought. You're a nihilist." To which Harlan replies, "Nobody's been one for years." Cannon, reassessing Harlan, says, "You *are* surprising. I didn't think you'd know what it meant." At which point Julia takes a long look at Harlan and says, "Just don't be an egg-head. You're stacked all wrong."[24]

Taking Cannon to be cold, calculating and willing to use sex to get whatever she wants, Harlan attempts to exploit his idea of her idea of him. However, as Harlan will learn, Cannon is neither loose nor a typical pulp culture *femme fatale*. Wanting Harlan to think he's got the measure of her estimation of him, Cannon tells him that, in her opinion, he operates "at the instinctive level. And yet you demonstrate great imagination and some intelligence in your campaigns to satisfy these primitive urges." With another reference to pulp culture writing and the marginalization of women within the genre, Harlan replies, "Why don't you write a book?" Then, regarding women in general, Harlan says, "They yakked all the time except when they were being laid or asleep."[25] But Cannon is smart enough to know that Harlan is motivated by fear. Contradicting the era's image of the tough guy, fear, for Williams, is a common cause of crime as well as misogyny. At the same time, Julia is also afraid, less of Harlan than of what he represents, less of being caught then the retribution of the state.

With his investigation adhering to his belief in petty capitalism, Harlan is pulped both by his method and his madness. Neither born to wealth nor self-made, he becomes entangled in the rungs of a rotting economic ladder. Once a bystander, Harlan, having enclosed himself within the adversarial machinations of the culture, becomes a victim and a perpetrator. To find out if he is working alone – and has not, as he claims, sent a letter which, in the event of his death, is to be handed to the DA – Cannon and Tallant hold Harlan hostage. This allows Cannon to estimate Harlan's worth and continue her investigation into what makes her adversary tick. She concludes that Harlan has insulated himself against every emotion but greed, and that he mistakes insensitivity for courage. Critical of her adversary's notion of venture capitalism, Cannon admits that, though he has a certain amount of imagination and daring, Harlan is unable to see the flaws in his plan.

Underestimating Cannon's desire for revenge, Harlan sees a glimmer of hope in Tallant's propensity for violence. For Harlan believes that "[if] you get emotional you can always lose your head".[26] But it's Harlan who is emotionally strained. With only money capable of triggering an emotional response, Harlan believes being held hostage in a middle-class neighbourhood provides a degree of safety. For murder, according to Harlan, is unlikely to occur on the right side of the tracks. This misconception indicates the inflated value Harlan places on money and commodities, and how his middle-class aspirations lead to alienation and unreality. As reality seeps in, Harlan realizes that death with curtains isn't any different from death with Venetian blinds: "I was lying here watching myself disappear."[27] Or does Harlan recognize that, as a pulp culture male, an attempt is being made to pulp him from the era and the text.

An ardent fatalist, Julia knows that crime has its own momentum. After telling Harlan his mistake was not taking time to learn something about the people he was blackmailing, Julia takes the pulping process a step further, claiming that Harlan would not be so tough if he knew how one can be "destroyed by random little sequences of events".[28] Once again Harlan dares Cannon to write it down and enter a genre to which most women are denied access: "Maybe somebody would publish it." But Julia's point is more political than personal or literary: "We're all destroyed . . . for wanting too many things and not caring how we get them." She tells him that if he really thinks he's a tough guy, he "should wait and be tough after there's no longer any hope of winning".[29]

But Julia realizes that Harlan is dangerous because he is insensitive and has just enough intelligence to concoct a plan to wrest Julia's money from her. Explaining her situation to him, Julia tells Harlan that there's no point in discussing why she was unfaithful to her husband, because eventually "we'd run into language connected with emotion, which . . . would have no meaning to you".[30] Though she might well have been referring to an aspect of pulp culture crime writing and its flawed search for autonomy. Running intellectual rings around Harlan by chipping away at his tough-guy pose, Julia Cannon might well be one of the few feminists in male pulp culture fiction.

Tied to a bed, Harlan is a captive audience for Julia's thoughts. Believing she could get away with her crime, Julia, now having considered the odds, realizes there are too many factors out of her control. She tells Harlan to imagine a roulette wheel that spun for five months, or a year, or ten years, before it stopped:

With all your money bet on just one number, and with that

much time to examine the laws of probability, you must
inevitably come to doubt the wisdom of it. Add to that the fact
that you never really know for sure when the roulette wheel *has*
stopped.[31]

Aware that the police will catch up with her, and having
succumbed to Harlan on one occasion, Julia vows never again to
underestimate him. When the opportunity presents itself, Harlan
attacks Tallant, at which point Julia inadvertently kills her
accomplice rather than her adversary. Knowing she cannot get
away with her crime, and planning to kill herself, Julia lets Harlan
have the money. But at a price. For Julia tells Harlan she has
already offered the money to her former teacher, who is now
terminally ill. When the woman, who has a notary's commission,
refuses the money, Julia asks her to keep a letter implicating
Harlan, to be handed over to the police when her friend dies,
which might be weeks, months or years. She admits she could
have left the note beside her bed for the police to find in the
morning, but "you wouldn't have time to enjoy your wealth, or
to savour your emotion".[32]

In bequeathing this emotion to Harlan, Julia might have been
referring to pulp culture men in general: "You lead a very barren
life . . . I have just done what I could to rectify that, by arranging
for you to have . . . the only emotion – besides greed – that I
believe you are capable of feeling. Fear."[33] As a wave of paranoia
washes over him, Harlan frantically thumbs the phone book for
the woman's name, but realizes the letter is with the woman's
lawyer: "*All I have to do is . . . find the lawyer* – But first I'd better
get out of here. This place wasn't safe any more . . . and then I
would be able to think."[34]

The Big Bite can be read as a metaphor for the final days of
pulp culture fiction, or as a treatise on the futility of crime. For
Harlan is trapped by his alienation and retrograde sexual politics.
As a critique of pulp culture tough guys and the limitations of
criminal libertarianism, Williams raises the question: At whose

expense is wealth acquired? For *The Big Bite*, like much pulp culture fiction, mirrors the morality of capitalism, and the restrictions on independent thought and action during the Cold War era. It also illustrates how men respond when confronted by an intelligent woman, and how they act as independent agents in a paranoid era.

Beginning the final chapter of the pulp culture age, *The Big Bite* examines the extent to which the era's paranoia had become part of the state's intrusion into private as well as public life. While, for most, the fear of poverty superseded the fear of communism, committing a crime necessarily entails living with the profits and consequences of that crime. Just as anarchism combined with retrograde sexual politics leads to libertarian stupidity, so autonomy and consumerism results in lobotomized criminals who merely like to shop. As Julia says, people are "destroyed by wanting too many things and not caring how we get them". Written in an era of economic optimism, *The Big Bite* brings home the notion that autonomy, if it is to extend beyond the world of fiction, is possible only by altering a system that associates autonomy, desire and consumerism.

Charles Willeford

Best known for his post-pulp culture work, particularly his Miami-based Hoke Moseley novels which appeared in the 1980s, Charles Willeford produced a number of pulp culture classics. An ex-boxer, horse trainer, soldier, radio announcer, painter and poet, Willeford, born into a Southern family in 1919, was raised in Los Angeles, and went on to use the South as well as southern California as settings for his pulp culture fiction, with books such as *Pick-Up* in 1955, *High Priest of California* and *Wild Wives* (published in a single volume) in 1956, *Lust Is A Woman* and *Honey Gal* in 1958 and *The Woman Chaser* in 1960. Publishing newsstand editions with Beacon and Belmont, Willeford, despite a willingness to cross genres, was never as prolific a writer as

Williams. Nevertheless, by the time of his death in 1988, he had notched up twenty-seven books, including four volumes of autobiography – *Cockfighter Journal, A Guide for the Undehemorrhoided, I Was Looking for a Street* and *Something About a Soldier* – as well as a handful of novels that bordered the pulp culture era – *Understudy for Love* in 1961, *No Experience Necessary* and *The Cockfighter* in 1962. Having adapted his style to the demands of the market, Willeford was one of a handful of writers capable of taking hardboiled crime fiction through the following decades.

Published two years after the opening of Lawrence Ferlenghetti's City Lights bookstore and in the same year as the Six Gallery poetry reading (featuring Kenneth Rexroth, Allen Ginsberg and Jack Kerouac) which signalled the beginning of the San Francisco poetry renaissance, *Pick-Up* features Harry and Helen, two alcoholics who have rejected the trapping of bohemian as well as bourgeois existence. Derivative though it may have been, Willeford showed little interest in cultural movements, preferring to investigate marginality and the effects of alcoholism, alienation and racism.

With its stripped-down prose, *Pick-Up* combines David Goodis's romanticism, Horace McCoy's portrayal of alienated outcasts and Charles Jackson's depiction of life as a "lost weekend". When, late one evening, Helen wanders into a downtown greasy spoon and cannot pay for her coffee, Harry, a short-order cook, picks up her tab and they retire to a nearby bar. Neither Harry nor Helen entertain notions of upward mobility but, unlike pulp cultists who contend that liberation can be achieved through the acquisition of wealth, they believe autonomy is possible only when drinking, preferably in each other's company. Consequently, their resignation holds them together. Though not at first glance a political novel, their attitude constitutes a political position in which alcohol is a means of escape and drunkenness a state from which they derive a perspective of the world. No wonder, for Harry, "The fact that

she was an alcoholic didn't make any difference to me."[35] For, as
Harry admits, "Gin was my weakness, not women."[36]

So natural is the "pick up" that it belies the puritanical
meaning of the word. But the book's title, which also refers to
the desired effect of alcohol, is meant to shock as well as entice.
For *Pick-Up*, with its street-level notion of coupling, serves notice
that this is not a cosy middle-class novel, but a sign-of-the-times
polemic.

As for Helen, she's attracted to Harry because he's "somebody,
underneath . . . and not just another man".[37] In carrying the
baggage of their pasts, they promise each other never to use the
word love, which they believe has been rendered meaningless by
advertising. Harry is astounded when Helen agrees:

> I never thought I'd hear a woman say that . . . Love is in what
> you do, not in what you say. Couples work themselves into a
> hypnotic state . . . by repeating to each other over and over
> again that they love each other . . . They also say they love a
> certain brand of tooth paste and a certain brand of cereal in
> the same tone of voice.[38]

As world weary as they are innocent, when Harry asks if she will
stay with him, Helen replies, "You didn't have to ask me like
that. I thought there was an understanding between us."[39]
Confiding in each other, Harry tells her he's a failure, but
Helen reminds him that, to her, such things do not matter. Nor
the fact that neither has had sex for a considerable time: for
Harry it's been two years, while Helen hasn't been with anyone
for years, ever since she was raped by her husband on their
wedding night, an event so traumatic it resulted in a suicide
attempt.

Well educated, Helen gained a college degree so she might
escape her domineering mother, while Harry has studied
painting at the Art Institute in Chicago and in Los Angeles.
About his painting, Harry the romantic says, "I used painting as
a substitute for love . . . It turned into an unsuccessful love affair,

and we broke it off. I'm over it now . . . and certainly the world of art hasn't suffered."[40]

When Helen tells him he could do anything to which he puts his mind, Harry counters with a cultural critique: "The Great American Tradition: *You* can do anything you think you can do! . . . Can a jockey last ten rounds with Rocky Marciano? Can Marciano ride in the Kentucky Derby? Can a poet make his living by writing poetry? The entire premise was so false it was stupid to contemplate."[41] Pressing her point, Helen asks Harry to paint her portrait. Though reluctant, Harry agrees, and finds that, once he begins, he's no longer drinking. But when her portrait is finished, Harry is overcome with despair: "[W]hat a rotten, stinking world . . . we live in . . . We aren't going to beat it by drinking and yet, the only way we can possibly face it is by drinking!"[42]

With suicide the first step on their road to recovery, Harry cuts Helen's wrists and then his own. Rudely awakened the next morning, their failure makes them wish they had a religion in which to seek refuge. But, for Harry, religion "isn't fair to those who find it impossible to believe, those who have to be convinced, shown, who believe in nothing but the truth".[43] Their agnosticism leads them to a hospital where they ask for treatment. It's there that Harry comes across an article in an art magazine by his former teacher who, stating that art must have subsidy to survive, asks why Harry Jordan gave up painting. It's not reading his name that stuns Harry, but the article's non-libertarian subtext: "I hadn't given up painting for economic reasons. No real artist ever does."[44] Convinced his life has taken a step without him, Harry feels he and Helen would be better off at home.

Unlike many women portrayed in pulp culture fiction, Helen is neither a *femme fatale* nor a manipulative man-hater. With Harry looking for work, Helen, unable to tolerate being left alone, goes to a bar where she's picked up by three marines. Harry finds her and takes her home, realizing that Helen's drinking has reached such proportions that only part-time employment will allow him enough time to look after her. When he next returns from work, Harry finds Helen has disappeared again. This time he finds her drinking with a sailor. Harry lashes out at the sailor, slicing his face with a broken bottle. Back home, Harry and Helen are at rock bottom, Harry's resignation having reached new heights:

> It might be interesting for that part of me that used to think things out, to sit somewhere and watch Harry Jordan . . . go through the motions. The getting up in the morning, the shaving, the shower, walking, talking, drinking . . . Let the body function and the senses sense. The body felt elation . . . My mind felt nothing.[45]

Harry tells Helen his death is imminent: "There isn't any driver . . . and the controls are set . . . I don't know how long they're going to last."[46]

That night Helen awakes and allows Harry to strangle her. With Helen dead, Harry turns on the gas. But his suicide fails because he forgets to close the transom. Arrested, he willingly confesses. Surprisingly, in the prison hospital, Harry is asked if he thinks Helen might have had any Negro blood. Harry, rather than replying, prefers to give a selected account of his life prior to meeting Helen, including his time in the army, his life with his wife and child in Chicago, and his teaching career.

More a victim of the era than a criminal, Harry, under observation, endures a series of humiliations. Helen's wealthy mother visits him only to spit in his face. A young woman in the stenography pool bribes an orderly so she can be alone with Harry in the hope of having sex with him. When Harry is offered $1000 from a men's magazine for the story of his relationship with Helen, he refuses, saying, "Everybody seemed to believe that money was everything, that it could buy integrity, brains, art, and now a man's soul."[47]

Just as he's due to appear in court, Harry is told he will be set free. For Helen was found to have died of a coronary thrombosis brought on by malnutrition. Though bruises were found on her neck, Harry's actions, incredibly enough, did not cause or even hasten her death. Furthermore, the DA was aware of this from the beginning but wanted a full psychological report on Harry before releasing him. As though in a dream, Harry drifts from the courthouse to the cafe where he and Helen met, to the bar where they drank, to his old rooming house. Though free, Harry has been handed a life sentence.

But the reader is unprepared for the final lines of the book:

I left the shelter of the awning, and walked up the hill in the rain.
Just a tall, lonely Negro.
Walking in the rain.[48]

Recalling *Just Walking In The Rain* – a song written and recorded by a black quartet, The Prisonaires, two years prior to the publication of *Pick-Up*, and later recorded by white crooner Johnnie Ray – Harry's final lines require one totally to rethink the narrative. In assuming the protagonist to be white, one's own racial bias is called to account as well as that of the era in which the book is set. Moreover, the reader must now consider how being black affects the narrative and Harry's place in it, including his silence regarding his blackness, which he maintains until he's destroyed by his freedom.

In re-investigating this narrative, one must examine the relationship between sex and race, particularly the era's fears about miscegenation. Equally, since no one in the novel comments on Harry's skin colour, one must also consider the difference between the alienation induced by racism and that caused by the bankrupt values of the Cold War era. Though this might intrude on the poignant banality of the novel, it means that *Pick-Up* must be re-read before it can be discarded. Willeford undercuts the notion that such writing, published in cheap paperback format, is mere pulp, or throwaway, fiction. His final lines are no afterthought. Despite being a pulp culture romance, *Pick-Up* is a critique of capitalism, racism, the work ethic, the role of the artist and the myth of black sexuality. Inserting a black protagonist into a literary landscape with which he's rarely associated turns *Pick-Up* into a razor-sharp narrative that rips open the genre, exposing the possibility that racial inequality, as much as economic inequality or war, might eventually destroy the era.

The Woman Chaser represents the final days of pulp culture fiction. Set in a post-Chandler Los Angeles, with a population divided between "feebs" – or the feeble-minded – and "insiders" – "who are wise to themselves and to things as the way they are"[49] – Willeford's novel satirizes a culture based on cars, movies and an anonymous labour force. Concerning Richard Hudson, a manipulative and Oedipal car salesman and scriptwriter who eventually destroys himself as well as his text, *The Woman Chaser* bridges pulp culture fiction, petty capitalism, consumerism, crime and sexual politics. It's a critique of southern California culture that recalls F. Scott Fitzgerald's Pat Hobby stories, Horace McCoy's *I Should Have Stayed Home* and Steven Fisher's *I Wake Up Screaming*. At the same time, *The Woman Chaser*'s structural self-consciousness prefigures subsequent post-modernist texts.

Relocated to LA to buy and manage a used-car lot for his San Francisco employer, Richard Hudson's deterioration begins when his obsession with the movies supersedes his ability to sell used cars. Yet, by the time the narrative has been recycled, Hudson still hasn't a clue: "Someday I may discover the exact point . . . or the error, if it was an error that I made, or someone else made, or just exactly what it was that happened to me."[50] Cleverly disguised as a *roman à clef*, Hudson speculates on the personal nature and meaning of his narrative:

> [M]aybe this is a conventional story after all. But not really, because it is too personal. It happened to me and therefore it is important to me . . . But everything a man does affects

somebody else . . . Some of my story is too personal to write in
the first person, and some of it is too personal to write in the
third person. Most of it is too personal to write at all.[51]

Personal it may be, but the politics of *The Woman Chaser* are the
product of the narrator's warped libertarianism and retrograde
sexual politics. Half aware of his own duplicity, Hudson takes
perverse pleasure in citing the unwritten laws of automobility,
particularly the one requiring LA inhabitants to own 2.5 cars
and live twenty miles from their place of work. With automobility
and economic mobility inextricably linked, Hudson is able to
profit from such laws, and from the feebs who, caught in LA's
sprawl, flock to his used-car lot.

A petty entrepreneur, Hudson is not as empathetic as he
claims. Feigning concern, Hudson says, "a wave of pity would hit
me when I screwed some aircraft mechanic out of his money for
a used car. But I did."[52] When it comes to making money, Hudson
pities no one, not even his salesmen who, on his orders, must
dress in Santa Claus costumes and swelter in the mid-August
sun. Nor his boss. For Hudson knows that if he makes enough
money, he could "cut Honest Hal's throat and take the entire
pie. Is not this the American way?"[53]

With a more honest, if not realistic, view of LA than either
Raymond Chandler or Ross Macdonald, Willeford nevertheless
portrays Hudson's step-father, Leo Steinberg – a Hollywood
director with artistic leanings – as a victim of an economic, rather
than political, blacklist. For *The Woman Chaser* is about profit
and loss rather than political subversion. And, as Elmore
Leonard's *Get Shorty* attests, Hollywood is overflowing with
would-be Hudsons who have excess capital to invest. Though he
could have invested his money in stocks, Hudson, trusting no
one else, knows movies are a potentially lucrative form of venture
capitalism.

Living in the apartment above the garage next to his mother's
spacious house, Hudson's furnishings indicate his taste and

pretentiousness: Herman Miller furniture, Henry Miller water-colours and a record collection – this last bought for a pittance from a music critic who lost everything in a divorce and eventually drowned himself. Another literate pulp culture protagonist, Hudson's book collection includes *Ulysses, The Trial, Practical Clinical Psychiatry, Crime and Punishment, Seven Pillars of Wisdom, Self Analysis*, the complete works of Edgar Rice Burroughs, Fitzgerald's Pat Hobby stories, and the collected poetry of T. S. Eliot, Dylan Thomas and Ezra Pound. Despite admitting that he buys pulp novels in drugstores for light reading, Hudson's tastes are hardly as daring as he believes them to be.

Hudson's hiring of ex-Sergeant Major Bill Harris to assist him at the car lot is characteristic of Willeford's interest in the connection between military and civilian life. Significantly, Willeford would remain in the air force until 1956, a year after the publication of *Pick-Up* and only four years before the publication of *The Women Chaser*. Though it's not certain who he's addressing, Hudson contrasts a retired officer, who will insist on telling you how to run your business, and a retired master sergeant, who is the perfect worker, willing to take orders without complaint. Despite his master sergeant and well-padded bank account, Hudson remains depressed, less for himself than for others, prompting him to ostentatiously announce that he's become "a walking allegory looking for the hidden meaning in the life of others".[54]

Previously too busy for women, Hudson now pursues them, starting with Leo's teenage daughter whose conquest he cloaks in educational and humanitarian terms. Though Hudson's advice to Becky might suggest he has the teenager's interests at heart, Hudson's reasons for having sex with her have more to do with the free market than free thinking: "[I]f it wasn't me it would soon be someone else, some unskilled but fast-talking ... boy who would make out with her by working the word 'love' into his pitch." Hudson, ever the humanitarian, decides if he's to be the one, to "manage it bluntly, brutally ... No tenderness, no subtlety, no shaded nuances, or romance."[55]

Believing workers are stupid precisely because they are workers, Hudson's eventual pulping results as much from his retrograde sexual politics as his snobbery. Referring to his secretary, Hudson says, "Laura wilted, retreating into a natural state of feminine inferiority women affect when they don't know what else to do." Confusing inferiority with fear, Hudson has a perverse interest in viewing women like Laura as a source of amusement: "I wondered why this woman . . . wanted to be so intelligent. Women are made for bed, and men are made for war. Life would be so simple if both sexes could only remember these basic facts of life."[56] When Laura tells him she's a virgin and wants to remain so, Hudson takes her home, peppering their journey with insults. At his apartment, Hudson's cold shower takes the form of a reading from *Ash Wednesday*. Overcome with compassion for Laura, Hudson returns to her apartment where he finally gets his way.

But Hudson's life undergoes an abrupt change when he spots a large, frizzy-haired woman in a housecoat walking down Wilshire Boulevard with her children. Looking at her, Hudson imagines her husband – most likely a pathetic feeb who is working himself to death in the aircraft industry:

> To support such a family he would have to work two shifts. To love such a family he would have to work three shifts. They would live in a project house . . . At home he would be unable to sleep, rest, watch television, or even go to the bathroom comfortably . . . After eight hours at home . . . the sound of riveting would be soothing to him.[57]

Hudson realizes he must make a movie that tells the true story of the American worker, which encapsulates his essential feebishness.

So intoxicated is he that, like an alcoholic searching for an AA meeting, Hudson ransacks the area for the nearest Toastmasters club where he listens to a first-time speech from a young corporate capitalist. With his phoney compassion resurfacing, Hudson envisages the young man in fifteen years' time, with a top position and a desire to perpetuate the system. Overwhelmed, Hudson rushes to his car and bursts into tears: "[T]he foolish waste, the dullness of their lives, ... the stupidity of such an existence, and underlying everything... they didn't *know!*"[58] That is, they cannot perceive their own feebishness, nor do they possess Hudson's dubious faith in the redeeming qualities of the creative act. Clutching his project, Hudson goes to his step-father, and together they plan the film. Using non-name actors on a low budget, his film, *The Man Who Got Away*, will be about a truck driver who, working overtime, runs down and kills a small child. Pursued by the police, he becomes the most wanted and well-known person in California.

Working on his screenplay in a hotel room, Hudson is visited by Harris. When Hudson admits he's having problems getting started Harris, who claims to have done a great deal of writing in the service – "Nothing creative . . . getting over ideas to others" – tells Hudson it's a matter of rewriting:

> After you get enough pages done, you have something to read. If you can read it you can revise it. If you revise it enough times, you come up with something pretty good. All writing is like that; it couldn't be any other way. So if you know what your story is, go ahead and put it down as best you can. You can always revise the lousy draft. And you aren't going to get a perfect script the first time.[59]

Ironic that a retired serviceman should offer such a pragmatic description of writing that contradicts bourgeois notions about artistic inspiration and the separation of art from ordinary work. For Harris, placing persistence over inspiration, demystifies and politicizes the act of writing. Moreover, Harris's comments constitute one of pulp culture's most accurate accounts of the writing process. Now able to proceed, Hudson's script gradually takes shape, and within ten hours he has already finished a rough draft.

Finding the lead actor in a small theatre group, Hudson cynically casts the trucker's wife by visiting Farmers Market and picking the first woman who spends $50 on groceries. With his treatment of actors no different from his treatment of other feebs, Hudson's finished product stuns Leo:

> It will make people angry . . . Is that bloodthirsty mob the American people? . . . The ending . . . there isn't any real answer . . . The movie is cynical, Richard. It's bitter . . . I don't believe in my heart . . . that the world is . . . like this. And yet your movie makes me believe it! Who did this to you? Why are you so unhappy?[60]

For the first time, Leo perceives his step-son as he actually is.

But Hudson's own dissolution begins after meeting the head of the studio – THE MAN. Still overrating his artistic ability, Hudson realizes that he, in comparison, is an immature feeb:

> I had fooled Leo and I had fooled myself, but THE MAN and Leo Steinberg were adults, something I would never be. I didn't want to be an adult – I didn't want to lose my dream . . . The dream is better; it makes living worthwhile . . . People like THE MAN and Leo Steinberg feed on men like me.[61]

An artistic success, the movie is twenty-four minutes short of the required ninety minutes. When THE MAN says he wants to edit and sell the film to television as part of a series tackling social issues, Hudson will not hear of it, making him, like his step-father, a victim of his artistic success. But, unless there is an ulterior motive, the studio's concern about the length of Hudson's film – sixty-six minutes – does not correspond with an era in which many films, particularly B features and *films noirs*, had running times well under ninety minutes.[62]

Angry because Leo has sided with THE MAN, a drunk Hudson returns home, his hatred of art surfacing when he takes a knife to his step-father's prize possession – a Roualt clown painting that Leo had hocked to raise money for the film. Fired up by his final cut, Hudson returns to the studio to burn his script and finds Laura who tells Hudson she's pregnant. Hudson celebrates the news by hitting her in the stomach, after which he sets fire to his script. Seeking refuge in a bar, Hudson picks up a woman collecting for the Salvation Army. Treating her as God's prostitute, he bribes her to go to his room. Though they share a bed, Hudson hasn't the heart to have sex with her. The next morning he returns to the car lot, fires Bill, puts on a Santa Claus costume and listens to the police siren in the distance.

Realizing he's a minor hustler with a knowledge of film no greater than his knowledge of used cars, Hudson remains cynical, bitter and psychologically twisted. Able to relate to others only by manipulating, seducing and abusing them, he realizes that, had his step-father not been in the profession, he would never have been able to make his film. Whereas a feeb, according to *The Man Who Got Away*, can achieve notoriety only through an inadvertent act of destruction, an insider can do the same through venture capitalism, art and a criminal instinct. Despite his slashing of Leo's painting, Hudson's crimes are aimed at people rather than property. When the smoke clears, all Hudson has left is his narrative, the skills for which have been taught to him by a man who, in his opinion, is no more than a drone.

Moving through various strata of the culture, *The Woman Chaser* expands the genre to include any fiction that contains an element of personal betrayal or political duplicity. In portraying Hudson's megalomania, Willeford associates a particular personality with crime, placing the person, through narrative voice and memoir form, into a political field. Willeford would continue this investigation through a career spanning fifty years, from the Depression through to the 1980s, with subjects as diverse as art forgery, cockfighting and life in the armed forces. For Willeford's writing, like that of Chester Himes, can be read as a history of modern marginality and a critique of American culture.

*

The "pulping" of the president comprised pulp culture's final hurrah. It also provided evidence that pulp culture paranoia had neither been misplaced nor was it the product of a paranoid imagination. With the speed of a bullet, there was a sense that history had changed course, and a realization that those who governed were, to a large extent, unaccountable, and engaged in secret, often illegal, activities.[63] Even though 1963 saw the publication of such paranoid classics as Charles Willeford's *The Machine In Ward Eleven*, Walter Tevis's *The Man Who Fell to Earth*, Jim Thompson's *The Grifters*, Charles Williams's *Dead Calm* and Robert Edmond Alter's *Swamp Sister*, it appeared that pulp culture fiction had been overtaken by real events.

Falsifying history is an act less typical of a true-crime assassin than a consortium interested in revising the dominant narrative. Outside the domain of pulp culture crime writing, the paranoia and intrigue generated by the assassination quickly became the province of conspiracy fiction. Though pulp culture writers could speculate upon the discrepancies found in the official texts, they had neither the resources nor the time to investigate them. Too bad, for conspiracy narratives or tabloid conjecture regarding JFK's formalin-preserved brain,[64] would once have been the stuff of pulp culture fiction. Yet only those courting bad taste could take their narrative to its conclusion.[65]

Not even Jim Thompson's most deranged protagonists would have dared such iconoclasm. For the paranoia that had once formed the basis of pulp culture fiction was now the subtext of the nation and part of a spectacle whose fragmented narrative has yet to be revised. Meanwhile, though the doors have been locked and the protagonists have been pulped, similar crimes continue. Regarding this co-option of paranoia or the ambiguity of individualism, Jim Thompson, in his story "The Flaw in the System", connects the Cold War to a parallel narrative:

They'd invented a system for beating our system . . . We've discouraged individuality, anything in the way of original thinking. All decisions are made at the top and passed down. Honesty, loyalty – we didn't feel that we had to worry about those things. The system would take care of them. The way the system worked – supposedly – a man simply *had* to be loyal and honest.[66]

Undaunted but no less paranoid, a post-pulp culture Thompson envisages the end of the narrative with a final paragraph in which individuals, systems, texts as well as the Cold War, are pulped once and for all:

There would be no refuge from the coming terror. No place to hide. No familiar thing to cling to. Something would become nothing, robbed of its intrinsic beauty and safety, and all else. There would only be a smoking, steaming blown-apart, crushed together mishmash where brother was himself eaten by brother while eating brother, ad nauseum, ad infinitum.[67]

Though the era of pulp culture ended with a bang, it would whimper along for a number of years. Likewise, crime fiction derived from that era would become a specialized interest and an increasingly self-conscious genre. This was exacerbated by crime writers opting to follow in the tracks of Raymond Chandler rather than the soon-to-be-neglected Jim Thompson, Dashiell Hammett rather than the less sophisticated David Goodis. Moreover, paperback fiction had become commonplace enough that the political edge of crime fiction had been blunted through overexposure. Now more a classless than a class-based phenomenon, crime fiction had begun to pander to a more middle-class readership. Similarly, fictional private eyes were more likely to be downwardly mobile misfits than ambivalent working-class heroes. Nevertheless, the influence of pulp culture fiction on contemporary crime writers like James Ellroy, Derek Raymond, Jerome Charyn and Elmore Leonard is undeniable, particularly in their portrayal of the gritty reality of urban life.

Though these days it might be read otherwise – particularly when one considers the inflated prices that original copies of these books now fetch – pulp culture fiction was rarely nostalgic. The product of a particular time in America's history, the phenomenon of pulp culture fiction can never be repeated. With pastiche a dominant literary mode, and crime fiction an ever-interesting genre that reflects the state of society, pulp culture fiction remains a benchmark from which to judge the quality of crime fiction, its politics, and its interpretation of how to survive on the mean streets of twentieth-century America.

APPENDIX I:

Primary Pulp Culture Texts
Due to the nature of the genre, the following list can only be approximate. When dealing with out of print books, the most recent, or most readily available, edition is listed. Moreover, where possible, US and UK editions are listed.

Leigh Brackett
The Tiger Among Us, 1957, Simon & Schuster, 1989, UK.

Gil Brewer
13 French Street, 1951, Chivers, 1988, UK/US. Simon & Schuster, 1988, UK.

Howard Browne (aka **John Evans**)
Halo in Blood, 1946, Oldcastle, UK, 1989. No Exit, 1988, UK. Quill, 1973, US.
Halo for Satan, 1948, Oldcastle, UK, 1989. No Exit, 1988, US/UK.
Halo in Brass, 1949, Bobbs and Merrill, 1949, US.
The Taste of Ashes, 1957, Simon & Schuster, US.

WR Burnett
The Asphalt Jungle, 1949, Pocket Books, 1949. US. Zomba, 1984, UK.
Vanity Fair, 1952, Pennant, 1953, US. Zomba, 1984, UK.

Raymond Chandler
Farewell, My Lovely, 1940, Random, 1992, US. Penguin, 1994, UK.
The High Window, 1942, Random, 1992, US. Penguin, 1994, UK.
The Long Goodbye, 1953, Random, 1992, US. Penguin, 1994, UK.

Kenneth Fearing
The Big Clock, 1946, Chivers Press, 1976, UK/US. Xanadu, 1990, UK.

Robert Finnegan
Many A Monster, 1949, Penguin, 1949, UK. Bantam, 1949, US.

David Goodis
Dark Passage, 1946, Zebra, 1988, US. Zomba, 1983, UK.
Nightfall, 1947, Black Lizard, Creative Arts, 1987, US. Zomba, 1983, UK.

Cassidy's Girl, 1951, Random, 1991, US.
The Burglar, 1953, Random, 1991, US. Simon & Schuster, 1988, UK.
The Moon in the Gutter, 1953, Zomba, 1983, UK.
Street of No Return, 1954, Random, 1991, US.

Chester Himes
If He Hollers Let Him Go, 1946, Thunders Mouth, 1986, US. *Serpent's Tail*, 1995, UK.
A Rage in Harlem (For Love of Imabelle), 1957, Random, 1989, US. Allison and Busby, 1993, UK.
The Big Gold Dream, 1960, Allison and Busby, 1993, UK.
The Heat's On, 1961, Allison and Busby, 1993, UK.

Dolores Hitchens
Sleep With Strangers, 1956, Simon & Schuster, 1989, UK.

Dorothy B. Hughes
In A Lonely Place, 1947, Carroll and Graf, 1988, US.

Horace McCoy
Kiss Tomorrow Goodbye, 1948, Zomba, 1983, UK. Signet, 1949, US.
No Pockets in a Shroud, 1948, Zomba, 1983, UK. Signet, 1948, US.

Ross Macdonald
The Moving Target, 1949, Warner, 1990, US. Allison and Busby, 1993, UK.
The Drowning Pool, 1950, Warner, 1993, US. Allison and Busby, 1993, UK.
The Way Some People Die, 1951, Warner, 1990, US. Allison and Busby, 1993, UK.
The Ivory Grin, 1952, Warner, 1992, US. Allison and Busby, 1993, UK.
The Galton Case, 1959, Warner, 1990, US. Allison and Busby, 1993, UK.

William B. McGivern
But Death Runs Faster, 1948, Berkley, 1988, US.
The Big Heat, 1953, Berkley, 1987, US. Simon & Schuster, 1988, UK.
Odds Against Tomorrow, 1957, Berkley, 1988, US. Xanadu, 1991, UK.

Richard Matheson
The Shrinking Man, 1956, Lightyear, 1993, US. Sphere, 1989, UK.

Peter Rabe
Kill the Boss Goodbye, 1956, Random, 1993, US.

Mickey Spillane
I, the Jury, 1947, Panzler, 1994, US.
Kiss Me, Deadly, 1952, Thorndike, 1993, US.

Walter Tevis
The Hustler, 1959, Buccaneer, 1991, US. Sphere, 1990, UK.

Jim Thompson
Heed The Thunder, 1946, Random, 1994, US.
Nothing More Than Murder, 1949, Random, 1991, US.
Cropper's Cabin, 1952, Random, 1992, US.
The Killer Inside Me, 1952, Random, 1991, US. Zomba, 1983, UK.
Savage Night, 1953, Random, 1991, US. Corgi, 1988, UK.
A Hell of a Woman, 1954, Random, 1990, US. Corgi, 1988, UK.
A Swell-Looking Babe, 1954, Random, 1991.
The Nothing Man, 1954, Warner, 1988.
After Dark, My Sweet, 1955, Random, 1990.
The Kill-Off, 1957, Mysterious Paperback, 1987, US. Corgi, 1988, UK.
Wild Town, 1957, Vintage, 1993, US. Corgi, 1989, UK.
The Getaway, 1959, Random, 1990, US. Zomba, 1983, UK.
The Grifters, 1963, Random, 1990, US. Zomba, 1983, UK.

Lionel White
The Killing (Clean Break), 1955, Black Lizard, Creative Arts, 1988, US.
The Big Caper, 1955, Gold Medal, 1961, US.

Harry Whittington
Web of Murder, 1958, Random, 1993, US.

Charles Willeford
Pick-Up, 1955, Random, 1990, US.
High Priest of California, 1956, ReSearch, 1987, US. Gollancz, 1990, UK.
The Woman Chaser, 1960, Carroll and Graf, 1990, US.

Charles Williams
The Big Bite, 1956, Dell, 1956, US. Cassell, 1957, UK.
Operator, 1958, (*Girl Out Back*), Dell, 1958, US. Cassell, 1958, UK.
Stain of Suspicion, 1958, (*Talk of the Town*), Dell, 1958, US. Cassell, 1958, UK.

Cornell Woolrich
Deadline at Dawn, 1944, Graphic, 1949, US.

APPENDIX 2:
FROM PULP TO NOIR

The contribution of pulp culture writers to *film noir*

Edward Anderson
They Live By Night, 1948, based on his novel, *Thieves Like Us*, directed by Nicholas Ray.
Thieves Like Us, 1973, based on the novel, directed by Robert Altman.

Leigh Brackett
The Big Sleep, 1946, co-scripted and directed by John Huston.
The Long Goodbye, 1973, written and directed by Robert Altman.

Howard Browne
Capone, 1975, scriptwriter, directed by Steve Carver.
St Valentine's Day Massacre, 1967, scriptwriter.

WR Burnett
The Racket, 1928, co-scripted, directed by Lewis Mileston.
Beast of the City, 1932, screen story by the author, directed by Charles Brabin.
High Sierra, 1941, based on his novel, co-scripted, directed by Raoul Walsh.
This Gun for Hire, 1942, co-scripted, directed by Frank Tuttle.
Nobody Lives Forever, 1946, screenplay based on his novel, directed by Jean Negulesco.
The Asphalt Jungle, 1950, based on his novel, directed by John Huston.
I Died a Thousand Times, 1955, based on his novel *High Sierra*, screenplay by the author, directed by Stuart Hiesler.

James M. Cain
Double Indemnity, 1944, based on his novel, directed by Billy Wilder.
Mildred Pierce, 1945, based on his novel, directed by Michael Curtiz.
The Postman Always Rings Twice, 1946, based on his novel, directed by Tay Garnett (remade in 1981, directed by Bob Rafaelson).

Paul Cain
The Black Cat, 1934, screenplay (as Peter Uric), directed by Edward Ulmer.

Vera Caspary
Laura, 1944, based on her novel, directed by Otto Preminger.

The Blue Gardenia, 1953, based on her short story "Gardenia", directed by Fritz Lang.

Raymond Chandler
Double Indemnity, 1944, co-scripted, directed by Billy Wilder.
Murder My Sweet, 1944, based on his novel *Farewell, My Lovely*, directed by Edward Dmytryk.
The Big Sleep, 1946, based on his novel, directed by John Huston.
The Blue Dahlia, 1946, screenplay, directed by George Marshall.
The Brasher Doubloon, 1947, based on his novel *High Window*, directed by John Brahm.
Lady in the Lake, 1947, based on his novel, directed by Robert Montgomery.
Strangers on a Train, 1951, co-scripted, directed by Alfred Hitchcock.
Marlowe, 1969, based on his novel *Little Sister*, directed by Paul Bogart.
The Long Goodbye, 1973, based on his novel, directed by Robert Altman.
Farewell, My Lovely, 1975, based on his novel, directed by Dick Richards.

Kenneth Fearing
The Big Clock, 1948, from his novel, directed by John Farrow.
No Way Out, 1987, based on his novel *The Big Clock*, directed by Roger Donaldson.

Steve Fisher
I Wake Up Screaming, 1942, based on his novel, directed by H. Bruce Humberstone.
Johnny Angel, 1945, screenplay, directed by Edwin L. Marin.
Dead Reckoning, 1947, co-scripted, directed by John Cromwell.
Lady in the Lake, 1947, screenplay, directed by Robert Montgomery.
I Wouldn't Be In Your Shoes, 1948, screenplay, directed by William Nigh.
Roadblock, 1951, co-scripted, directed by Harold Daniels.
City That Never Sleeps, 1953, screenplay, directed by John H. Auer.
Vicki, 1953, based on his novel *I Wake Up Screaming*, directed by Harry Horner.

David Goodis
Dark Passage, 1947, based on his novel, directed by Delmar Daves.
Of Missing Persons, 1956, based on his novel, directed by Pierre Chenal.
The Burglar, 1957, co-scripted, directed by Paul Wendkos.
Nightfall, 1957, based on his novel, directed by Jacques Tourneur.
Shoot the Piano Player, 1960, based on his novel *Down There*, directed by François Truffaut.
And Hope to Die, 1972, based on his novels *Black Friday, Somebody's Done For* and *Raving Beauty*, directed by Rene Clement.

The Moon in the Gutter, 1984, based on his novel, directed by Jean-Jacques Beineix.
Street of the Damned, 1984, based on his novel *Street of the Lost*, directed by Gilles Behat.
Descente aux Enfers, 1986, based on his novel *The Wounded and The Slain*, directed by Francis Girod.
Street of No Return, 1989, based on his novel, directed by Samuel Fuller.

William Lindsay Gresham
Nightmare Alley, 1947, based on his novel, directed by Edmund Goulding.

Dashiell Hammett
City Streets, 1931, screen story, directed by Rouben Mamoulian.
The Maltese Falcon, 1941, based on his novel, directed by John Huston.
The Glass Key, 1942, based on his novel, directed by Stuart Heisler.

Chester Himes
Cotton Comes to Harlem, 1970, based on his novel, directed by Ossie Davis.
A Rage in Harlem, 1991, based on his novel, directed by Bill Dukes.

Dolores Hitchens
Bande à Part, 1964, based on her novel *Fool's Gold*, directed by Jean-Luc Godard.

Dorothy B. Hughes
Ride the Pink Horse, 1947, based on her novel, directed by Robert Montgomery.
In A Lonely Place, 1950, based on her novel, directed by Nicholas Ray.

Jonathan Latimer
The Glass Key, 1942, screenplay, directed by Stuart Heisler.
Nocturne, 1946, screenplay, directed by Edwin L. Marin.
They Won't Believe Me, 1947, screenplay, directed by Irving Pichel.
The Big Clock, 1948, screenplay, directed by John Farrow.
Night Has a Thousand Eyes, 1948, co-scripted, directed by John Farrow.
The Accused, 1949, co-scripted, directed by William Dieterle.

Ross Macdonald
Harper, 1966, based on his novel *The Moving Target*, directed by Jack Smight.
Blue City, 1986, based on his novel, directed by Michelle Manning.

Horace McCoy
Kiss Tomorrow Goodbye, 1950, based on his novel, directed by Gordon Douglas.
The Turning Point, 1952, screen story, directed by William Dieterle.
They Shoot Horses, Don't They?, 1969, based on his novel, directed by Sydney Pollack.
Un linceul n'a pas de poches, based on his novel *No Pockets in a Shroud*, 1974, directed by Jean-Pierre Mocky.

William P. McGivern
The Big Heat, 1953, based on his novel, directed by Fritz Lang.
Rogue Cop, 1954, based on his novel, directed by Roy Royland.
Shield for Murder, 1954, based on his novel, directed by Edmond O'Brien and Howard W. Koch.
Odds Against Tomorrow, 1959, based on his novel, directed by Robert Wise.

Daniel Mainwaring (Geoffrey Homes)
Out of the Past, 1947, based on his novel *Build My Gallows High*, directed by Jacques Tourneur.
Roadblock, 1951, co-screen story, directed by Harold Daniels.
The Hitch Hiker, 1953, screen story, directed by Ida Lupino.
Baby Face Nelson, 1957, screenplay, directed by Don Siegel.

Willard Motley
Knock on Any Door, 1949, based on his novel, directed by Nicholas Ray.

Jo Pagano
Try and Get Me, 1950, based on his novel *The Condemned*, directed by Cyril Endfield.

Mickey Spillane
I, the Jury, 1953, based on his novel, directed by Harry Essex.
The Long Wait, 1954, based on his novel, directed by Victor Saville.
Kiss Me Deadly, 1955, based on his novel, directed by Robert Aldrich.

Walter Tevis
The Hustler, 1961, based on his novel, directed by Robert Rosen.

Jim Thompson
The Killing, 1956, co-scripted, directed by Stanley Kubrick.
Paths of Glory, 1958, co-scripted, directed by Stanley Kubrick.
The Getaway, 1972, based on his novel, directed by Sam Peckinpah.
The Killer Inside Me, 1975, based on his novel, directed by Burt Kennedy.
Serie Noire, 1979, based on *A Hell of a Woman*, directed by Alain Corneau.

Coup de Torchon, 1982, based on his novel *Pop. 1280*, directed by Bertrand Tavernier.
The Kill-Off, 1989, based on his novel, directed by Maggie Greenwald.
After Dark, My Sweet, 1990, based on his novel, directed by Steven Foley.
The Grifters, 1990, based on his novel, directed by Stephen Frears.

Donald Tracy
Criss Cross, 1949, based on his novel, directed by Robert Siodmak.

Donald Westlake (Richard Stark)
Point Blank, 1967, based on his novel *The Hunter*, directed by John Boorman.
The Split, 1968, based on his novel *The Seventh*, directed by Gordon Flemying.
The Outfit, 1973, based on his novel, directed by John Flynn.
Made in U.S.A., 1966, based on *Rien dans le coffre*, directed by Jean-Luc Godard.

Lionel White
The Killing, 1956, based on his novel *Clean Slate*, directed by Stanley Kubrick.
Pierrot Le Fou, 1965, based on his novel *Obsession*, directed by Jean-Luc Godard.

Charles Willeford
The Cockfighter, 1974, based on his novel, directed by Monte Hellman.
Miami Blues, 1989, based on his novel, directed by George Armitage.

Charles Williams
Finally Sunday, 1983, from his novel *The Long Saturday Night*, directed by François Truffaut.
Dead Calm, 1989, based on his novel, directed by Phillip Noyce.
Hot Spot, 1990, from his novel *Hell Hath No Fury*, directed by Dennis Hopper.

Cornell Woolrich
Street of Chance, 1942, based on his novel *Black Curtain*, directed by John Hively.
Phantom Lady, 1944, based on his novel, directed by Robert Siodmak.
Black Angel, 1946, based on his novel, directed by Roy William Neill.
The Chase, 1946, based on his novel *The Black Path of Fear*, directed by Arthur Ripley.
Deadline at Dawn, 1946, based on his novel, directed by Harold Clurman.
Fall Guy, 1947, based on his novel, directed by Reginald LeBorg.
The Guilty, 1947, based on his short story "Two Men in a Furnished Room", directed by John Reinhardt.
I Wouldn't Be In Your Shoes, 1948, based on his novel, directed by William Nigh.

The Night Has A Thousand Eyes, 1948, based on his novel, directed by John Farrow.

The Window, 1949, based on his novel, directed by Ted Tetzlaff; *Rear Window*, 1954, based on his short story, directed by Alfred Hitchcock.

Nightmare, 1956, based on his novel, directed by Maxwell Shane.

The Bride Wore Black, 1967, based on his novel, directed by François Truffaut.

Twenty post-1945 *noir*-oriented films adapted from pulp culture novels or written by pulp culture authors

The Asphalt Jungle, 1950, directed by John Huston. From WR Burnett's novel. A despair-ridden hardboiler investigating the era's obsession with criminality and social decay. Hard-edged dialogue by Huston and Ben Maddow, and the director's concern with naturalism, turns an otherwise run-of-the-mill gangster film into a minimalistic and self-enclosed *film noir*. A sad portrait of a society in which crooks and ordinary citizens are equally corrupt.

The Big Clock, 1948, directed by John Farrow. Screenplay by Jonathan Latimer. From Kenneth Fearing's novel. Beginning in typical *film noir* fashion – a cityscape, a running figure, a voice over and a flashback – Farrow's film is noteworthy for its screenplay and cast – Ray Milland, Charles Laughton, Elsa Lanchester, Macready. Unlike other examples of *film noir*, *The Big Clock* steers clear of eccentric camera angles and low-key lighting. Yet wide angle close ups of Laughton gives *The Big Clock* an expressionistic quality. In examining pulp culture guilt and innocence, the plot tightens, making the film a study in claustrophobia and paranoia.

The Big Heat, 1953, directed by Fritz Lang. From William P. McGivern's novel. A nihilistic portrayal of middle-class life. Glen Ford as a deranged precursor to *Dirty Harry*, with Gloria Grahame as the *femme fatale*. Losing everything, Ford single-handedly fights organized crime. Ambiguous regarding McCarthyism, its extremism in pursuit of virtue is hardly a vice. Lang's direction, camerawork and lighting are particularly evocative.

The Big Sleep, 1946, directed by John Huston. From Raymond Chandler's novel. William Faulkner and Leigh Brackett contribute to a memorable script. Forget the plot. This is *film noir* pulp culture dialogue at its snappiest. Arguably the best Chandler on film. And establishes LA as the *noir* capital of the world.

The Blue Dahlia, 1946, directed by George Marshall. From a novel by Raymond Chandler, whose original script was supposedly too hot for the studio. William Bendix proves he is one of *film noir*'s great amnesiacs, perfectly complementing the emotionally crippled protagonist played by Alan Ladd. About corruption, the film's atmosphere outweighs the content and product.

Build My Gallows High, aka **Out of the Past**, 1947, directed by Jacques Tourneur. From Geoffrey Homes's novel. A subtle critique of McCarthyism with Robert Mitchum as the doom-ridden hero. Excessively plotted, its opening scenes recall *The Killers*. Eventually Mitchum allows himself to be destroyed by a corrupt woman – a device destined to become a *noir* cliché.

The Burglar, 1957, directed by Paul Wendkos. From a novel by David Goodis. Burglary as a family enterprise. From the film's tense opening to its tragic conclusion, the influence of Orson Welles is apparent. Fine performances from Jayne Mansfield and Dan Duryea. Though self-conscious, the film remains true to Goodis's novel. Less concerned with plot intricacies than emotional impact.

Cape Fear, 1962, directed by J. Lee Thompson. From John D. MacDonald's novel *The Executioners*. More frightening and carefully crafted than Martin Scorsese's remake. Wonderful score by Bernard Herrmann and a reptilian performance from Robert Mitchum. Another nightmare regarding the breakdown of post-war family life.

Criss Cross, 1949, directed by Robert Siodmak. From Don Tracy's novel. Burt Lancaster as the fatalistic protagonist: "[I]t was fate or a jinx or whatever you want to call it." Tragic, expressionistic, erotic, paranoid, claustrophobic, and a marvellous score by Rosza. *Criss Cross* is a *noir* classic.

Dark Passage, 1947, directed by Delmar Daves. From David Goodis's novel. Like *Lady in the Lake*, Daves keeps close to the novel. The viewer sees the world through Humphrey Bogart's eyes, and, in doing so, enters into a world of pulp culture paranoia. Though somewhat pristine, *Dark Passage* is about the creation of an alternative post-war narrative. With Bogart finding sanctuary in America's backyard. Daves tacks on an absurd Hollywood ending. Nevertheless, this remains a favourite *film noir*.

The Hitch Hiker, 1953, directed by Ida Lupino. From an unpublished story by Daniel Mainwaring (Geoffrey Homes). A rare example of a *film noir* directed by a woman. The underrated Lupino investigates the 1950s obsessional fear of strangers. "Commies", aliens and hitch hikers have become interchangeable. Yet Mainwaring's radical politics seep into his script. He will extend the themes established in *The Hitch Hiker* three years later in his script for *Invasion of the Body Snatchers*.

In A Lonely Place, 1950, directed by Nicholas Ray. From Dorothy B. Hughes's novel. A *noir*-romance with electrifying performances from Humphrey Bogart and Gloria Grahame. Though the film contains only a fraction of the novel's paranoia, it still conveys the era's sense of darkness, alienation, and what it was like to work in Hollywood during the McCarthy era.

The Killing, screenplay by Jim Thompson, 1956, directed by Stanley Kubrick. A faithful adaptation of Lionel White's novel *Clean Slate*. With its pseudo-documentary style, Kubrick's film recalls *The Asphalt Jungle*. Noteworthy for its manipulation of time, dialogue and division of criminal labour. Excellent performances from Sterling Hayden and the great Timothy Carey as a beatnik psycho horse killer.

Kiss Me Deadly, 1955, directed by Robert Aldrich. From Mickey Spillane's novel. Aldrich's film is equally deterministic and even more sinister than the novel. And, with its unrelenting violence, only slightly less warped. "Commies" beware, this is *noir* at its bleakest.

Mildred Pierce, 1945, directed by Michael Curtiz. From James M. Cain's novel. Despite low key lighting, dark interiors and night exteriors, Curtiz's film is not as *noir*-oriented as pre-pulp culture *Double Indemnity*. Yet this excellent domestic *noir* is unusual in deploying a woman – Joan Crawford type-cast to perfection – to play the role normally reserved for a free agent tough guy. Pierce personifies the era's domestic conflict – romance vs finance – and begs to be viewed through *fin de siècle* feminism and concerns regarding child abuse.

Nightfall, 1957, directed by Jacques Tourneur. From a novel by David Goodis. Tourneur deploys a gamut of *noir* devices: paranoia, flashbacks, misfortune, the city streets as a place of safety rather than danger. A metaphor for the era, *Nightfall* is about coming to terms with history, as Vanning attempts to comprehend his violent past and how it contributes to his present misfortune. One of the best Goodis adaptations.

Nightmare Alley, 1947, directed by Edmund Goulding. From William Lindsay Gresham's novel. The seedy side of the mystic arts and carnival life – always an intriguing backdrop for *film noir*. Here shadows and low-key photography remind the viewer once again of expressionism's influence on *film noir*. With its geeks, mind readers and hustlers, it's a film concerned with class, deception, corruption, and the price of success. Tyrone Power, as the fake spiritualist, is so miscast that he becomes genuinely frightening.

Odds Against Tomorrow, 1959, directed by Robert Wise. From William P. McGivern's novel. Recalls earlier social issue films and gangster movies like *The Asphalt Jungle* and *White Heat*. Made at the end of the pulp culture era, and alongside an emerging civil rights movement, this is one of the last real *films noirs.* Joseph Brun's night-for-night location shots are exceptional. Likewise his use of light, shadow and sharp angles. Interesting, if warped, sexual politics – a homosexual crook, fear of miscegenation, and Gloria Grahame as the ultimate *femme fatale* who, before making love, demands that Robert Ryan describe what it's like to kill someone.

The Postman Always Rings Twice, 1946, directed by Tay Garnett. Faithful to James M. Cain's novel. Conveys a sense of evil, corruption and treachery. Excellent performances from John Garfield and Lana Turner as the couple whose pulp culture love exceeds society's boundaries. Unlike other Cain heroines, Cora is a *femme fatale* with whom it is easy to identify. The film also flirts with surrealism, as Garfield and Turner take a midnight swim to wash away their sins. The era's claustrophobia is conveyed with a minimum of camera movements, while the narrator looks back on his life, and tries to understand how his past has created the present.

They Live By Night, 1948, directed by Nicholas Ray. From Edward Anderson's Depression novel, *Thieves Like Us.* Young lovers – "This boy and this girl were never properly introduced to the world we live in" – caught in a web of violence, and on the run in a country so close to economic collapse that only crime offers the hope of autonomy. Poetic and violent, this is *film noir* at its most romantic, shot by Murnau veteran Paul Ivano. Unlike the young females in *Gun Crazy* and Robert Altman's *Thieves Like Us*, Cathy O'Donnell's portrayal of Keechie suggests a saintliness out of tune with the era in which she lives. The pulp culture theme of misunderstood youth resurfaces in other Ray films, most notably *Rebel Without a Cause.*

NOTES

I. Better Dead Than Read

[1.] Hardboiled writing might be defined as a hard-edged, often objective style and attitude that is found in many, but not all, thrillers, mysteries, crime and low-life fiction.

[2.] "It does not matter much to me that I don't know if Hammett was a Communist Party member: most certainly he was a Marxist." Lillian Hellman, *An Unfinished Woman*, Quartet, London, 1979, p. 212.

[3.] Mickey Spillane, *Kiss Me, Deadly*, Corgi, London, 1953, p. 221.

[4.] Ibid., p. 43.

[5.] See Ernest Mandel's *Delightful Murder*, Pluto Press, London, 1984; Tzvetan Todorov's "The Typology of Detective Fiction", in *The Poetics of Prose*, Blackwell, Oxford, 1977; and Fredric Jameson's essay, "On Raymond Chandler", in *The Poetics of Murder: Detective Fiction and Literary Theory*, ed. Glenn W. Most, William Stowe, 1983, pp. 122–48. Surprisingly, Fourth Internationalist Mandel ignores the political and literary significance of the paperback phenomenon. Similarly, Todorov, a post-structuralist with an appreciation of various types of crime fiction, ignores the politics of the genre; while Jameson, a post-modern Marxist, makes no mention of Chandler's expropriation of the genre, his less than flattering portrayal of blacks and women; nor recognizes Marlowe as a dubious moral arbiter and petit bourgeois whose battle against corruption never exceeds local power.

[6.] While smart corporate money hedged its bets when using words like revolution, Pocket Books would remain a generic term even though its monopoly on paperback publishing would last only until the early 1940s.

[7.] See Geoffrey O'Brien, *Hardboiled America*, Van Nostrand Reinhold, New York, 1981. Also the source for much of the information in this section.

[8.] The term pulp fiction relates to the cheap wood-pulp paper on which magazines carrying such stories were printed. Beginning when *Argosy* turned to adult adventure stories in 1896, the "pulps", their profit margins derived from cheap paper and a large readership, quickly replaced the dime novel as the most popular form of reading entertainment. See Lee Server, *Danger Is My Business*, Chronicle, San Francisco, 1993.

[9.] Kenneth Fearing, *New and Selected Poems*, Indiana University Press, Bloomington, 1974, p. 126.

[10.] Ibid., "Foreword: Reading, Writing and Rackets", p. ix.

[11.] The Marshall Plan's precursor, the Blum-Byrnes accord, was partly responsible for French interest in pulp culture–Série Noire writing. The accord made economic aid dependent on limiting domestic films shown in French cinemas, which, in turn, paved the way for Hollywood films, including examples of *film noir*. See Serge Guilbaut's *How New York Stole the Idea of Modern Art*, University of Chicago Press, Chicago, 1983, pp. 133–8.

[12.] Mickey Spillane, *One Lonely Night*, Corgi, London, 1951.

[13.] By 1953, 1.6 per cent of the US adult population owned more than 80 per cent of the corporate stock and 90 per cent of the corporate bonds, and, by 1958, some 30 per cent of the population were living below the poverty line.

[14.] Advertisements for Community silverware and Cannon percale sheets, *Life Magazine*, 15 October 1945.

[15.] Robert Finnegan, *Many A Monster*, Bantam, New York, 1949, p. 3.

[16.] Jim Thompson, *The Killer Inside Me*, Zomba, London, 1983, p. 237.

[17.] David Madden, *Tough Guy Writers of the Thirties*, Southern Illinois University Press, 1977, p. xix.

[18.] *Many A Monster*, p. 1.

[19.] Unattributable quote, Jameson in "On Raymond Chandler", in *The Poetics of Murder*, p. 126.

[20.] Jim Thompson, *The Getaway*, Zomba, London, p. 105.

[21.] Ibid., p. 109.

[22.] Ibid., p. 107.

2. A Knife That Cuts Both Ways

[1.] David Goodis, *Dark Passage*, Zomba, London, 1983, p. 295.

[2.] Jim Thompson, *The Killer Inside Me*, Zomba, London, 1983, p. 181.

[3.] Chester Himes, *If He Hollers Let Him Go*, Sphere, London, 1967, p. 8.

[4.] Where possible I avoid distinguishing between popular and classical definitions of paranoia. To do otherwise would have necessarily placed undue attention on the classical definition, and would have conflicted with this study's emphasis on popular culture.

[5.] See Richard Maltby, "The Politics of the Maladjusted Text", in *Movie Book of Film Noir*, ed. Cameron, Studio Vista, London, 1992, p. 39.

[6.] Against a backdrop of growing paranoia, NSC 68 proposed making foreign markets accessible while expanding the arms industry through military Keynesianism. Weighing tolerance against suppression, taxes were to be increased and social programmes decreased. Meanwhile, labour unions, civic enterprises, churches and the media would be protected from subversive influences. This even though diplomatic historian Richard Immerman claimed fears of a Soviet attack were "the product of a paranoid imagination". Noam Chomsky, *Deterring Democracy*, Verso, London, 1991, p. 31.

[7.] Wade Miller, *Fatal Step*, Signet, New York, 1948, p. 30.

[8.] In 1835, de Tocqueville noted that African Americans were already condemned by law and public opinion to the lowest rung of the socioeconomic ladder. Just above them were Europeans driven to the New

World by poverty or misbehaviour. To de Tocqueville, these groups constituted a threat to a democratic republic, and he advocated an armed force to suppress such elements and ensure democracy. See Elizabeth Wilson, *The Sphinx In The City*, Virago, London, 1991, pp. 6–7.

9. See Jonathan Bushsbaum, "Tame Wolves and Phoney Claims", in *Movie Book of Film Noir*, p. 90.

10. See Gilles Deleuze and Félix Guattari, *Anti-Oedipus*, Viking, New York, 1977, p. 274.

11. Ibid., p. 278.

12. Ibid. Cited by D. Thomas, "Psychoanalysis and Film Noir", in *The Movie Book of Film Noir*, p. 71.

13. See John Ranleigh, *The Agency*, Sceptre, London, 1987; John Stockwell, *The New Centurions*, South End Press, Boston, 1991.

14. Nelson Algren, *Never Come Morning*, Corgi, London, 1964, pp. 35–6.

15. Raymond Chandler, *Farewell, My Lovely*, Penguin, London, 1978, p. 7.

16. David Goodis, *The Moon in the Gutter*, Zomba, London, 1983, p. 403.

17. Letter to Bill Sherman, quoted by Adrian Wootton, "Missing Person", in *For Goodis Sake*, ed. Adrian Wootton and Taylor, BFI, London, 1989, p. 4.

18. *Dark Passage*, p. 263.

19. Ibid., p. 339.

20. Ibid.

21. Ibid., p. 348.

22. Ibid., p. 383.

23. David Goodis, *Nightfall*, Zomba, London, 1983, p. 3.

24. Ibid., p. 27.

25. Ibid., p. 66.

26. Ibid., pp. 78–9.

27. Ibid., p. 91.

28. See Philippe Garnier, *Goodis: la view en noir et blanc*, Editions du Seuil, Paris, 1984.

29. David Goodis, *Cassidy's Girl*, Black Lizard, Berkeley, 1987, p. 148.

30. Ibid., p. 141.

31. Ibid., p. 4.

32. Ibid., p. 5.

33. Ibid., p. 33.

34. Ibid., pp. 42–3.

35. Ibid., p. 15.

36. Ibid., p. 146.

37. Ibid., p. 154.

38. Ibid., p. 63.

39. Ibid., pp. 66–7.

40. Ibid., pp. 87–8.

41. Ibid., p.86.

42. Ibid., p. 98.

43. Ibid., p. 121.

44. Ibid., p. 129.
45. Ibid., p. 150.
46. Ibid., p. 152.
47. Ibid.
48. *The Moon in the Gutter*, p. 429.
49. Ibid., p. 473.
50. Ibid., p. 446.
51. Ibid., p. 474.
52. Ibid., p. 492.
53. Ibid., p. 513.
54. Ibid.
55. Ibid., p. 408.
56. Ibid., p. 511.
57. David Goodis, *Street of No Return*, Black Lizard, Berkeley, 1987, p. 88.
58. Ibid., p. 92.
59. Ibid., p. 166.
60. Chester Himes, *The Quality of Hurt*, Paragon House, New York, 1990, p. 61.
61. Ibid., p. 3.
62. Chester Himes, *My Life of Absurdity*, Paragon House, New York, 1990, p. 109.
63. Ibid., p. 110.
64. See *The Quality of Hurt*, p. 77.
65. Chester Himes, *If He Hollers Let Him Go*, Sphere, London, 1967, p. 9.
66. *The Quality of Hurt*, p. 73.
67. *If He Hollers Let Him Go*, p. 12.
68. Ibid., p. 8.
69. Ibid., p. 9.
70. Ibid., p. 8.
71. Ibid.
72. Ibid., pp. 9–10.
73. *My Life of Absurdity*, p. 102.
74. Ibid., p. 126.
75. See Bruce Franklin, *Prison Literature in America*, Lawrence Hill, Westport, 1978, p. 224.
76. Chester Himes, *A Rage in Harlem*, Allison & Busby, London, 1985, p. 9.
77. See Wepman, Newman and Binderman, *The Life: The Lore and Poetry of the Black Hustler*, Holloway House, Los Angeles, 1976.
78. *A Rage in Harlem*, p. 44.
79. Ibid., pp. 49–50.
80. Ibid., p. 56.
81. Ibid., p. 105.
82. Chester Himes, *The Big Gold Dream*, Allison & Busby, London, 1988, p. 6.
83. Ibid., p. 10.

[84.] Ibid., p. 19.
[85.] Ibid., p. 20.
[86.] Ibid., p. 23.
[87.] Ibid., p. 73.
[88.] Ibid., p. 43.
[89.] Ibid.
[90.] Ibid., p. 46.
[91.] Ibid., p. 59.
[92.] Ibid., pp. 50–51.
[93.] Ibid., p. 57.
[94.] Ibid., p. 71.
[95.] Ibid., p. 62.
[96.] Ibid., pp. 62–3.
[97.] Chester Himes, *The Heat's On*, Allison & Busby, London, 1992, p. 14.
[98.] Ibid., p. 16.
[99.] Ibid., p. 23.
[100.] Ibid., p. 53.
[101.] Ibid., p. 55.
[102.] Ibid., p. 57.
[103.] Ibid., p. 38.
[104.] Ibid., p. 85.
[105.] Ibid., pp. 136–7.
[106.] Ibid., p. 138.
[107.] Ibid., p. 145.
[108.] Ibid., p. 146.
[109.] Ibid., p. 158.
[110.] Ibid., p. 174.
[111.] See Jim Thompson, *Roughneck*, Mysterious Press, New York, 1989, pp. 161–3.
[112.] Michael J. McCauley, *Sleep With The Devil*, Mysterious Press, New York, 1991, p. 72.
[113.] Jim Thompson, *Fireworks*, ed. Polito and McCauley, Donald I. Fine, New York, 1988, p. 41.
[114.] Jim Thompson, *Pop. 1280*, Zomba, London, 1988, p. 471.
[115.] See Jim Thompson, *Bad Boy*, Donald I. Fine, New York, 1986, pp. 387–9.
[116.] Ibid.
[117.] Jim Thompson, *Heed The Thunder*, Vintage, New York, 1993.
[118.] Ibid.
[119.] Ibid.
[120.] Jim Thompson, *Nothing More Than Murder*, Black Lizard, Berkeley, 1985, p. 210.
[121.] Jim Thompson, *Cropper's Cabin*, Black Lizard, Berkeley, 1987, p. 144.
[122.] *The Killer Inside Me*, p. 158.
[123.] Ibid., p. 166.
[124.] ibid., p. 132.

125. Ibid., p. 235.
126. Ibid., p. 145.
127. Ibid., p. 180.
128. Ibid., p. 204.
129. Ibid., p. 237.
130. Ibid., p. 245.
131. Ibid.
132. Ibid., p. 248.
133. Jim Thompson, *Wild Town*, Corgi, London, 1989, p. 119.
134. Ibid., p. 163.
135. Ibid.
136. Jim Thompson, *A Hell of a Woman*, Black Lizard, Berkeley, 1984, p. 102.
137. Ibid., pp. 181–2.
138. Jim Thompson, *Savage Night*, Black Lizard, Berkeley, 1985, p. 179.
139. Ibid., p. 31.
140. Ibid., pp. 146–7.
141. Jim Thompson, *A Swell-Looking Babe*, Black Lizard, Berkeley, 1986, p. 184.
142. Ibid., p. 61.
143. Ibid., pp. 139–40.
144. Jim Thompson, *The Nothing Man*, Donald I. Fine, New York, 1986, pp. 186–7.
145. Ibid., p. 187.
146. Jim Thompson, *After Dark, My Sweet*, Black Lizard, Berkeley, 1986, p. 46.
147. Ibid., p. 123.
148. Ibid., p. 129.
149. Jim Thompson, "A Horse in the Baby's Bathwater", in *Fireworks*, p. 288.
150. Jim Thompson, *The Kill-Off*, Donald I. Fine, New York, 1986, p. 45.
151. Ibid., p. 57.
152. Ibid., p. 64.
153. Jim Thompson, *The Grifters*, Zomba, London, 1983, p. 231.
154. Jack Finney, *The Body Snatchers*, First Edition, New York, p. 136.

3. Taking Out Contracts

1. Kenneth Fearing, "Foreword: Reading, Writing and Rackets", in *New and Selected Poems*, Indiana University Press, Bloomington, 1956, p. x.
2. In 1932, J. Edgar Hoover boasted about the value of the FBI's Uniform Crime Report which, compiled from figures submitted by local police departments, had been launched to meet the need for national crime statistics. Its purpose, according to Hoover, was to determine whether the US was in the midst of a crime wave. Not surprisingly, throughout all the years in which the FBI would chart trends and geographical variations, crime never failed to increase. See Churchill and Vander Wall, *Agents of*

Repression, South End Press, Boston, 1988, p. 1.

3. Putting the Cold War in a historical context, Noam Chomsky offers the following reminder: "As Gaddis and other serious historians recognize, the Cold War began in 1917, not 1945." Noam Chomsky, *Rethinking Camelot*, Verso, London, 1993, p. 21. Meanwhile, Victor Navasky outlines the post-war parameters of the Cold War, saying it "was really three simultaneous conflicts: a global confrontation between rival imperialisms and ideologies . . .; a domestic clash in the United States between hunters and hunted . . .; . . . a civil war amongst the hunted . . ." Victor Navasky, *Naming Names*, John Calder, London, 1982, p. 3.

4. On 21 December 1919, Attorney General Palmer's men rounded up 249 aliens of Russian birth including Emma Goldman and Alexander Berkman and deported them to the Soviet Union. On 2 January 1920, the FBI arrested an estimated 10,000 people in twenty-three cities, many of them immigrants who could speak no English. From July 1919 to June 1920, warrants were issued for 6,000 alien radicals, 4,000 of whom were arrested but fewer than 1,000 deported.

5. Jack London, *The Assassination Bureau, Ltd.*, Mayflower, London, 1966, pp. 26–7.

6. Philip Durham, "The Black Mask School", in *Tough Guy Writers of the Thirties*, Southern Illinois University Press, Carbondale, p. 56.

7. Ibid., pp. 56–7.

8. Carol See, "The Hollywood Novel", in *Tough Guy Writers of the Thirties*, p. 199.

9. Cited by David Geherin, *The American Private Eye*, Ungar, New York, p. 33.

10. Frederick Nebel, "Spare the Rod", in *Six Deadly Dames*, Gregg Press, Boston, 1980, p. 97.

11. Raymond Chandler, *The Long Goodbye*, Penguin, London, p. 237.

12. Ernest Mandel, *Delightful Murder*, Pluto Press, London, 1984, p. 31. By 1938, profits from drug dealing in the US had exceeded one billion dollars per year.

13. Ibid., p. 91. After the 1949 and 1953 recessions, youth unemployment would rise to 15 and 20 per cent, and to 30 per cent in black and Hispanic communities.

14. Ibid. Helping entrepreneurs avoid high taxation, social security contributions, and state regulation.

15. The proportion of military spending in the US's GNP, excluding the war years, went from 1.5 per cent of the economy in 1939 to 11.4 per cent in 1946 to 13.6 per cent in 1953. Ernest Mandel, *Late Capitalism*, Verso, London, 1987, p. 276.

16. In 1946 Hoover reported that the FBI during the Second World War had investigated 19,587 cases of alleged subversion or sabotage, 2,447 of which turned out to be bona fide in his view. Of these, 611 were convicted, their aggregate sentences totalling 1,637 years and their fines

totalling $251,709. See *Agents of Repression* p. 31. When Party membership fell from 74,000 in 1947 to 54,000 in 1950, Hoover claimed there remained 486,000 fellow travellers, each a potential spy. Meanwhile, Hoover "was very cool to the whole idea [of going against . . . the national crime syndicate] . . . He ordered the FBI files, containing the very information we needed on organized crime, close to us . . ." See *Agents of Repression*, p. 9.

17. Dalton Trumbo, *The Time of the Toad,* Journeyman, New York, 1982, pp. 25–6.
18. *New and Selected Poems*, p. ix.
19. Cited in *The American Private Eye*, p. 5.
20. Raymond Chandler, *The High Window*, Penguin, London, p. 101.
21. Raymond Chandler, *Farewell, My Lovely*, Penguin, London, 1978, p. 243.
22. From a letter of 7 May 1948 to Frederick Lewis Allen, in *Raymond Chandler Speaking*, ed. Gardiner and Walker, Houghton Mifflin, Boston, 1977, p. 219.
23. *Farewell, My Lovely*, p. xx.
24. ibid., p. 39.
25. *Selected Letters of Raymond Chandler*, ed. McShane, Columbia University Press, 1981, p. 333.
26. *Farewell, My Lovely*, pp. 78–9.
27. Ibid., pp. 118–19.
28. Ibid., p. 61.
29. Ibid., p. 58.
30. Ibid., p. 80.
31. Ibid., p. 142.
32. *The Long Goodbye*, p. 212.
33. ibid., p. 200.
34. *Farewell, My Lovely*, p. 1.
35. Ibid., p. 127.
36. Raymond Chandler, *Red Wind*, cited by Michael Sorkin, *Exquisite Corpse*, Verso, London, 1991, p. 54.
37. *Farewell, My Lovely*, pp. 201–2.
38. *The Long Goodbye*, p. 9.
39. *Delightful Murder*, p. 121.
40. Cited in *Delightful Murder*, p. 37.
41. *Farewell, My Lovely*, p. 201.
42. *The Long Goodbye*, pp. 232–3.
43. Ibid., pp. 76–7.
44. Ibid., p. 79.
45. Ibid., p. 87.
46. Ibid., p. 39.
47. Ibid., p. 88.
48. Ibid., p. 110.
49. Ibid., p. 135.

50. Ibid., p. 149.
51. Cited in *Delightful Murder*, p. 37.
52. Ross Macdonald, *Self-Portrait*, Capra Press, Santa Barbara, 1981, pp. 27–8.
53. Ibid.
54. Ross Macdonald, *The Moving Target*, Allison & Busby, London, 1986, p. 103.
55. *Self-Portrait*, p. 120.
56. Ibid., p. 28.
57. Ibid., pp. 106–7.
58. Ross Macdonald, *The Drowning Pool*, Allison & Busby, London, p. 2.
59. Ross Macdonald, *The Ivory Grin*, Allison & Busby, London, p. 248.
60. Ibid.
61. Ibid.
62. Ibid., p. 11.
63. Ibid., p. 10.
64. Ibid., pp. 107–8.
65. Ibid.
66. Ibid., p. 21.
67. Ibid.
68. Ibid.
69. *The Drowning Pool*. p. 37.
70. Ibid., p. 43.
71. Ibid., p. 85.
72. Ross Macdonald, *The Way Some People Die*, Allison & Busby, London, 1992, p. 8.
73. Ibid., p. 118.
74. Ibid., p. 182.
75. *Self-Portrait*, p. 20.
76. Ibid.
77. Ibid., p. 18.
78. Ibid.
79. Ross Macdonald, *The Galton Case*, Allison & Busby, London, 1989, p. 21.
80. *The Moving Target*, pp. 84–5.
81. Harold Browne writing as John Evans, *Halo in Blood*, Quill, New York, 1973, p. 26.
82. Harold Browne, *The Taste of Ashes*, p. 53.
83. Harold Browne, *Halo in Brass*, Pocket Books, New York, 1950, p. 88.
84. Harold Browne, *Halo for Satan*, Quill, New York, 1973, p. 53.
85. *Halo in Blood*, p. 15.
86. Ibid., p. 30.
87. Ibid., p. 25.
88. Ibid., p. 28.
89. Ibid., p. 156.

90. Ibid., p. 157.
91. Ibid., p. 98.
92. Ibid., p. 179.
93. Ibid., p. 68.
94. Ibid., p. 118.
95. Ibid., p. 33.
96. Ibid., p. 54.
97. Ibid., p. 142.
98. Ibid.
99. Ibid., p. 163.
100. Ibid., p. 123.
101. Ibid., p. 107.
102. Ibid., p. 218.
103. Ibid., p. 230.
104. Ibid., p. 233.
105. Ibid., p. 236.
106. Ibid., p. 237.
107. *Delightful Murder*, pp. 66–7.
108. *The American Private Eye*, p. 121.
109. Ibid.
110. Mickey Spillane, *One Lonely Night*, Corgi, London, 1951, p. 51.
111. Mickey Spillane, *The Snake*, Corgi, London, 1965, p. 104.
112. Mickey Spillane, *I, The Jury*, Signet, New York, 1968, p. 11.
113. Ibid., p. 7.
114. *One Lonely Night*, p. 102.
115. *I, The Jury*, p. 27.
116. *Delightful Murder*, p. 86.
117. *The American Private Eye*, p. 130.
118. Ibid., p. 127.
119. Ibid., p. 123.
120. Karl Marx, *Theories of Surplus Value*, Part I, cited in *Delightful Murder*, pp. 10–11.
121. Raymond Chandler, *The Big Sleep*, p. 21.
122. ibid., p. 214.
123. *The Drowning Pool*, p. 7.
124. *The Moving Target*, p. 17.
125. As consumer credit went from $7.7 billion in 1946 to $50 billion in 1958, and mortgage credit increased from $27 billion in 1946 to $175 billion in 1961. Ernest Mandel, *Marxist Economic Theory*, Merlin, London, 1977, p. 527. Moreover, between 1951 and 1956, wholesale prices stabilized, increasing by only 3.8 points from 1951 to 1964 and rising substantially only in the boom year of 1956. Retail prices within that period went up by 17.6 points. See *Late Capitalism*, p. 428.
126. *The Way Some People Die*, p. 5.
127. *The Galton Case*, p. 6.

[128.] As of 1970, firemen received an average yearly pay of $9,423, and firewomen $7,809; while policemen made, on average, $8,989 and policewomen $5,582 per annum. See Harvey Braverman, *Labour and Monopoly Capital*, Monthly Press, New York, 1974, p. 369.

[129.] Not in 1946, when 36 per cent of family units had income before taxes of less than $2,000. See Howard Zinn, *Postwar America*, p. 90. Or when private indebtedness had increased three and a half times. See *Late Capitalism*, p. 418. Or when disposable income, from 1947 to 1955, rose from $160 billion to $275.3 billion (ibid., p. 448). For this was an era in which 1.6 per cent of the adult population owned more than 80 per cent of corporate stocks and nearly 90 per cent of the corporate bonds, when the highest fifth of society received 45 per cent of all income, while the lowest, whose share of the wealth would remain unchanged throughout the era, received 5 per cent. See *Postwar America*, p. 91.

4. Femme Fatality

[1.] These quotes appeared on the covers of the following editions: *The Body Snatchers*, First Edition, New York, 1955; *The Weeping and the Laughter*, Popular Library, 1951.

[2.] Gil Brewer, *13 French Street*, Simon & Schuster, London, 1988, p. 156.

[3.] With so many returning servicemen, 1946 – the year Dorothy B. Hughes's *Ride The Pink Horse*, Vera Caspary's *Stranger Than Truth* and Margaret Millar's *Wall of Eyes* were published – marked a highpoint for the number of divorces in the US. In 1947 – the year of Hughes's *In A Lonely Place* and Millar's *Fire Will Freeze* – women would make up only 31.8 per cent of the workforce. See Harvey Braverman, *Labor and Monopoly Capital*, Monthly Review Press, New York, 1974, p. 391. By 1955, 60 per cent of women attending college had dropped out to marry or because they believed education would prevent them from marrying. By the time Patricia Highsmith's *Deep Water* and Caspary's *The Husband* were published in 1957, teenage pregnancies had hit an all-time high – ninety-seven out of every one thousand girls having given birth. By 1958, the year of Highsmith's *A Game For the Living*, the number of women attending college had dropped from 47 per cent in 1920 to 35 per cent. By 1960, and the publication of Dolores Hitchens's *Sleep With Slander*, working women comprised 36 per cent of the workforce, their income a third that of men. Of those women at work, 43 per cent had school-aged children, but nursery places were available for only 2 per cent of those employed. Meanwhile, 14 million women were engaged before their seventeenth birthday, and the average age of marraige for women had fallen below twenty. See Betty Friedan, *The Feminine Mystique*, Penguin, London, 1965.

[4.] McGivern, *The Big Heat*, Simon & Schuster, London, 1988, p. 12.

[5.] Harold Browne, *The Taste of Ashes*, Simon & Schuster, New York, 1957,

p. 23.
6. Richard Matheson, *The Shrinking Man*, Gold Medal, Fawcett, 1956, p. 12.
7. Ibid., p. 13.
8. Ibid., p. 189.
9. Ibid.
10. The image of the golden-era family is, for the most part, a social creation used for specific political aims. The nuclear families of 1950s suburbia relied on state-sponsored roads and highways and an elaborate system of federal financing of home mortgage loans. See Michael S. Kimmel, "In the Family Room" (a review of Stephanie Coontz's *The Way We Never Were*), in *The Nation*, 1 March 1993, p. 279. Meanwhile, between 1945 and 1960 some $116 billion would be borrowed to cover home mortgages.
11. Ibid., p. 164.
12. Ibid., p. 45.
13. *The Big Heat*, p. 13.
14. Dashiell Hammett's more humane attitude to women might have been one reason why early *Black Mask* publisher Eltinge Warner disliked his work. Though Hammett's 1924 once-rejected *Black Mask* story, "Women, Politics and Murder", is less a re-reading of the genre than a story using each category as a backdrop for violence. See William F. Nolan's *Black Mask Boys*, Mysterious Press, New York and London, 1985, p. 24.
15. Ibid., p. 40.
16. *Black Mask Boys*, p. 22.
17. On 17 June 1957, the Supreme Court overturned a contempt conviction of a man who had refused to answer questions put to him by the House Committee on Un-American Activities, imposed restraints on investigations by state legislatures, ordered the federal government to reinstate an alleged security risk, and reversed the Smith Act conviction of California communists. See *Oxford Companion to the Supreme Court*, ed. James Hall, Oxford University Press, New York, 1992, p. 172.
18. Popular fascination with middle-class juvenile delinquency corresponds with the increased buying power of teenagers. According to *Life* magazine, teenagers in the late 1950s owned 10 million phonographs, over a million TV sets and 13 million cameras. Teenagers and their parents, according to *Life*, spent some $10 billion dollars yearly, which amounts to $1 billion more than the total sales of General Motors. See Paul Goodman, *Growing Up Absurd*, Panther, London, 1970, p. 89.
19. Leigh Brackett, *The Tiger Among Us*, Simon & Schuster, London, 1989, p. 7.
20. Betweeen 1950 and 1960, suburbs grew forty times faster than central city areas. See Mike Davis, *Prisoners of the American Dream*, Verso, London, 1986, p. 191.
21. Ibid. Between 1950 and 1960 automobile registrations increased by 22 million.

22. *The Tiger Among Us*, p. 7.
23. Ibid., p. 11.
24. Ibid., p. 12.
25. Ibid., p. 25.
26. Ibid., p. 27.
27. At a time when 31 per cent of the US were living in poverty, 42 per cent had graduated high school and 8 per cent graduated from college. See *Growing Up Absurd*, p. 52. When, of those entering college in 1950, only 14 per cent came from working-class families. See *Prisoners of the American Dream*, p. 192. And when, in 1959, hospital workers were making $59 per week and migratory farm workers $900 per year. Ibid., p. 52.
28. *The Tiger Among Us*, p. 107.
29. Ibid., p. 126.
30. Ibid., p. 187.
31. Assigning qualities according to gender is an arguable and even a politically retrograde business. Nevertheless, it is not a subject that has not gone unstudied. Regarding such qualities in the world of painting, Germaine Greer writes, "Many women must have wondered if there was a female art and true female imagery, while painstakingly working on parodic versions of the fashions set by the male art pundits." Germaine Greer, *The Obstacle Race*, Picador, London, 1981, p. 321.
32. Dolores Hitchens, *Sleep With Strangers*, Simon & Schuster, London, 1989, p. 8.
33. Ibid., p. 22.
34. Ibid., p. 64.
35. Ibid., p. 67.
36. Ibid., p. 53.
37. Ibid., p. 77.
38. Ibid., p. 79.
39. Ibid., p. 39.
40. Ibid., p. 83.
41. Ibid., p. 52.
42. Ibid., p. 69.
43. Ibid., p. 112.
44. Ibid., p. 98.
45. Ibid., p. 147.
46. Ibid., p. 115.
47. Ibid., p. 171.
48. Though pulp culture lesbianism was considered pathological, it would be exploited in a number of male-oriented soft-core titles, particularly in the 1960s.
49. *Sleep With Strangers*, p. 184.
50. Ibid., p. 127.
51. Dorothy B. Hughes, *In A Lonely Place*, Bantam, New York, 1979, p. 78.
52. Ibid., p. 79.

53. Ibid., p. 87.
54. Ibid., p. 15.
55. Ibid., p. 11.
56. Ibid., p. 38.
57. Ibid., p. 13.
58. Ibid., p. 81.
59. Ibid., p. 9.
60. Ibid., p. 57.
61. Ibid., p. 55.
62. Ibid., p. 57.
63. Ibid., p. 66.
64. Ibid., p. 62.
65. Ibid., p. 58.
66. Ibid.
67. Ibid., p. 71.
68. Ibid., p. 72.
69. Ibid., p. 97.
70. Ibid., p. 98.
71. Ibid., p. 99.
72. Ibid., p. 124.
73. Ibid., p. 24.
74. Ibid., p. 33.
75. Ibid., p. 47.
76. This is particularly true of David Goodis's and Jim Thompson's work. By the end of the era, even their narratives would be reduced to pulp, resembling the state of Dix's story at the conclusion of *In A Lonely Place*. The pulping of such narratives can be seen in several of the genre's writers, but is best illustrated by William Burroughs, whose would-be pulp culture narratives such as *Junky* and *Queer* would be forsaken for work dominated by his renowned cut-up technique. On a fictional level, this could be equated to the emphasis on the text and its destruction in Charles Willeford's *The Woman Chaser*. Even Philip Marlowe – the knight in shining armour – is put through the pulp culture wringer. Likewise, Raymond Chandler's writing deteriorates as the era progresses.

5. Profits of Crime

1. Atilla Kotányi, "Gangland and Philosophy", in *Situationist International Anthology*, ed. Knabb, Bureau of Public Secrets, Berkeley, 1981, p. 59.
2. Writing of another era in which state crime flourished, Michel Foucault notes the tendency to displace criminality: "Replacing the adversary of the sovereign, the social enemy was transformed into a deviant who brought with him the multiple danger of disorder, crime and madness." Michel Foucault, *Discipline and Punishment: The Birth of the Prison*, Allen Lane, London, 1977, pp. 299–300.

3. WR Burnett, *Vanity Fair*, cited by Wingrove, Introduction, *4 Novels by WR Burnett*, Zomba, London, 1983, p. ix.

4. Horace McCoy, *Kiss Tomorrow Goodbye*, in *4 Novels by Horace McCoy*, Zomba, London, 1983, p. 81.

5. Ibid., p. 314.

6. Paul Cain, "Parlor Trick", in *Seven Slayers*, Black Lizard, Berkeley, 1987, p. 39.

7. Joyce Carol Oates, *Tough Guy Writers of the Thirties*, Southern Illinois University Press, Carbondale, p. 110.

8. James M. Cain, *The Postman Always Rings Twice*, Pan, London, 1981, p. 123.

9. Cited by Geoffrey O'Brien, *Hardboiled America*, Van Nostrand Reinhold, New York, 1981, p. 74.

10. Raymond Chandler, *The Long Goodbye*, Penguin, London, 1994, p. 111.

11. "The people of the business world are probably more criminalistic . . . than are people of the slums. The crimes of the slums are direct physical actions . . . The victim identifies the criminal definitely or indefinitely . . . The crimes of the business world, on the other hand, are indirect, devious, anonymous, and impersonal . . . The perpetrators thus do not feel the resentment of their victims and the criminal practices continue and spread." Edwin Sutherland and Donald Cressey, *Principles of Criminology*, JP Lippincott, Chicago, 1960, pp. 46–7.

12. Away from pulp culture, Soviet *criminalists* Belkin and Korukhov note crime's sociohistoric network: "No matter how fleeting the crime may be, it is never a one-time deed. It is, rather, a complex system of deeds and actions committed by the perpetrator before, during, and after the criminal deed. The deeds and actions of the victims, and also of other individuals who were intentionally or unintentionally drawn into the criminal event, should likewise be added to the above mentioned deeds and actions." Belkin and Korukhov, *Fundamentals of Criminalistics*, Progress Press, Moscow, 1987, p. 10.

13. Harry Whittington, *Web of Murder*, Vintage, New York, 1993, p. 22.

14. Criminologists Edwin Sutherland and Donald Cressey outline this aspect of the state's narrative and its legal terrain: "[T]he 'spirit of combat' in legal trials continues to make it necessary for some lawyers to practice fraud and misrepresentation by misstatement and concealment of whole truth if they are to win cases. Such practices generally are not grounds for disbarment . . . but, again, they illustrate our criminalistic traditions." See *Principles of Criminology*, pp. 43–4.

15. James Ross, *They Don't Dance Much*, Harrap, London, 1986, p. 98.

16. Cornell Woolrich, *Deadline at Dawn*, cited by Richard Rayner, in his Introduction to Cornell Woolrich, *Rear Window and Other Stories*, Simon & Schuster, London, 1988, p. ix.

17. Cornell Woolrich, *The Black Curtain*, Simon & Schuster, New York, 1941, p. 3.

18. Whose "influence – economic, political, even spiritual – is felt in every city, every State house, every office of the Federal government . . .". Urging the nation to "guard against the acquisition of unwarranted influence, whether sought or unsought, by the military-industrial complex", Eisenhower, himself a perpetrator, warned the "potential for the disastrous rise of misplaced power exists and will persist". Hofstadter, "Dwight D. Eisenhower, Farewell Address", in *Great Issues in American History*, Vintage, New York, 1982, p. 544.

19. According to Edwin Sutherland and Donald Cressey, it is merely "a diagnosis of convenience arrived at by a process of exclusion. It does not refer to a specific behavioral entity. It serves as a scrapbasket to which is relegated a group of otherwise unclassified personality disorders and problems." See *Principles of Criminology*, p. 125, citing Preu, "The Concept of Psychopathic Personality".

20. Albert Camus, who modelled *L'Etranger* on *The Postman Always Rings Twice*, believed that objective realism, in "reducing man either to elementals or to his external reaction and . . . behavior", had more to do with automation than autonomy: "Its technique consists in describing men by their outside appearances, in their most casual actions, of reproducing, without comment, everything they say down to their repetitions, and finally by acting as if men were entirely defined by their daily automatisms . . . This type of novel, purged of interior life, in which men seem to be observed behind a pane of glass, logically ends, with its emphasis on the pathological, by giving itself as its unique subject the supposedly average man . . . The simpleton is the ideal subject for such an enterprise since he can only be defined by . . . his behavior. He is the symbol of the despairing world in which wretched automatons live in a machine-ridden universe." Albert Camus, *The Rebel*, cited by Robert I. Edenbaum, "The Poetics of the Private Eye", in *Tough Guy Writers of the Thirties*, pp. 94–5.

21. As Michel Foucault notes, "[Crime] should be seen not so much as a weakness of disease, as an energy that is reviving, an 'outburst or protest in the name of individuality', which no doubt accounts for its fascination . . . It may be, therefore, that crime constitutes a political instrument that could prove . . . precious for the liberation of society . . ." *Discipline and Punishment*, p. 289.

22. There were 3,616 people executed between 1930 and 1958.

23. Kenneth Fearing, *The Big Clock*, Perennial Library, New York, 1980, p. 174.

24. William McGivern, *Odds Against Tomorrow*, Xanadu, London, 1991, p. 46.

25. Ibid., p. 99. In 1952, approximately 60 per cent of blacks did not vote for a president. See Manning Marable, *Black American Politics*, p. 248. "In Mississippi at the height of Reconstruction, when federal troops enforced Negro rights in the South, 67 per cent of the Negro population were

registered to vote, as compared with 55 per cent of the white population; by 1955, the registration figure for Negroes was down to 4 per cent while that of whites was 59 per cent." Howard Zinn, *Postwar America*, p. 127.

[26.] *Odds Against Tomorrow*, p. 122.

[27.] Ibid., p. 134.

[28.] Ibid., pp. 155–6.

[29.] Ibid., p. 159.

[30.] Ibid., p. 171.

[31.] Ibid., p. 178.

[32.] Ibid., p. 147.

[33.] William McGivern, *But Death Runs Faster*, Berkeley, New York, 1988, pp. 18–19.

[34.] In reality, the work of true-crime writers – many of whom doubled as pulp culture crime fiction writers – faced similar devaluation as payment to *True Detective* authors dropped from $300 per 5,000 words during the Depression to $250 for articles of the same length in 1988. Marc Gerald, *Murder Plus*, Pan, London, 1993, p. 4.

[35.] *But Death Runs Faster*, p. 21.

[36.] Ibid.

[37.] Ibid., p. 18.

[38.] Ibid., pp. 25–6.

[39.] Ibid., p. 32.

[40.] Ibid.

[41.] Ibid., p. 53.

[42.] Within a year of V-J Day, more than five million workers were on picket lines. By the end of January 1946 "the industrial core of the U.S. was virtually at a standstill as the auto, steel, electrical and packinghouse workers were simultaneously on strike". Mike Davis, *Prisoners of the American Dream*, Verso, London, 1986, p. 86.

[43.] *But Death Runs Faster*, p. 62.

[44.] Ibid., p. 71.

[45.] Ibid., p. 102.

[46.] Ibid., p. 103.

[47.] Ibid., p. 118.

[48.] Ibid., pp. 119–20.

[49.] Ibid., p. 106.

[50.] Ibid., p. 139.

[51.] Ibid., p. 138.

[52.] Ibid.

[53.] Ibid., p. 140.

[54.] Ibid., p. 141.

[55.] Gil Brewer, *13 French Street*, Simon & Schuster, London, 1988, p. 5.

[56.] Ibid., p. 3.

[57.] Ibid., p. 17.

[58.] Ibid.

59. Ibid., p. 25.
60. Ibid., p. 27.
61. Ibid.
62. Ibid., p. 48.
63. Ibid., p. 49.
64. Ibid., pp. 55–6.
65. Ibid., p. 56.
66. Ibid., p. 64.
67. Ibid., p. 65.
68. Ibid.
69. Ibid., p. 75. In 1954, Stouffer's opinion survey, *Communism, Conformism, and Civil Liberties*, found Americans primarily worried about personal financial and health problems: loan repayments, overdemanding children, mortgages, college finance, hospital bills, and so on. Less than 1 per cent mentioned communism or civil liberties. Hardly any American could claim that they'd met a communist. Dale Carter, *The Final Frontier*, Verso, London, 1988, pp. 98–9.
70. *13 French Street*, p. 78.
71. Ibid., p. 111.
72. Ibid., p. 124.
73. Ibid., p. 126.
74. Ibid., p. 144.
75. Ibid., p. 154.
76. *The Final Frontier*, pp. 97–9.
77. Between 1951 and 1958, 112 nuclear weapons tests were carried out by the United States. In "Operation Cue" some 200 companies decorated the blast area with consumer products to test their durability and reliability while television and press men crouched in trenches two miles from Ground Zero waiting to publicize the results. *The Final Frontier*, pp. 98–9.
78. Jean-Luc Godard would base his 1965 film *Pierrot Le Fou* on Lionel White's novel *Obsession*.
79. Lionel White, *The Killing*, Black Lizard, Berkeley, 1988, p. 23.
80. Ibid., p. 33.
81. Ibid., pp. 34–5.
82. Because the success of their crime depends on it being subdivided and timed for maximum efficiency, the robbery is the criminal equivalent of Taylorism, or scientific management, in which workers are told what to do and how to do it and any deviation is said to be fatal to success. Despite the deployment of Taylorist techniques, the inability to predict external influences shows how difficult it is for ordinary people to control their lives, much less production, profits and the redistribution of wealth. Moreover, without democratic participation and access to the means of criminal production, robbing those who rob does not generate wealth, but only redistributes it amongst a privileged few whose money has already been stolen.

[83.] This at a time when Ralph Nader's "Unsafe At Any Speed" challenged the automative industry: "It is clear that Detroit today is designing automobiles for style, cost, performance and calculated obsolescence, but not – despite the 5,000,000 reported accidents, nearly 40,000 fatalities, 110,000 permanent disabilities and 1,500,000 injuries yearly – for safety." Ralph Nader, "Unsafe At Any Speed", in *The Nation Anthology*, Pluto, London, 1991, p. 235. Having become a full-fledged car culture, automobile credit multiplied eightfold between 1947 and 1957. In 1957 65 per cent of all new cars were bought by instalments, while within twenty years of the end of the Second World War, the short-term consumer debt rose from $5 billion to $74 billion. *The Final Frontier*, pp. 98–9.

[84.] Lionel White, *The Big Caper*, Gold Medal, London, 1961, pp. 77–8.

[85.] Ibid., p. 154.

[87.] Cited by Vaneigem, *The Revolution of Everyday Life*, Rebel Press, London, 1983, section 7.1.

[88.] Peter Rabe, *Kill The Boss Goodbye*, Vintage, New York, 1993, p. 120.

6. Beaten To A Pulp

[1.] Jack Finney, *The Body Snatchers*, First Edition, New York, 1955, p. 7.

[2.] On taking office John F. Kennedy increased the military budget by $9 billion even though as of 1960, military spending stood at $45.8 billion – 49.7 per cent of the budget. Meanwhile, nuclear testing meant that within a 250-mile radius of the Nevada test site, 170,000 people were exposed to contamination. With approximately 250,000 servicemen taking part in atomic war games in Nevada and the Marshall Islands during the 1950s and early 1960s, "it is reasonable to estimate that at least 500,000 people were exposed to intense, short-range effects of nuclear detonation". Another million Americans have worked in nuclear weapons plants since 1945, some having "contaminated" their environments with secret, deadly emissions, including radioactive iodine". While storm fronts frequently "dumped carcinogenic, radio-isotope 'hot spots' as far east as New York City". From an unpublished report by a Carter administration taskforce. Cited by Mike Davis, "Ecocide in Marlboro County", p. 67, *New Left Review*, London, July/August 1993.

[3.] The 1950s had been a decade when the dominant narrative had all but subsumed the nation. According to an editorial page article in the *New York Herald Tribune* of 6 November 1957, those under thirty had become a "non-generation, a collection of people who, for all their apparent command of themselves, for all their sophistication, for all their 'maturity', know nothing, stand for nothing, believe in nothing". CLR James, *Facing Reality*, Correspondence, p. 59.

[4.] Walter Tevis, *The Hustler*, Pan, London, 1985, p. 67.

5. Ibid., p. 166.

6. According to Guy Debord, "Kennedy remained an orator even to the point of proclaiming the eulogy over his own tomb, since Theodore Sorenson continued to edit speeches for the successor in the style which had characterized the personality of the deceased". Guy Debord, *Society of the Spectacle*, section 61, Black and Red, Detroit, 1977. Kennedy's pursuit of the spectacle was apparent in his urging of Congress to invest in fallout shelters and prepare for the spectacle of nuclear war. "Fallout Shelters and the Geopolitics of Hibernation", in *Situationist Anthology*, p. 76. By May 1961, JFK has approved a secret plan for military action in Viet Nam and Laos.

7. A veteran of the detonation of a 74-kiloton hydrogen bomb in July 1957 recalled his encounter with human guinea pigs in the Nevada desert: "We'd only gone a short way when one of my men said, 'Jesus Christ, look at that!' I looked where he was pointing, and what I saw horrified me. There were people in a stockade – a chain-link fence with barbed wire on top of it. Their hair was falling out and their skin seemed to be peeling off. They were wearing blue denim trousers but no shirts." Quoting Gallagher in "Ecocide in Marlboro County", *New Left Review*, p. 64.

8. *Fortune* magazine, as early as 1954, maintained that the average middle-class consumer was no longer the businessman but the machinist in Detroit. It failed to say that such machinists composed only 15 per cent of auto-workers and were almost entirely white." See Kim Moody, pp. 54–5.

9. British critics Nicholas Blake and Q. D. Leavis, discounting the economics and politics of publishing, claim "low-brow thrillers" for the working class and "detective fiction" for the middle and professional classes.

10. Charles Williams, *Operator*, Pan, London, 1958, pp. 18–19.

11. Ibid., p. 81.

12. Charles Willeford, *High Priest of California*, Gollancz, London, 1990, pp. 184–5.

13. This in an era which saw California complete the largest highway network since the German autobahns of the 1930s. In 1949, Rapid Transit – Now planned to combine a rail rapid-transit system with a radial downtown-centred freeway grid and, in doing so, protect the Central Business District; but a coalition of developers and outside business interests maintained the plan was socialist. See Mike Davis, *City of Quartz*, p. 122.

14. Charles Williams, *The Big Bite*, pp. 41–2.

15. Ibid.

16. Charles Willeford, *The Woman Chaser*, Carroll & Graf, New York, 1990, p. 38. The only writer to tackle the politics of oil was Jim Thompson in books like *Bad Boy*, *Roughneck*, *South of Heaven* and *Texas by the Tail*. This at a time when cheap oil sustained the genre and the culture, even at the

expense of foreign governments: "With no capital and credit, Pop became a dealer in leases, or . . . lease louse. There were thousands like him in the oil country cities. Middlemen of middlemen – men so far removed from the principals in a deal that they frequently did not know the latters' identities." Jim Thompson, *Bad Boy*, hardcore pp. 372–3.

17. Charles Williams, *Stain of Suspicion*, Pan, London, 1966, p. 146. Despite racial infractions, the South was, according to Glazer and Lipset, "the most anti-McCarthy section of the country", a situation which historian C. Vann Woodward found difficult to comprehend. Though the latter points to "the region's particularly rich historical experience with its own assortment of demagogues – Populist and other varieties – and the subsequent acquirement of some degree of sophistication and some minimal standards of decency in the arts of demagoguery". Additionally, in the foreign policy crisis prior to the Second World War, the South, according to Woodward, "was the least isolationist and the most inter-nationalist and interventionist part of the country". C. Van Woodward, *The Burden of Southern History*, Vintage, New York, 1961, p. 158.

18. Charles Willeford, *I Was Looking for a Street*, p. 138.

19. *Operator*, p. 152.

20. Ibid., p. 39.

21. *The Big Bite*, p. 70.

22. Ibid., p. 59.

23. Ibid., p. 106.

24. Ibid., pp. 107–8.

25. Ibid., p. 111.

26. Ibid., p. 147.

27. Ibid.

28. Ibid., p. 150.

29. Ibid.

30. Ibid., pp. 151–2.

31. Ibid., p. 155.

32. Ibid., p. 184.

33. Ibid.

34. Ibid., p. 188.

35. Charles Willeford, *Pick-Up*, Black Lizard, Berkeley, 1987, p. 8.

36. Ibid., p. 4.

37. Ibid., p. 17.

38. Ibid.

39. Ibid., pp. 17–18.

40. Ibid., p. 23.

41. Ibid., p. 24.

42. Ibid., p. 40.

43. Ibid., p. 47.

44. Ibid., p. 61.

45. Ibid., p. 94.

46. Ibid., p. 95.
47. Ibid., pp. 152–3.
48. Ibid., p. 164.
49. *The Woman Chaser*, pp. 14–15.
50. Ibid., p. 10.
51. Ibid., p. 11.
52. Ibid., p. 49.
53. Ibid., p. 16.
54. Ibid., p. 49.
55. Ibid., pp. 62–3.
56. Ibid., p. 99.
57. Ibid., pp. 65–6.
58. Ibid., pp. 68–9.
59. Ibid., p. 110.
60. Ibid., p. 159.
61. Ibid., p. 169.
62. At RKO, Edgar Ulmer's *Detour* clocks in at 68 minutes; Ida Lupino's *Hitch-Hiker*, 71 minutes; Wise's *The Set-Up*, 72 minutes; Montagne's *The Tattooed Stranger*, 64 minutes and Fleischer's *Follow Me Quietly*, 59 minutes. Likewise at Monogram productions, LeBorg's *Fall Guy* has a running time of 64 minutes and Reinhardt's *The Guilty* of 71 minutes. While Kubrick's *Killer's Kiss*, released by United Artists, runs for 67 minutes and Lewis's *My Name is Julia Ross*, released by Columbia, 64 minutes.
63. Though, thirty years on, the real narrative has yet to be written, John F. Kennedy's assassination has produced a plethora of texts, not least of which is the *Warren Commission Report*, the longest and most unreadable piece of pulp culture fiction ever written.
64. In 1972, pathologist and coroner Dr Cyril Wecht, obtaining a court order to examine what was left of President Kennedy's brain to ascertain from what direction, how many times and where the bullets had struck, found that the President's brain had disappeared.
65. Would-be pulp culture writer Terry Southern's facetious comments proved accurate: "I began to indulge in a compelling fantasy . . . the idea that the assassination would set off an *uncontrollable* of indiscriminate assassinations – long-range snipers knocking off dignitaries as they stepped from the plane." *The Realist Anthology*, p. 137. While *The Realist* satirized the Warren Commission's lack of evidence by taking Gore Vidal's remark that Jackie Kennedy found LBJ unacceptable to an extreme: "That man was crouching over the corpse, no longer chuckling but breathing hard and moving his body rhythmically . . . I realized – there is only one way to say this – he was literally fucking my husband in the throat. In the bullet wound in the front of his throat. He reached a climax and dismounted. I froze. The next thing I remember, he was being sworn in as the new President." Ibid., in "Parts Left Out of the Kennedy Book", p. 190.

66. Jim Thompson, "The Flaw in the System", in *Fireworks: The Lost Writings of Jim Thompson*, pp. 229-30.
67. Ibid., p. 350.

INDEX

Ace (publishers) 6
Agee, James 50
Aldrich, Robert 2, 198, 202
Algren, Nelson 19
Alter, Robert Edmond 189
Altman, Robert 195, 196, 203
Anderson, Edward 10, 113, 133,
    195, 203

Baldwin, James 34
Basie, Count 23
Beineix, Jean-Jacques 31, 197
Belafonte, Harry 141
Belkin and Korukhov 218
Bellem, Robert Leslie 68
Berkman, Alexander 210
Black, Jack 133
Black Mask 4, 10, 37, 67–68, 96,
    112, 113, 133, 145, 150, 210,
    215
Blake, Nicholas 223
Boucher, Anthony 96
Brackett, Leigh 3, 8, 13, 106, 113–
    119, 124, 130–131, 192, 195,
    200
Brande, Dorothea 4
Braverman, Harvey 214
Brewer, Gil 13, 107, 132, 133,
    149–156, 161, 192
Brocklebanks, Katherine 112
Browne, Howard (John Evans) 13,
    71, 89–95, 109, 192, 195
Burnett, WR 132–135, 156, 192,
    195, 200
Burroughs, Edgar Rice 184
Burroughs, William S. 217
Bushsbaum, Jonathan 206

Cain, James M. 107, 114, 133, 136,
    170, 195, 202, 203
Cain, Paul (George Sims) 6, 114,

133, 135–136, 138, 195
Caldwell, Erskine 170
Camus, Albert 20, 34, 219
Carter, Dale 221–222
Caspary, Vera 8, 106, 108, 195–
    196, 214
Chaber, ME 18
Chandler, Raymond 5, 10, 13, 66,
    68, 69, 71, 72–81, 82–84, 89,
    90, 92, 96, 98–99, 119, 124,
    136, 182, 183, 190, 192, 196,
    200, 204, 217
Charyn, Jerome 190
Chomsky, Noam 205, 210
Christie, Agatha 4
Churchill-Vander Wall 210, 211
Cold War 1–3, 6, 14–17, 33, 45,
    66, 71, 77, 84, 96, 99, 100, 108,
    109, 111, 126, 133, 138, 140,
    148, 167, 176, 181, 189, 190,
    210
Conroy, Jack 10, 113
Coontz, Stephanie 215
Crews, Harry 171
Crumley, James 12
Cullen, Countee 35

Daly, Carroll John 67, 112
Daves, Delmar 196, 201
Davis, Mike 215, 216, 220, 222,
    223
Davis, Mildred 8
Davis, Norbert 68
Debord, Guy 223
Dell (publishers) 4, 6, 23, 140
Deleuze, Gilles and Guattari, Félix
    17–18
de Tocqueville, Alexis 206
Dewey, Thomas B. 71, 114
Duhamel, Marcel 37
Durham, Philip 210

Edenbaum, Robert I. 219
Eisenhower, Dwight D. 138, 162, 219
Eliot, T. S. 184
Ellison, Ralph 34
Ellroy, James 12, 190
Ellsworth, F. 112

Faulkner, William 20, 113, 149, 200
Fearing, Kenneth 6–7, 14, 65, 70–71, 133, 139–140, 192, 196, 200
Ferlenghetti, Lawrence 177
Finnegan, Robert 9, 10, 63, 133
Finney, Jack 17, 64, 106, 164
Fisher, Bruno 135
Fisher, Steven 66, 112, 182, 196
Fitzgerald, F. Scott 182, 184
Fleischer, Richard 225
Foucault, Michel 217, 219
Foxx, Red 41
Franklin, Bruce 207
Friedan, Betty 111, 214
Furthman, Jules 113

Garnier, Philippe 206
Gault, William Campbell 71
Geherin, David 210
Gerald, Marc 220
Ginsberg, Allen 177
Godard, Jean-Luc 119, 197, 199, 221
Goines, Donald 20
Gold Medal (publishers) 6, 9, 31, 109, 110, 150
Gold, Mike 113
Goldman, Emma 210
Goodis, David 3–6, 9–10, 12–14, 17–18, 20, 21–34, 35, 63, 107, 133, 163, 171, 177, 190, 192, 196–197, 201–202, 217
Goodman, Paul 215, 216
Gresham, William 6, 14, 133, 197, 202

Grubb, David 133
Gruber, Frank 112
Guilbaut, Serge 205

Haley, Bill 1
Hall, James 171
Halliday, Bret 71
Hammett, Dashiell 1–3, 5, 21–23, 34, 66–68, 70, 71, 76, 83, 84, 190, 197, 204, 215
Hano, Arnold 20
Hawkes, Howard 113
Haywood, Gar 20
Hemingway, Ernest 20, 112
Hiassen, Carl 171
Highsmith, Patricia 108, 214
Hilton, James 4
Himes, Chester 6, 10–14, 18, 20–22, 42–57, 63, 82, 163, 166, 188, 193, 197
Hitchens, Dolores 3, 8, 13, 106, 119–124, 130, 131, 193, 197, 214
Homes, Geoffrey (Daniel Mainwaring) 3, 6, 15, 107, 133, 135, 198, 201
Hoover, J. Edgar 96, 98, 104, 209, 210–211
Hopper, Dennis 171, 199
Hughes, Dorothy B. 3, 6, 8, 13, 106, 124–131, 152, 193, 197, 201–202, 214
Hughes, Langston 35
Huston, John 195–197, 200
Huxley, Aldous 5

Iceberg Slim 20
Immerman, Richard 205

Jackson, Charles 177
Jameson, Fredric 204, 205
Jordan, Louis 41
Joyce, James 20

Keene, Day 191

Kennedy, Jacqueline 225
Kennedy, John F. 6, 164, 166, 189, 222, 223, 225
Kerouac, Jack 114, 177
Knight, Edward 133
Knight, Stephen 97
Kimmel, Michael S. 215
Kromer, Tom 10, 113
Kubrick, Stanley 156, 198, 199, 202, 225

Lang, Fritz 196, 198, 200
Latimer, Jonathan 5, 68, 75, 135, 197, 200
Lawrence, D. H. 5
Leavis, Q. D. 223
LeBorg, Reginald 225
Leonard, Elmore 12, 183, 190
Lewis, Joseph 225
Lion Books 20, 29
London, Jack 10, 66, 113
Lupino, Ida 198, 201, 225

McBain, Ed 139
McCarthy, Joseph 1-3, 5, 18, 48, 88, 114, 133, 167, 202, 224
McCarthyism 9, 10, 17, 71, 77, 85, 103, 111, 200, 201
McCauley, Michael 208
McCoy, Horace 3, 7, 15, 66, 67, 107, 133, 134, 135, 139, 193, 198
McCullers, Carson 150
McGivern, William 8, 10, 12, 13, 19, 107, 119, 132, 133, 140- 149, 150, 163, 193, 198, 200, 202
Macdonald, John D. 82, 149, 201
Macdonald, Ross (John Ross Macdonald, Kenneth Millar) 13, 15, 71, 82-89, 90, 91, 102, 166, 183, 193, 197
Madden, David 10
Malcolm X 141
Mandel, Ernest 98, 204, 210, 213

Marable, Manning 219-220
Marx, Karl 92-95, 213
Masur, Harold Q. 71
Matheson, Richard 109-111, 193
Millar, Margaret 8, 82, 214
Miller, Henry 184
Miller, Wade 16, 71
Montagne, Edward J. 225
Moody, Kim 223
Mosley, Walter 12, 20
Motley, Williard 34

Nader, Ralph 212
Navasky, Victor 210
Nebel, Frederick 85
NAL (New American Library) 7, 107
Nolan, William F. 215
Noyce, Phillip 171, 199

Oates, Joyce Carol 218
O'Brien, Geoffrey 204, 218

Pagano, Jo 172, 198
Palmer, A. Mitchell 210
Pinkerton Agency 65
Pocket Books 4, 140, 204
Pound, Ezra 184
Prather, Richard 71
Prisonaires, The 181

Rabe, Peter 163, 193
Rand, Ayn 96
Ranleigh, John 206
Ray, Johnny 181
Ray, Nicholas 124, 195, 197, 198, 201, 203
Raymond, Derek 190
Realist, The 225
Reinhardt, John 248
Rexroth, Kenneth 177
Rimbaud, Arthur 20
Roosevelt, Franklin D. 15
Roscoe, Mike 68

Ross, James 75, 133, 137

Sartre, Jean-Paul 5
See, Carolyn 132
Série Noire (publishers) 37
Server, Lee 204
Shaw, Joseph 112, 150
Sherman, Bill 206
Signet (publishers) 6
Sorkin, Michael 211
Southern, Terry 225
Spicer, Bart 71
Spillane, Mickey 1-3, 10-13, 15,
    66, 70-71, 95-100, 139, 194,
    198, 202
Steinbeck, John 20
Stockwell, John 206
Sutherland, Edwin and Cressey,
    Donald 218, 219

Tevis, Walter 6, 164, 165, 166,
    189, 194, 198
Thomas, Deborah 206
Thomas, Dylan 184
Thompson, Freddie 47
Thompson, Jim 3-6, 9, 11-14,
    17-18, 20-21, 35, 46-63,
    106, 109, 133, 135, 137, 149,
    156, 163, 166, 171, 189-190,
    194, 198, 202, 217, 223, 224
Todorov, Tzvetan 17
Tourneur, Jacques 25, 196, 198,
    201, 202
Tracy, Donald 135, 199, 201
Trail, Armitage 132

Truffaut, François 171, 196, 199,
    200
Trumbo, Dalton 70

Ulmer, Edgar 135, 225

Vidal, Gore 225

Wald, Jerry 23
Warner, Eltinge 168
Welles, Orson 171, 201
Wendkos, Paul 29, 196, 201
Westlake, Donald 199
White, Lionel 13, 19, 132, 133,
    156-162, 163, 194, 199, 202
Whitfield, Raoul 67, 68
Whitman, Walt 50
Whittington, Harry 137, 149, 194
Willeford, Charles 6, 13, 82, 133,
    164, 166, 167, 168, 169, 176-
    188, 189, 194, 199, 214, 217,
    223
Williams, Charles 3, 64, 133, 137,
    149, 164, 166-169, 170-176,
    177, 189, 194, 199
Wilson, Elizabeth 206
Wise, Robert 140, 198, 202
Wodehouse, P. G. 92, 93, 94
Wolfe, Thomas 20, 50, 149
Woodward, C. Van 224
Woolrich, Cornell 14, 15, 107,
    112, 133, 138, 194, 199-200
Wright, Richard 26, 34

Zinn, Howard 214, 220